Acrobat® 6
and PDF
Solutions

Taz Tally, Ph.D.

SYBEX® San Francisco • London

Associate Publisher: Dan Brodnitz
Acquisitions Editor: Bonnie Bills
Developmental Editor: Pete Gaughan
Production Editor: Susan Berge
Technical Editor: C. Scott Miller
Copyeditor: Linda Recktenwald
Compositor: Happenstance Type-O-Rama
Graphic Illustrator: Tom Webster
CD Coordinator: Dan Mummert
CD Technician: Kevin Ly
Proofreaders: Laurie O'Connell, Nancy Riddiough
Indexer: Rebecca R. Plunkett
Cover Design, Photo, Illustration: John Nedwidek, Emdesign
Cover Photos, People: Kerry Swartz

Software License Agreement: Terms and Conditions

To my wonderful Jaz, without whom life would not be anywhere near as interesting, funny, delightful, and just generally grand.

 # Acknowledgments

This book would not have happened without the dedicated work of many publishing professionals, whom I would like to thank: acquisitions editor Bonnie Bills, for helping to conceive and plan this book, and for her encouragement and patience during a rough period in my life; developmental editor Pete Gaughan, for his invaluable organizational and formatting direction, his excellent writing insights, and his efforts in keeping the book on schedule; production editor Susan Berge, for her encouragement, her project orchestration skills, and her ability to keep all the parts and concurrent process straight; technical editor Scott Miller, for his terrific content insights and suggestions; copyeditor Linda Recktenwald, for making my writing clearer and more readable; compositor Maureen Forys, for making all of our work appealing and approachable; our proofreaders, for helping to improve the quality and consistency of this book; the CD team, Dan Mummert and Kevin Ly, for adding another media dimension to this project; and last but not least, associate publisher Dan Brodnitz, for making the whole project possible.

Foreword

Trends—such as management philosophies and cool vacation destinations—can come and go, but one trend that has stood the test of time and will most likely endure is the PDF file format. Why? Quite simply, because it works, and more importantly because it helps you work.

When you use PDF files, you don't have to worry about the silly techno mumbo jumbo stuff under the hood of your computer. What is this silly stuff? It's all the things you're asked when you send someone a file that is *not* a PDF file: What program was used (PageMaker vs. QuarkXPress)? Which version was used (Word 98, Word 2001)? Which fonts were used (Arial vs. Helvetica)? What file formats are the pictures (BMP vs. TIFF)? What is the font technology (TrueType vs. Type 1)? Which computer and operating system was used (Windows vs. Mac OS 9 or OS X)?

Instead of getting bogged down with all that, PDF files allow people to say just "send me a PDF," or in the new digital vernacular, "PDF it to me." One day those phrases will be as ubiquitous and popular as "Scotch tape" and "Xerox."

However, like most wonderful things in life, there is a catch. The catch is that the creation of PDF files is not as simple and elegant as their usefulness. As a result, inexperienced people (not bad people) create bad PDFs.

What are bad PDFs? Bad PDFs may not open, can look bad on the screen, or may not print correctly. Bad PDF files can be created with the wrong tools, or with the right tools but incorrect settings. The solution to bad PDFs is simply to learn the basics of good file preparation. That's what this book is all about.

Like your author Taz Tally, I spend a great deal of time training people to create and work with PDF files. And the results are amazing. With a few rounds of "No, no, no—don't do that" and "Watch and do this," the creation of PDF files can shift from a company-wide problem to a company-wide solution.

This book has something for everyone. Depending on your experience and your use for PDF files, you may find some sections more useful than others. For anyone having problems sending PDFs, I recommend reading the sections on creating good PostScript files and creating PDF files. For anyone who has to mark up pages, I suggest the section on collaboration. For those interested in PDF for presentations, see the chapter on creating presentations (but remember that the PowerPoint file may be smaller and easier to print than the PDF). For anyone doing printing, I recommend reading the chapter on preflighting and outputting PDF files.

Just as trends can come and go, so can the so-called experts—but Taz is not one of those. I have known Taz for a long time and have edited many of his books. Although I make fun of the "Tazman" because he sometimes makes up his own words, I can say without hesitation that his knowledge and ability to train can only be found in a short list of trainers in the world. (And after reading the edited drafts I am pretty sure the editors have replaced the made-up words.)

However, the greatest advantage of Taz's training is his unabashed style. It does not matter whether you are watching him as he blazes through a hands-on demo from behind his computer or reading one of his books. Taz will communicate what works best, explain why it works best, and in a step-by-step fashion show you how to do it. And the best advantage of reading his books is that you don't have to go to Starbucks and drink the garbage-can-sized venti coffee to keep up with him.

Enjoy the book, and may all your PDFs be good PDFs!

—HOWIE FENTON
   Senior Technical Consultant
   Digital Technologies
   National Association of Printing Leadership (NAPL)

Contents

Chapter 9   **Collaborative Publishing and Interactivity**   **259**

Introduction

If we all used the same type of computer, the same operating system, and the same application to create, edit, and distribute our documents, and we published our documents in the same format and on the same media, we might not need Acrobat technology…and if only pigs could fly! Acrobat technology—Distiller specifically—allows us to convert just about any digital document we create into a common (application-, OS-, and computer-independent) file format, PDF. PDF, in turn, can be distributed and manipulated, using the Reader and Acrobat applications, in just about any way we can imagine.

Unfortunately, many people are unaware of most of Acrobat's robust capabilities. Most folks understand that they can create and receive PDFs and that these files can be viewed and printed by others as well. What is not commonly known is that PDF documents can and should be tailor-made for specific uses. And most people are unaware of the vast range of uses for PDF documents, such as forms, presentations, interactive multimedia, collaborative publishing, and secure document control, just to name a few. Further, many do not know how or when PDFs can or should be manipulated and edited to suit their needs.

Like other books in the *Solutions* series, *Acrobat 6 and PDF Solutions* is designed to provide rapid and ready access to the information and techniques you want, when you need them. Each technique or capability covered in this book is designed to be a stand-alone tutorial as much as possible. Advanced techniques and capabilities that require some basic knowledge include specific references to the background information you will need.

Who Should Read This Book

Anyone who wants to distribute their documents to others or who wants to use their documents in a variety of ways (multipurposing) will benefit from the knowledge and use of the various Acrobat technologies. Whether you need to send a copy of your latest design to your boss upstairs (who may be challenged by just turning on their computer), or you are looking for a medium within which to manipulate and distribute your documents to a worldwide audience, Acrobat and PDF technologies can be a big bonus for you.

Perhaps you would like to convert your print documents into multimedia master-pieces, presentations, or forms; or participate in a group publishing project, but have neither the time for nor the interest in learning a whole raft of new applications to accomplish these tasks—then Acrobat may be the tool for you, and I'll show you why (and how!). If you want to learn specific Acrobat- and PDF-related tasks and techniques, then this is the book for you. If you want to learn how to turn your PDF document into an interactive form, you need only turn to that chapter (Chapter 8 in this case) and start learning the step-by-step techniques involved in creating interactive PDF forms. If you already know the basics about Acrobat and PDF and would like to know how to better take advantage of the myriad of Acrobat capabilities, this is the book for you.

How This Book Is Organized

Acrobat 6 and PDF Solutions takes you easily from the basics that you need to know about PDF files to the most advanced and detailed improvements and adjustments you can make to your documents. Along the way you'll learn the quickest and most common settings in Acrobat, as well as how to navigate and perform tasks quickly.

Part I: Creating Proper PDF Files These chapters focus on the often ignored parts, processes, and techniques involved with creating a pre-PDF document, as well as the PDF itself. The emphasis is on controlling the content and quality of both the original, native, page-layout document and the final PDF file.

Chapter 1: Acrobat Parts and Workflow In this chapter I sort out the various and expanding components of Acrobat technology. I distinguish between Distiller, Acrobat Standard and Pro, and Adobe Reader and Elements. Also covered are key peripheral components and concepts such as native vs. PDF files, file manipulation vs. editing, PostScript printer drivers and files, and PostScript and PDF workflows.

Chapter 2: Creating Pre-PDF Documents The focus here is on document construction and preflighting concepts and techniques. This information will provide you with the insights and tools you need to construct, prepare, and test high-quality native page-layout documents, which will in turn allow you to create high-quality PDF documents. Topics include fonts, graphics, master pages, style sheets, and pre-flighting tools.

Chapter 3: Creating Quality PostScript Files Many well-constructed documents have been sidetracked on their way to becoming a PDF file at the PostScript file-creation step. Here you will learn how to control what goes into the PostScript file destined to become a PDF. Topics include working with PostScript printer drivers, colors and color separations, font management, page setups, and other job-specific settings. Streamlining this process with print styles is also covered.

Chapter 4: Creating the PDF You Want PDF documents can, and often should, be customized for specific uses. In this chapter you learn the details of optimizing your PDF creation process to create PDF documents tailored to suit your needs. Various creation processes are discussed, with a focus on setting up and using Distiller; you'll see which PDF creation processes and settings are appropriate to use in various circumstances.

Part II: Fundamentals of Acrobat Here I focus on the core PDF management and manipulation tools common to both Acrobat Standard and Professional versions. The many powerful capabilities for which Acrobat is becoming better known, such as presentations, forms, collaborative publishing, interactive multimedia, as well as Web and e-mail tools, are featured.

Chapter 5: Controlling Acrobat and Access to Your PDFs Learn how to set up and use Acrobat's powerful document access and security features. See how to control what your PDF will look like; who can see and do what with your PDFs; and how to track PDF access and use, including the use of digital signatures.

Chapter 6: Using Acrobat and Navigating PDFs The focus here is learning how to set up, use, and navigate around and through a PDF document, including cool new navigational stuff such as split screens and digital loupes so that you can spend most of your time on the fun stuff. You will also learn how to improve access to your PDFs for visually and motor-skill-challenged users.

Chapter 7: PDF Document Management Learn how to take ultimate advantage of the page-based nature of PDF documents with page manipulation such as cropping, rotating, extracting and even creating combination size and orientation PDFs. In addition, you will learn about comparing documents, adding repetitive page elements (such as watermarks), PDF layering, and utilizing Acrobat's flexible and powerful search functions.

Chapter 8: Building Presentations and Forms PDF documents can be used as an effective medium for information transfer. Here you will learn how to build or convert PDF documents for use as presentations in a few short steps. Also see how to build and utilize Acrobat's powerful forms tools to help you acquire and distribute data.

Chapter 9: Collaborative Publishing and Interactivity Interactivity is one of the hallmarks of Acrobat technology. Here you will learn to use Acrobat's vast array of collaborative publishing tools, including bookmarks, articles, and commenting, to work effectively in a group. You will also have the opportunity to get the hang of linking interactive sounds and movies to your PDFs to add other media dimensions.

Chapter 10: Acrobat E-mail, eBook, and Web Features Acrobat was designed with the Web in mind, so it has a whole raft of web and e-mail functions, some of which are linked to common applications such as Microsoft Office. Here you can find out how to collaborate via e-mail, e-mail from within Acrobat, and even convert whole websites into PDF documents. Acrobat has become an eBook reader, so you will learn how to access, manage, and even share and purchase eBooks via Acrobat.

Part III: Advanced Acrobat We focus on some of the more advanced topics and capabilities, many of which appear only in Acrobat Pro version. With Acrobat version 6, Acrobat Pro supports a complete prepress tool set, including support for PDF/x, preflighting PDFs, and more output features such as color separation and bleed previews and printing. And finally you will learn how to automate many of Acrobat's tools, functions, and features to enhance your productivity.

Chapter 11: Preflighting PDFs Preflighting a PDF allows you to check the viability of a PDF for specific uses. Here you will learn how to use Acrobat 6's extensive prepress preflight capabilities including its PDF/x specific tools. You can also preflight for the accessibility of the PDF for visually and motion-impaired users.

Chapter 12: Editing PDFs In this chapter you will learn how to simplify a PDF by removing unused or unwanted document components. In addition, you will see how to access and edit any component of a PDF document including text, graphics, and document structure. You will even learn how to add text and alternative text to your PDF documents.

Chapter 13: Outputting PDFs and Their Contents Here we cover the complete range of Acrobat 6 output capabilities including previewing color proofs (including separations), changing the format of an entire PDF document, printing setup and options, importing and exporting text and graphic components including table contents. A special section covers the interactivity between Acrobat and Photoshop.

Chapter 14: Automating Acrobat Tasks Once you learn the Acrobat capabilities and techniques you need to meet your needs, you will likely want to learn how to perform tasks, particularly repetitive ones, quicker. With Acrobat's batch functions and actions you will see how many tasks can be performed quickly and dependably.

On the Companion CD

The accompanying CD-ROM provides a great collection of resources for your PDF work.

Fantastic software demos I've assembled trial versions of the best PDF workflow software: Enfocus PitStop, a PDF production tool; Markzware FlightCheck, a popular preflighting application; StaffingTools online PDF training; and Virginia Systems Sonar Bookends for indexing and Sonar Bookends Activate for automatic hyperlinking.

Chapter files In several chapters, the hands-on, step-by-step instruction also includes starter and demonstration files so you can experiment with Acrobat's versatility.

Bonus appendices Appendix A has some key information that adds depth to some of the topics covered in the main text: online references you can use to expand your Acrobat know-how, and a list of Acrobat shortcuts.

Chapter 4 in the book provides a good introduction to the content and use of Distiller and its settings. Appendix B on the CD goes beyond that with more comprehensive coverage of all 72 of Distiller's settings, for those who are hungry to understand and/or exercise all of the controls and options Distiller offers...feast away!

How to Contact the Author

Sybex strives to keep you supplied with the latest tools and information you need for your work. Please check their website at www.sybex.com for additional content and updates that supplement this book. Enter the book's ISBN—4273—in the Search box (or type **acrobat and solutions**), and click Go to get to the book's update page.

You can contact me via e-mail at ttallyphd@aol.com and taztally@alaska.net or though my website, www.tazseminars.com. You can find a complete listing of all my digital training and educational resources at www.graphicauthority.com/home.htm and on the NAPP (National Association of Photoshop Professionals) website, www.photoshopuser.com.

About the Author

Dr. Taz Tally is the founder of Taz Tally Seminars, a consulting and training company that specializes in electronic publishing. Taz is the author of *Avoiding The Scanning Blues*, a comprehensive guide to desktop scanning, which was chosen as a featured selection of the DoubleDay book club, as well as *Electronic Publishing: Avoiding The Output Blues*, a textbook on electronic publishing fundamentals and PostScript file preparation. He is also a frequent contributor to *Photoshop User* magazine, for which he writes a regular pre-press column.

Taz has produced numerous instructional videos and CDs on scanning, prepress, Photoshop, Microsoft Publisher, font management, and keyboard shortcuts, and was the co-developer and instructor for the video training series DeskTop to Print. Taz has invented and produces a 10-step scanner and digital camera calibration target and kit. Taz is a frequent presenter at seminars and trade shows throughout the U.S., including Graph-Expo, and appears as a member of the Photoshop Dream Team at the biannual Photoshop World conventions.

Taz is perhaps best known for his entertaining, content-rich seminars and his ability to present complex materials in a simple, easy-to-understand fashion. Taz is currently writing books on Digital Photography, Photoshop, and OSX, and is developing an on-line training print curriculum for Sessions.edu.

When Taz is not touring the country by plane or motor home presenting his seminars, he splits time between houses in Homer, Alaska, and Ft. Myers, Florida, with his fabulous partner Jaz and their Cardigan Welsh corgi, Zip. In their "spare time," Taz and Jaz generally head off to the outdoors. They can be found hiking or mountain biking in Alaska, skiing the powder snow in Utah, or diving with the whales in the waters off Hawaii.

Taz is available for custom training and consulting.

Contact Taz and Jaz at Taz Tally Seminars:

16175 John Morris Road #10

Ft. Myers, FL 33908-3030

239-433-0622 (Office)

239-267-8389 (Fax)

ttallyphd@aol.com or jazkatz@aol.com

Creating Proper PDF Files

PDF (Portable Document Format) documents have become a universal digital document format. There are several workflow pathways to creating a PDF document—and some work better than others. The secret to creating high-quality, useful PDF documents in any workflow requires paying attention to the content, quality, and characteristics of your document and its text and graphic components at each step along the way. The old adage "garbage in, garbage out" applies to PDFs—image quality can be preserved but not enhanced during the PDF creation process.

Acrobat Parts and Workflow

Adobe Acrobat is not about creating original documents. Acrobat is a software technology designed to make the conversion, distribution, and use of digital documents easier, more compatible, expandable, and more flexible. Acrobat technology comprises several components including AdobeReader, Acrobat (Professional and Standard) Distiller, and the PDF document itself. Workflow, simply stated, is what you do and the order in which you do it. Successful creation and use of PDF documents and Acrobat technology require that certain functions, such as original page layout document construction and preflighting, be properly completed prior to the creation of a PDF document. In addition, the most successful PDF-oriented workflows require that PDF documents be formatted for specific types of uses.

1

Chapter Contents

Working in native documents vs. PDF files

Acrobat technology and PDF parts

PostScript parts

PDF document workflow

Working in Native Documents vs. PDF Files

Document applications such as Adobe InDesign and QuarkXPress and their files are used for document design and creation, while Acrobat technology and Portable Document Format files (PDFs) are typically intended to be used to present and distribute/share document information. The documents created in application-specific formats—"native" files—are a starting point in a publishing workflow; PDF documents are typically created toward the end of a workflow. As such, the basic natures of native documents and PDF files are quite different.

Name: Ch 1 Acrobat
Workflow.qxd

Ch1 Acrobat Workflow.pdf

Native files are *document-based*, which means that each page is connected to and integrated with all the other pages in a document. For instance, text flows easily from one document page to another. Native document files also tend to have their various font files and graphic components as linked *external* files, which makes them easily available for editing.

PDF files, on the other hand, are *page-based*, which means that each document page is a separate entity from all the other PDF document pages, with no connection between them. In fact, each page *element*—such as each word of text—is a separate page item unrelated to any other item on the page. The process of *distilling*, which converts a native file into a PDF, by its very nature separates each page and page element into its own discrete and disconnected component.

Note: This is why it is a slow and often cumbersome process to select, never mind edit, specific portions of text in a PDF document. This is also why you want to pay close attention to the construction of the original native page layout document, so that little if any editing of the PDF document is required.

The distilling process also involves the inclusion in the PDF file of all linked external page elements such as external high-resolution graphics files and (if properly distilled) used font files, creating a self-contained document. This internalization of page elements makes for a nice complete package but also makes access to those elements for editing purposes more difficult.

These fundamental differences between open and editable document-based native files and the more self-contained, less-editable, page-based PDF documents are really at the heart of the various purposes for which each document format is intended. Figure 1.1 compares the key characteristics of native and PDF files. Native files such as those from Quark, PageMaker, Frame, and InDesign are highly editable; PDFs are secure but not as editable.

Manipulation vs. Editing

When you work with PDF documents, it is appropriate, and indeed wise, to distinguish between editing and manipulation. In this context, editing refers to changing the basic components or elements of a document, such as its text and graphics components. Manipulation refers to actions such as rotating (90° increments), rearranging, combining, and linking pages and documents. Native applications are generally excellent for document creation and editing, while Acrobat and PDF files are best for document manipulation.

Creating and editing text, typesetting, copying, pasting, reordering, formatting, tagging, and hyperlinking Any major creation or editing of text in a document should occur in your original page layout document. Any text that is copied and pasted or edited automatically causes the reformat and reflow of the text. To attempt this in a PDF file would be difficult and slow at best and hair-pulling frustration at worst.

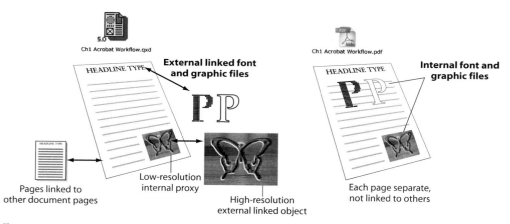

Figure 1.1 Native file (left) vs. PDF document file (right) characteristics

Creating, editing, and placing graphics; and assigning colors As with text components of an original document, all graphic components should be properly formatted (resolution, dimensions, color mode, and graphic file format) and placed in the page layout at 100%. Likewise, colors should be properly chosen and assigned (RGB vs. CMYK± Spot colors) in the original page layout document.

Manipulating pages: linking, rotating, positioning If, on the other hand, your goal is to rotate some pages in a document and completely reorganize the order after all the text had been set and then link some pages to one another or to other documents, now you are in the comfort zone of Acrobat and PDF. First, you cannot rotate some pages in QuarkXPress and not others, and even if you wanted to do so, documents filled with text and graphics often prevent you from changing the orientation of a page. As anyone knows who has done any reordering of pages in a document with active linked text pages, extensive page reordering often results in document corruption and operator frustration. And linking native file documents or pages to one another—never mind to documents of other types or formats—is not at all something that these applications are designed for. But for Acrobat and PDF, such page-based manipulations and linking are easy as pie.

The first key point to be made is that you should plan to perform various functions in the file/document formats that lend themselves to those functions. You should perform any internal creation and extensive editing of document components in a native file document such as QuarkXPress or InDesign, while any post-creation, page-based manipulation such as rotations, linking, and reorganization should be completed on PDFs.

This does not mean that you can't edit a PDF file. On the contrary, as you will see, PDF files are certainly editable, and in some cases you can even edit items such as imbedded vector graphics right in the PDF file. However, extensive editing, especially of text, can be slow and cumbersome. Most of your basic document construction should be accomplished prior to creating the PDF, leaving the more PDF-compatible document-based functions for Acrobat.

Acrobat Technology and PDF Parts

There are now five basic components to Acrobat technology:

- Acrobat Distiller
- The PDF document file
- Adobe Reader
- The Acrobat application itself, which now comes in two flavors: Standard and Professional
- Acrobat Elements (new in Acrobat 6)

Acrobat technology, like most other Adobe products, is also extensible and supports a variety of Adobe and third-party plug-in technologies.

Acrobat Distiller

Acrobat Distiller is the application used to convert a native file document, such as an InDesign or QuarkX-Press document, into a PDF document. In order for Distiller to work its conversion magic, you must convert the original document file into a PostScript file that contains PostScript language code (described later in this chapter). This conversion is done with a PostScript printer driver. Distiller then converts the PostScript code into a PDF document file. This process is known as *distilling* (and is sometimes referred to as *normalization*) and creates the viewable and editable version of the PostScript file that you and I recognize as a PDF file.

Normalization, which occurs during distilling, is the term used to describe the process of creating a PDF file because the process not only converts PostScript code into a PDF file, it simplifies and standardizes (normalizes) the PostScript code into a more universally editable, manageable, and useful form. Choosing the proper PostScript printer driver, creating a complete PostScript file, and choosing the best distilling settings are all key steps in creating a successful PDF file.

Adobe Elements

Acrobat Elements is a new application released with Acrobat 6. Elements is basically an easy-to-use version of Distiller, a "Distiller Lite" if you will. Elements is designed to be used in corporate environments where individual, strict control over distilling variables and characteristics may not be as important as, say, a prepress environment. This is currently a site-licensed product with the smallest license available being 1000 seats. I suspect that the initial distribution of this product will be limited due to the large seat requirement and that we may well see a modification of this policy in the future.

PDF Document

Ch1 Acrobat Workflow.pdf

The Portable Document Format (PDF) file is of course the heart of Acrobat technology. PDF is a PostScript-based format designed to be platform-, application-, and version-independent. Its core function has always been "universal" document distribution, although many more spectacular capabilities have been added and improved upon over the years, including forms, multimedia, and collaborative publishing.

It is important to note that the basic PDF file was intended for, and the default settings are set for, low-resolution, on-screen, composite viewing and printing. So if you are intending to use a PDF for another purpose—such as high-resolution, color-separated, PostScript commercial printing—you need to be prepared to steer the PDF away from its default uses and settings and toward the specific demands of those uses.

Adobe Reader

 This is the application formally known as Acrobat Reader (I prefer the original name as it is more specific). Adobe Reader is a free application distributed by Adobe. Reader is made for basic viewing, searching, and printing of PDF files and does not provide more advanced functions, such as document page manipulations, editing, and collaborative publishing, or the addition of interactive or multimedia functions. Most of these capabilities can be viewed in Reader but not created or edited. The free nature of Adobe Reader has been largely responsible for the rapid and wide proliferation, acceptance, and adoption of PDF-based technologies. However, most people who adopt Acrobat technology and PDF into their standard workflow will not be satisfied with Reader; they will want to acquire Acrobat itself with all of its wonderful capabilities.

Acrobat the Application

It is a bit confusing that Acrobat is both the name of the overall technology and the name of the main core application. Early on, this application was called Acrobat Exchange; the name was changed in version 4 to just Acrobat. In this book when I refer to "Acrobat," I will always be referring to the application itself. When I am making reference to the overall technology, I will refer to "Acrobat technology."

Acrobat provides the same basic viewing and printing functions as Reader but includes a whole variety of PDF manipulation, management, and editing capabilities, such as document page manipulation, editing, collaborative publishing, or the addition of interactive or multimedia functions. Historically, Acrobat has been available in only one form. Starting with Acrobat 6, there are now two flavors known as *package options*: Acrobat Standard and Acrobat Professional.

Acrobat Standard

 It would be incorrect to think of Acrobat Standard as "Acrobat Lite," because it is anything but a light version (Acrobat Professional is more of an enhanced version).

Both Standard and Professional versions arrive with Distiller. Standard supports all the basic tools that Acrobat has to offer:

- Creation
- Viewing
- Navigation
- Cataloging and searching
- Reviewing, comparing, and commenting
- Security
- Administrative
- E-book
- Multimedia

Most business users will find that the Standard version will meet all of their needs.

Acrobat Professional

 Acrobat Professional contains all of the Acrobat Standard document management, editing, and manipulation features. In addition, Professional supports a range of functions that Adobe considers to be more professional tools for graphic artists, prepress, and engineering professionals, such as these:

- One-button PDF creation from Vision, Project, and AutoCAD
- Grids and guides, layer management, Loupe tool, and Pan and Zoom
- Measurement, clouding, and arrow commenting tools
- Forms creation, PDF comparison, PDF/x support, and preflighting
- Color management and job ticket
- Previewing color separations, overprinting, and simulating printing substrates.
- Printing color separations

Plug-ins

 Acrobat technologies are expandable through the use of plug-ins, which add capabilities to the applications. Currently most plug-ins are created for either Reader or for Acrobat Standard or Professional, with the Acrobat versions having the lion's share of them. The plug-ins are normally stored in a Plug-ins folder associated with the specific application.

You can find a list of the plug-ins under either the Application or File menu, depending upon which operating system you are using. Figure 1.2 shows one of the plug-in lists in Acrobat Professional (available by choosing the About Adobe Plug-Ins or About Third-Party Plug-Ins menu option). When you view the list of plug-ins, Acrobat will in most cases provide an explanation of the use of each plug-in and a list of other plug-ins that may be required for the fully functional use of that plug-in.

The third-party plug-in capability allows other manufacturers to further enhance Acrobat technology. An example is Enfocus' PitStop, which provides robust preflight and editing capabilities to Acrobat. We will cover this plug-in and its use in Chapter 11, "Input and Output of PDF Documents and Contents."

PostScript Parts

I've already discussed the fact the PDF files are based upon the document language called PostScript. PostScript is our preferred language because it is sophisticated and powerful enough to allow us to perform tasks such as scaling, stretching and rotating type, stroking and filling graphics, working with both pixel- and vector-based images, and performing sophisticated printing chores such as separating colors. PostScript, which was developed by Adobe, has become the graphics industry standard language for creating and outputting complex pages and is the foundation of a PDF file.

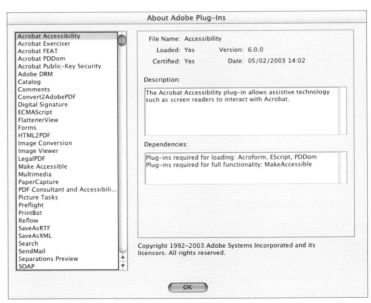

Figure 1.2 Plug-in list in Acrobat Professional on Mac OS X, showing plug-in descriptions and dependencies

The PostScript Language

The PostScript language is the background code describing what is in the document, much like HTML code is the behind-the-scenes code that creates a web page. Below is a section of PostScript code—Distiller converts this code into a viewable and editable PDF file.

```
/Adieresis/Aring/Ccedilla/Eacute/Ntilde/Odieresis/Udieresis/aacute
/agrave/acircumflex/adieresis/atilde/aring/ccedilla/eacute/egrave
/ecircumflex/edieresis/iacute/igrave/icircumflex/idieresis/ntilde/oacute
/ograve/ocircumflex/odieresis/otilde/uacute/ugrave/ucircumflex/udieresis
/dagger/degree/cent/sterling/section/bullet/paragraph/germandbls
/registered/copyright/trademark/acute/dieresis/notequal/AE/Oslash
/infinity/plusminus/lessequal/greaterequal/yen/mu/partialdiff/summation
/product/pi/integral/ordfeminine/ordmasculine/Omega/ae/oslash
/questiondown/exclamdown/logicalnot/radical/florin/approxequal/Delta/
guillemotleft
/guillemotright/ellipsis/space/Agrave/Atilde/Otilde/OE/oe
/endash/emdash/quotedblleft/quotedblright/quoteleft/quoteright/divide/
lozenge
/ydieresis/Ydieresis/fraction/Euro/guilsinglleft/guilsinglright/fi/fl
/daggerdbl/periodcentered/quotesinglbase/quotedblbase/perthousand
/Acircumflex/Ecircumflex/Aacute/Edieresis/Egrave/Iacute/Icircumflex/
Idieresis/Igrave
/Oacute/Ocircumflex/apple/Ograve/Uacute/Ucircumflex/Ugrave/dotlessi/
circumflex/tilde
/macron/breve/dotaccent/ring/cedilla/hungarumlaut/ogonek/caron
```

The PostScript File

Ch1 Acrobat Parts.ps

The PostScript code is contained in a PostScript file. You create this PostScript file by printing (or saving) a file to disk rather than sending it directly to a printer. A PostScript file, although it is straight ASCII and can be edited within a plain-text editor, will typically have a .ps (Macintosh) or .prn (Windows) file extension.

The PostScript Printer Driver

AdobePS 8.5.1

A little known and understood but very important part of the PDF workflow is the printer driver used to output your document file. The printer driver ultimately determines the final code that is placed in the print/save to disk file. It is imperative that you begin your document construction process by choosing a PostScript printer driver rather than a non-PostScript printer driver *before* you start constructing your document. The reason for this is twofold:

- The printer driver will determine the code that leaves your document when you print or save a file to disk.
- Printer drivers work backward as well as forward—that is, they feed document information such as page size and margins back into the document. If you wait until after your document is constructed to choose a PostScript printer driver, you may receive a rude awakening when your document is reformatted before your eyes and document elements such as text and graphic boxes are relocated on your page.

Note: Windows users should pay special attention to this, because the default printer driver is a non-PostScript printer driver. I keep a Post-it note on my Windows monitor that reads "Printer Driver!" to remind me to select a PostScript printer driver prior to creating my documents.

Printer drivers are located in various places depending upon which computer operating system you are using. If you are working on Mac OS version 9.2 or earlier, you will find the printer drivers listed in the Chooser under the Apple menu. In Mac OS X you select the printer driver in the Printer utility, and in Windows XP you do so through the Printer And Faxes control panel. Some versions of operating systems also allow you to change printer drivers through the Page Setup and Print dialog boxes. Check to see which of these accesses work for you.

Figure 1.3 shows several versions of printer drivers that I have on one of my Macs (OS 9.2). Note that I have placed the version number labels on each icon. The reason for this is that some versions of printer drivers produce better PostScript code than other printer drivers. The version of PostScript created becomes increasingly important as the complexity of printing you intend to perform increases. When you are engaged in high-resolution, color-separated PostScript printing at a commercial print shop, the version of PostScript you use may make the difference between a job printing properly or not at all.

Note: Along with selecting the proper PostScript printer driver, you must also use the proper a PPD (PostScript Printer Description) file that matches your output device. For instance, even if the correct PostScript driver is selected (like AdobePS), if the PPD that is selected in the native program is a grayscale printer (like Laserwriter II), the resulting PDF may have most or all of the graphics rendered in grayscale.

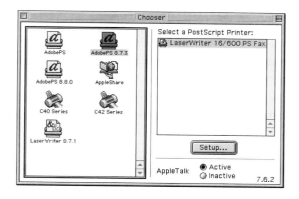

Figure 1.3 PostScript printer driver versions

You can download PostScript printer drivers for free from the Adobe website, www.adobe.com.

> **Note:** If you intend to send your PDF files to a commercial printer, get their recommendation as to which PostScript printer driver to use.

PDF vs. PostScript Document Workflows

As you will see, there are many processes, or workflows, for creating PDF documents. Various specific workflows may work better than others, depending upon the application you work with and your workflow objectives. In this section I will map out a complete, standard, high-quality PDF document-creation workflow. In Chapter 4, "Distilling to the PDF You Want," I will consider some alternative workflows and discuss where the various workflows might be used.

In the early days of desktop publishing we employed a straight PostScript workflow in which documents were converted to PostScript code via a printer driver and sent only to print, either directly to a printing device or via a PostScript file. This was a print-only workflow. In addition, the PostScript file, while complete (if it was made properly—more on this later), was not viewable or editable and it was large.

Modern PDF workflow provides us with same completeness of the PostScript file but with a viewable, editable, flexible, inclusive and usually much smaller file, which can be made and reused for many purposes.

> **Note:** Successive versions of the PDF format and concurrent Acrobat program upgrades have expanded the Distiller Job Setting options and uses for which PDFs may be applied (like forms, commenting, JavaScripting, layers, XML utilization, e-books, previewing options, and transparency compatibility with illustration programs).

A high-quality PDF workflow begins by paying attention to the parts and pieces, such as text and graphics, that will ultimately go into your PDF file. You must then pay attention to how these document elements are integrated into a final document ready for conversion to PDF. Attention to detail at each step along the way will ensure the creation of a high-quality and appropriately converted PDF document.

Figure 1.4 shows how a standard, high-quality PDF workflow includes and goes beyond a PostScript workflow.

The following steps are an overview of the key stages to a PDF workflow. In Chapters 2–4 I will discuss the details of each of these key steps in this PDF workflow, as well as some variations on this standard PDF workflow.

Image creation The quality of the final PDF document begins with the initial capture and/or creation of the graphics. During this stage you must pay attention to graphics quality, dimensions, resolution, color space, and format. If you intend to use your graphic for more than one type of output (and therefore make more than one kind of PDF), then you must make sure that the graphics you create will be usable on all of your output devices.

Document construction At this stage you need to choose a page layout application that is best suited for the kinds of documents you are creating and your output devices. Word processors are fine to use for simple documents that are to be viewed or printed at low resolution. But more complex documents destined for high-quality output devices are best created with page layout applications. You must also pay attention to the fonts you select, the graphics format you choose, and your color assignments. Various font architectures, file formats, and color modes are best suited for various uses and output devices. For instance PostScript fonts, TIFF and EPS graphic file formats, and CMYK and spot colors are best used for commercial printing, while TrueType (as well as PostScript) fonts, JPEG and GIF graphic file formats, and RGB colors are more appropriate for Web use.

Preflighting Before you create the PostScript file that will become your PDF document, you need to make sure all the document components are present and properly formatted. As you know, native page layout documents tend to have their key document components, such as font and graphic files, linked externally. You want to make sure that those links are in place so that these critical components are included in the PostScript file and ultimately in the PDF. You should check other key characteristics such as document dimensions, color spaces, and bleeds as well. Paying attention here to make sure your document is correct can save lots of time, money, and disappointment later in the workflow.

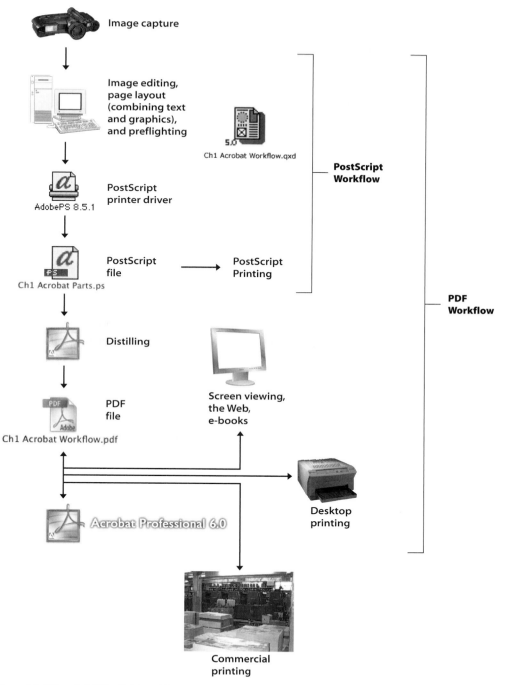

Image capture

Image editing,
page layout
(combining text
and graphics),
and preflighting

Ch1 Acrobat Workflow.qxd

5.0

**PostScript
Workflow**

PostScript
printer driver

AdobePS 8.5.1

PostScript
file

Ch1 Acrobat Parts.ps

PostScript
Printing

**PDF
Workflow**

Distilling

PDF
file

Ch1 Acrobat Workflow.pdf

Screen viewing,
the Web,
e-books

Acrobat Professional 6.0

Desktop
printing

Commercial
printing

Figure 1.4 PDF vs. straight PostScript workflow

PostScript file creation The printer driver determines the actual PostScript code that is included in the PostScript file and therefore the code that is used in the creation of the PDF document. Some printer drivers create high-quality PostScript code, others produce poor-quality code, and still others create no PostScript code at all. So it is crucial to use the proper PostScript printer driver when creating a PostScript file. In addition at this stage you need to check to be sure you are using the correct document setup and make sure all document components make it into the PostScript file.

Distilling Once you have created a high-quality PostScript file, you want to determine how that PostScript file will be converted into a PDF. Distiller, the application that actually creates the PDF document, can be configured to create a wide variety of PDF documents—for on-screen viewing, viewing on the Web, e-books, desktop printing, commercial printing, and even specific print workflows. So setting up the proper Distiller settings for the specific use you intend for the PDF is a key function at this stage if you want to end up with the PDF document you expect. Fortunately for most of our readers, Job Option Settings are savable and transferable, which means that vendors with specific format requirements can distribute their customized Job Option Settings files to the customers they work with.

PDF creation In this chapter I have discussed the top of the heap in terms of creating a predictable, high-quality PDF using a professional page layout application, a good-quality PostScript printer driver, and Distiller. There are other methods that provide shortcuts and/or other tools. Knowing which method works for your workflow and document use will be critical to your success.

PDF alteration: manipulation, enhancement, and editing PDFs can be manipulated, enhanced, and edited in a variety of ways. Acrobat itself provides a wide range of PDF manipulation, enhancement, and editing tools. Other applications or plug-ins can also be used to alter your PDF file. Some alterations involve changing the content of the PDF and some do not. Deciding where (in the PDF or native document) and how to alter the contents and/or characteristics of your PDF document is an important part of an efficient PDF workflow.

PDF use As I have discussed, PDFs can be created with very specific uses in mind. And as you will see as you move deeper into this book, PDF documents can be altered to enhance their use for specific needs, such as forms, presentations, and collaborative publishing. After you have created and altered a PDF, it is critical to *not* use your PDF for purposes for which it is not suitable, such as using a low-resolution RGB web-intended PDF for commercial printing.

Creating Pre-PDF Documents

2

The text and graphics you choose and place in the document, how you construct your initial document, and how you handle your document after it is constructed and then converted into a PDF file all strongly affect the quality of your PDF document. In this chapter we focus on the details of putting a document together for various uses and preflighting that document before converting it to PDF.

Chapter Contents

Using the Proper Page Layout Application

Choosing the right text and graphics components to place in your page layout file starts with choosing the proper page layout application. For some purposes the use of a word processing program is adequate; for others you will want to learn and use a professional page layout application. You will also want to choose the best graphics components and font files for your needs.

Most file-creation applications fall into one of three categories: word processors, graphics creation tools, and page layout applications. For the best and most dependable results, it is best to use an application for the purpose it is primarily intended:

- Word processors for creating and editing text, including tables and tagged contents.
- Graphics applications for creating and editing graphics
- Web design applications for combining and arranging text and graphics for online distribution. for online distribution
- Presentation applications for combining text and graphics for on-screen and online presentations and multimedia
- Page layout applications for combining text and graphics in a printed document

Many document editing and output problems start when you choose the wrong tools for creating your document in the beginning of the process. The more sophisticated and complicated your document is, and the more demanding your output device is, the more important your document tool choices become. Table 2.1 lists some of the commonly available file-creation programs and their recommended uses.

Word Processing Applications

In this age of marketing hype and feature explosion, the distinctions have been blurred between the various types of applications and their uses. This blurring is clearly evident in the confusion over word processors and page layout applications. Word processors such as Microsoft Word and Corel WordPerfect have been given the ability to let you place graphics, add charts, and even add movies and sounds. With all of these added capabilities, and the marketing hype that accompanies these additional features, you would have to forgive people if they mistook such applications for full-blown prepress page layout and/or multimedia applications.

Word and WordPerfect are still darn good word processors (although they would work better and faster without all that add-on baggage, but that is another story). If you need to type, edit, and reorganize text, including tables, you should do it in these applications; the word processing features in other applications, such as InDesign and QuarkXPress, don't match up to the power of Word and WordPerfect. However, if you intend to participate in page layout where you will be combining lots of text and graphic elements, you will benefit from the capabilities that a page layout application has to offer.

Application	Use
Microsoft Word	Word processing
Corel WordPerfect	Word processing
Microsoft PowerPoint	Onscreen presentations
Apple Keynote	Onscreen presentations
Adobe PhotoShop	Painting program: Creating, editing, processing and converting pixel-based images such as photographs
Adobe Illustrator	Drawing program: Creating and editing vector-based images such as line art and logos
Macromedia FreeHand	Drawing program: Creating and editing vector-based images such as line art and logos
CorelDRAW	Drawing program: Creating and editing vector-based images such as line art and logos
Microsoft Publisher	Page layout tool for output on composite desktop printers
Adobe InDesign	Page layout tool for PostScript and commercial printing
Adobe FrameMaker	Page layout tool for PostScript and commercial printing (especially for long structured documents)
QuarkXPress	Page layout tool for PostScript and commercial printing
Adobe PageMaker	Page layout tool for PostScript and commercial printing
Microsoft FrontPage	Web page/site composition
Macromedia Dreamweaver	Web page/site composition
Adobe GoLive	Web page/site composition
Macromedia Fireworks	Web graphics creation (pixel-based)
Macromedia Flash	Web graphics creation (vector-based)
Adobe ImageReady	Web graphics creation (pixel-based)

Page Layout Applications

If your purpose is primarily word processing on the desktop, sharing the document from one computer to another, and maybe printing it on a low-resolution desktop printer, you will likely have success with Word or WordPerfect. But if you intend to frequently combine text and graphics or you intend to print your documents at higher resolutions, on expensive stock, or through a third party, there are far more appropriate tools: page layout applications such as Adobe InDesign, FrameMaker, and QuarkXPress. These applications were designed to provide users very sophisticated controls and options for combining text and graphics. Because of their excellent output-to-print capabilities (such as color separations, bleeds, and trapping), commercial printers have built their workflows around them. To state it simply, a PDF you create from QuarkX-Press or InDesign will be far more likely to be received favorably by a commercial printing company than one from a word processor.

Note: The bottom line suggestion here is to use the right tool for the job. Text processing is best performed by word processors. Sophisticated page design and layout are best accomplished with dedicated page layout applications. And more demanding output, such as PostScript-based commercial printing, is best attempted with applications that provide the tools and quality demanded by these uses.

Web Design Applications

Match the tools you use to create your initial documents to your most demanding final output. If you intend to create and output your final PDF document in a commercial print environment, then use a PostScript-oriented page layout application such as InDesign or QuarkXPress. If you intend for your document to end up as a web page, then use a web-oriented layout application such as Macromedia Dreamweaver, Adobe GoLive, or Microsoft FrontPage.

Just as QuarkXPress and InDesign excel in the PostScript printing world, applications such as Dreamweaver and GoLive excel in the web world of HTML. Although you will find that word processor and print-oriented page layout applications offer web-export capabilities, these applications simply do not offer the quality of web page design and implementation that dedicated web applications do. Once again, use the right tool for the right job to get the best results.

As we will see later in this book, using Acrobat, you can convert web pages to PDF document pages. However, if creating a PDF document is your intention, you are better served to start with a PostScript page layout application, such as InDesign, rather than its web cousin GoLive, because you will have a wider range of document design, construction, and output options.

Presentation Applications

Presentation applications such as Microsoft PowerPoint and Apple's Keynote are created primarily to produce documents destined for on-screen use. Like word processors, presentation applications are sometimes used for printing. Once again this may work out okay on a low-resolution desktop printer or on an RGB film output device. But ugly problems nearly always erupt when these files end up inside a PDF file (or alone) at a printing company. There is a myriad of problems with this approach, not the least of which is the fact that most PowerPoint graphics files are low-resolution RGB images, while most commercial-quality printers use high-resolution CMYK files.

On the other hand, many presenters are successfully converting their presentations into PDFs for their presentations. As you will see in Chapters 8 and 9, presentation documents can be easily converted into PDFs or created directly from various PDFs, and they can be easily posted and distributed on the Web. PDF-based presentations are cross-platform compatible and the fonts are embedded. PDFs accommodate pages of different sizes within the same document and enable cross-document linking and search functions. Also, Acrobat enables the generation of many interactive controls for navigating the document and launching programs, multimedia, sounds, and flash files.

Graphics Applications

Graphics creation and editing applications such as Adobe PhotoShop, Illustrator, Corel-DRAW, and Macromedia FreeHand, like word processing programs, are sometimes touted (thanks to evil marketing managers) and therefore used as page layout applications. Yes, you can combine text and graphics in Illustrator and FreeHand. Heck, they even have style sheets...wow! But once again, the core strength of these applications is creating and editing graphics, *not* combining them with text to construct final page layout documents. It is worth noting that the reverse is also true. In recent years, page layout applications have been imbued, some of us think burdened, with graphics editing capabilities. My suggestion: Leave the graphics creation and editing to the graphics applications, and leave the page layout to the page layout applications.

Two Key Page Layout Tools

Regardless of the tool you use to construct your original document, there are two tools that you should use to help improve the consistency and editability of your original document and later the searchability of the PDF document. These tools are master pages and style sheets.

Master Pages

Master pages are basically template pages that contain any page elements that will be repeating from one document page to another. These page elements commonly include, but are not restricted to, headers, footers, page numbers, company logos, and automatic text boxes, which flow text from one page to the next. Using master pages to place repeating page elements will dramatically improve the consistency and speed of creation of your documents. This consistency will also aid in the printing (as Xobjects) and searchability of your document once it is converted into a PDF document. Figure 2.1 shows an example of items that might commonly be placed on a master page.

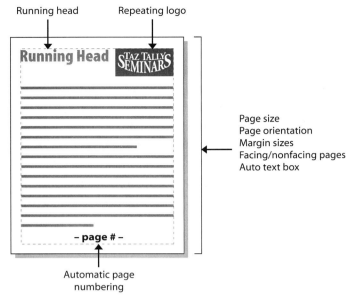

Figure 2.1 Example of master page elements

Style Sheets

Style sheets are templates for the look, known as formatting, of the text used in your document. Text formatting includes defining such character formatting as font type-face, style, size, and color, as well as paragraph formatting including leading (the space between lines in a paragraph), indents, and space before and after paragraphs. Any text formatting that is used repeatedly in your document should be configured and applied through style sheets. Text controlled through style sheets includes chapter titles, all heads and subheads, all types of body copy, tables, and basically any formatted text that is used more than once in a document.

Look at this book's pages and see how many different styles of formatted text would be assigned and controlled by a separate style sheet. For instance, in this section of Chapter 2 the headings "Master Pages" and "Style Sheets" are controlled by style sheets that format the text to indicate these are subsections within "Two Key Page Layout Tools."

Figure 2.2 shows a list of the style sheets used to create this book. Like master pages, style sheets are used to increase the speed, consistency, and editability of a document. They can also be used to automate many text processes, such as creating a table of contents (TOC). In addition, once your style sheet–controlled document has been converted into a PDF file, its style sheets can be used for searches and for creating bookmarks and other internal hyperlinks such as from a style sheet–controlled TOC to their related heads and subheads in the related sections of the PDF document (you will see how this is done in Chapter 9, "Collaborative Publishing and Interactivity").

> **Note:** At the beginning of my document construction process I draw a thumbnail of the various document page templates that I will be using to create my document (like the one in Figure 2.1). On each of these I note master page elements and the style sheet–controlled type that I will be using to create these pages. I then assign keyboard shortcuts to the most commonly used style sheets to allow me to assign them quickly. I also assign following style sheets (style sheets that automatically apply themselves to the next paragraph) to speed the process of assigning style sheets. This initial process really helps me get organized and saves a lot of time by eliminating the need to reconstruct and/or manually format and reformat copy. The result will ultimately be a much more consistent, flexible, and usable PDF document.

Selecting and Preparing the Best Graphics

Regardless of whether you use your PDFs on the Web, in desktop work, or in high-quality print output, you will want to pay attention to the quality of your graphics so that your PDFs will view well, at least on screen. If you plan to output your PDFs on high-resolution devices such as commercial printing presses, you will want to pay particular attention to the dimension, resolution, color space, and file format in which you save your graphics. Following is an overview of some of the key issues to attend to when creating and formatting your graphics.

Figure 2.2 Style sheets used in this book

Controlling Image Quality

To assure good-quality images, you should make key fundamental adjustments (in a graphics application, of course) including setting the overall brightness and contrast control and performing basic color corrections for color images. You initially control brightness and contrast by setting the proper highlight and shadow starting points (usually with an editable histogram, like the one in Figure 2.3) and then fine-tuning between those (typically with a curve tool, like the one in Figure 2.4). You perform basic color correction by making RGB values equal in neutral areas of your image (as in Figure 2.5). See the recommended reading list in the appendix for more complete information on image correction.

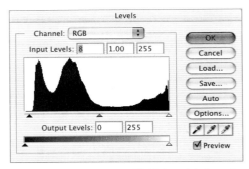

Figure 2.3 Histogram setting of highlight and shadow points

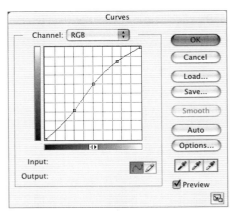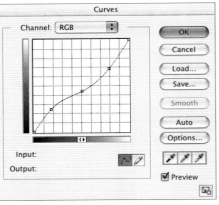

Figure 2.4 Raise the curve to lighten and apply an "S" shape to increase contrast; lower the curve to lighten and flatten the shape to lower contrast.

Figure 2.5 Equalize RGB values at a neutral location in your image to remove color cast.

Creating Images at Final Dimensions

For the best quality and results and easiest and fastest output when printing, you should place images in their page layout documents at 100 percent size. If possible, it is best to scan or capture the images at the proper dimension in the beginning. When this is not possible and you find yourself scaling images later, you should return to your graphics application—before inserting your graphic into the page layout and prior to outputting to PostScript and PDF—and resize your image there so that it will be placed in your page layout application at 100 percent. Figure 2.6 shows the image-sizing process in PhotoShop. After resizing the image dimensions, you will want to update the link to this graphic (as described in the later section "Establishing and Maintaining Links").

> **Note:** Most professional page layout applications provide a hot link from placed graphics to their original graphics application (such as PhotoShop for pixel-based images or Illustrator for vector-based images), which streamlines any resizing or updating of the placed images.

Make sure that when you scale an image (particularly up), you maintain the resolution of the image. See the next section for a discussion of resolution requirements.

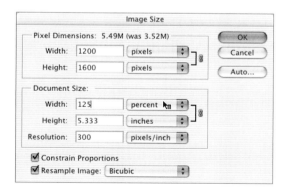

Figure 2.6 Resize images and control resolution in a graphics application, and then place at 100 percent in a page layout application.

Note: I realize that you may not always have the time to create the "best quality and results." And cutting some corners, such as scaling your graphics in your page layout application, may often produce acceptable results—I cut corners sometimes too. However, in this chapter, I am noting those key issues and methods that will produce the best quality and results when you want or need to.

Setting Appropriate Image Resolution

Images of a wide range of resolutions (from 72 ppi to more than 2000 ppi) all typically look fine on screen because screen resolutions tend to be low (72–96 ppi). It is during printing that you often see a degradation of image quality (the common blockiness known as pixelization or rasterization). The resolution of your images should be determined by the demands for the highest-quality output device you will be using. Table 2.2 lists typical resolution (in pixels per inch, or ppi, commonly referred to as dpi) requirements for various categories of output devices. Note the high-resolution requirements for commercial printing.

▶ **Table 2.2** Resolution Requirements of Various Output Device Categories

Device	Resolution
Monitors	72–96 ppi
Desktop inkjet printers	150–200 ppi
Desktop laser printer	125–200 ppi
Wide format printing	300 ppi (8″×10″ image)
Commercial printing (≤133 lpi)	200 ppi
Commercial printing (150–200 lpi)	300 ppi

Note: For printing devices that use lines screens (LPI), if you provide 100 percent scaled images with resolutions of 2x lpi, you will have plenty of resolution to support high-quality printing.

Remember that if you scale your image up in a page layout document, the effective resolution of your graphic will drop by a similar percentage to the scaling. For instance, if you scale an image up 200 percent, your effective resolution will drop by 50 percent. So, if your original image was 300 ppi, its final resolution will be 150 ppi after scaling. If you intend to output this image at 175 lpi, it would no longer offer enough resolution to support this high-quality output. This is one of the key reasons why you want to make sure that you scale and control the resolution of your image when you capture your image or in the original graphics application before final placement and output (see Figure 2.6).

Note: Throughout this book I will use the proper image, or input, resolution terminology of pixels per inch (ppi). You will commonly find image resolution referred to as dots per inch (dpi). Images are constructed of pixels, not dots. Dpi is appropriate for referring to print or output resolution where you actually print your images with spots and dots. LPI is short for lines per inch, and refers to the number of halftone dots (which form rows or lines of dots) per inch used when printing an image. It is often useful to clearly distinguish between input and output resolution to prevent confusion. My books *SilverFast: The Official Guide* (Sybex, 2003) and *Avoiding the Output Blues* (Prentice-Hall, 1999) have complete discussions of this topic.

Assigning the Appropriate File Format for Output

File formats can be thought of as containers that hold the pixels and vector components or building blocks of your images. Like the shoes you choose to wear for different occasions or uses, it is often necessary to match the containers (file formats) with specific uses. As with resolution, the device to which you intend to output your PDF should determine the file format you choose for your graphic images. Here again, on-screen viewing is the least demanding in terms of file format assignments. The most demanding is PostScript printing. The processing of the image during printing, known as RIPping, proceeds faster and more dependably if you use specific file formats such as TIFF and EPS. Table 2.3 includes some common file formats and their contents and uses.

▶ **Table 2.3** File Formats and Their Uses

Format	Uses
BMP	Pixel-based image format: Appropriate for non-PostScript desktop printing.
EPS	Vector-based and pixel-based (especially multi-tonal and/or pre-color separated), and pixel+vector-based images: Appropriate for commercial PostScript as well as general-purpose printing. Some RIPs will not process EPS files and will render only low-resolution versions during printing.
GIF	Lossless compressed pixel-based image format: Appropriate for web viewing. Not recommended for high-quality and/or PostScript printing; 8-bit pixel depth does not contain enough information for printing at high quality or resolution.
JPEG	Lossy compressed pixel-based image format: Appropriate for web viewing. Not recommended for high-quality and/or PostScript printing. Lossy compression may lower the print image quality too much.
TIFF	Very flexible pixel-based file format (recent versions support both pixel and vector components): Appropriate for commercial PostScript as well as general-purpose printing.
WFM	Combined pixel- and vector-based image format: Appropriate for non-PostScript desktop printing.

Note: RIP is an acronym for *raster image processing* or *processor*, used as either a verb or a noun. Ripping is the process through which a document is converted from a document code (for text and graphic elements) into printable elements. A RIP is a device that does this processing. So RIP is either a process or device that is used to convert a document into a printable page.

If your intended output includes PostScript printing devices, I recommend that you consider using TIFF and EPS exclusively. (For an explanation of "lossy" and "lossless" compression, see the later section "Compressing Images.")

Choosing Color Spaces and Color Assignments

You need to pay attention to two kinds of colors: captured colors and assigned colors. Captured colors are those captured with a scanner or digital camera. Colors typically are captured in red, green, and blue (RGB) components. RGB also refers to the color space and components used by monitors to create the colors you see on your screen. However, most printing devices reproduce colors using cyan, magenta, yellow, and black (CMYK) inks. So, your captured RGB colors need to be converted to CMYK prior to printing. The second category of color, assigned colors, are colors that you apply to objects such as borders, logos, line art, and backgrounds when you draw boxes, arrows, and other line-based images.

You typically have a choice of three types of color systems: RGB, CMYK, and spot colors. Spot colors, often referred to as Pantone colors, are special mixtures of a limited number of standardized color inks used to create custom ink colors. Spot colors should be assigned only when a device capable of printing separated colors, such as a commercial printing press, will be used to output your image and other graphics in PDF files.

Here again, as with resolution and file format, the type of output device you are using should determine the color you use when you assign your colors. Do you see a recurring theme here about image use (and particularly the demands of output devices) being a key factor in how you construct your files prior to converting them to PDF files? Some output devices, such as monitors and projectors, require RGB colors only, and in fact converting to or assigning CMYK or spot colors may slow them down and result in unwanted color changes. Other devices, such as commercial printing presses, demand that they be sent either CMYK or spot colors. An increasing number of desktop printing devices, while they print in CMYK, are set up to perform the RGB to CMYK conversion on-the-fly. Table 2.4 is a matchup of some common output devices and their pref, as well as those to avoid.

Device	Preferred Color Systems	Color Systems to Avoid
Monitor	RGB	RGB
Desktop printer	CMYK	RGB and spot
Commercial printer	CMYK and spot	CMYK and spot

Remember that many desktop printing devices prefer to be sent RGB (captured) images, which will be converted to CMYK values on-the-fly. But even with these devices it will be best to use CMYK colors when you assign (as contrasted with capture) colors. Also, desktop printers will typically convert spot colors into CMYK simulations, with unpredictable and often unsatisfactory results. Due to color shifts that can occur during the distilling process, it is best to standardize on the CMYK color mode when saving image files destined to be rendered as print-oriented PDFs. RGB images and spot colored graphics that are distilled frequently appear and print in paler tones than their originals.

Compressing Images

The primary role of compression is to reduce file size. File size reduction is important in some output/distribution environments, such as the Web. It is far less important, and in fact can lead to complications, in other output environments, such as commercial printing.

There are two types of compression, lossless and lossy:

Lossless compression, such as is found in GIF files with LZW compression, offers a maximum of 50 percent compression, and therefore file size, but protects your images and especially your contone (continuous tone) images from any data loss, and therefore image quality loss. .ZIP and .sit (StuffIt) are other common examples of lossless compression.

Lossy compression, used in JPEG file format images, offers far greater compression from 5/1 up to 100/1 of contone images but also results in loss of image data and, as a result, image quality. The greater the amount of compression applied to an image, the smaller its file size but the greater the potential damage to the image. And once again the use of your images should control if, what kind, and how much compression should be applied to your images. If the PDFs will be used only on the Web, you can apply more lossy compression without fear of too much visual degradation of your images.

In PDFs for desktop printing, you should reduce the amount of compression to limit the amount of damage that will be apparent in the final print. To print images on high-quality devices such as photo-quality printers or commercial printing presses, it is typically best to avoid compression altogether. Table 2.5 shows the various uses, image types, and recommended compression types, amounts, and file formats.

▶ **Table 2.5** Compression Recommendations

Image Use and Type	Type of Compression	Amount of Compression	File Format
Web: line art and flat colors	Lossless	2/1 max	GIF
Web: contone grayscale images	Lossless	2/1 max	GIF
Web: contone color images	Lossy	Moderate 10/1 max	JPEG
Desktop printing	Lossless	2/1 max	TIFF/EPS
Commercial/photo printing	None	0%	TIFF/EPS

Reducing Bit Depth of Images

In addition to using compression to control file size, you can also adjust the bit depth (also known as pixel, color depth, or density) of an image. Reducing the bit depth of an image reduces its file size but also decreases the number of tones in an image, which in turn reduces the number of shades of gray or color in an image. Decreasing the number of tones in an image can have a significant deleterious effect on the visual quality of your images. Images with more shades of gray or colors will show greater impacts than those with fewer shades/colors. In general monitors are more forgiving than print devices when rendering reduced bit depth images. When creating a PDF for print, your print image quality will be best served by using grayscale images with a minimum of eight bits per pixel and RGB color images with a minimum bit depth of 24. Table 2.6 shows some of the common file formats, their supported bit depths, and some print recommendations.

Bitonal vs. Multitonal Images

You typically work with two types of tonal images:

- Bitonal images, which have only two (bi) shades of gray (black and white line art is a common example)
- Multitonal images, such as continuous tone (contone) photographs, which have many (multi) shades of gray

Line art images lend themselves well to lossless compression. Contone images can be compressed with either lossless or lossy compression, but they tend to be damaged with the lossy compression, particularly at higher compression ratios.

File Format	Grayscale bit Depth	RGB Color Bit Depth	CMYK Supported	Print Recommendations
TIFF	8–16	24–48	Yes	Desktop and commercial
EPS	8–16	24–48	Yes	Desktop and commercial
JPEG	8	24	Yes but not recommended	Desktop
GIF	1–8	1–8	No	None

Note: The process of RIPping and printing will often show image quality degradation that is not apparent on a lower-resolution device such as a computer monitor. In addition, the presence of compression in an image, even lossless compression, can slow down, complicate, and even prevent the RIPping process. For this reason it is best to avoid the use of compression, especially when outputting to high-quality PostScript printing devices. And remember that even web images will clearly show the impact of too much applied lossy compression. The posterization commonly seen on web page images is typically the result of too much applied lossy compression. You must always balance the need for speed with the demands of image quality. Many graphics creation applications offer side-by-side image comparison screens, which allow you to preview various combinations of resolution, compression, and bit depth settings.

Establishing and Maintaining Links

Whenever you place a graphic in a page layout document, the original, high-resolution version of the graphic remains outside the document. Only a small, low-quality (low-resolution, low–bit depth) proxy version of the graphic, linked to the original, becomes part of the page layout document (see Figure 2.7). But it's the linked high-quality graphic that needs to be included in the PostScript file and PDF document. If the link between the proxy and the external graphic is broken, only the low-resolution proxy will be included in the PostScript and PDF. And, the missing high-quality graphic may not be discovered until long after the PDF has been created and moved.

Broken links can occur for a variety of reasons, including moved documents and/or moved or renamed graphics. The easy way to make sure the high-quality graphic-proxy links are maintained is to place the linked high-quality graphics in the same folder as the page layout document (see Figure 2.8). Then just move the whole folder whenever you want to move the document. With this method, any time that document is launched and printed or converted to a PDF document, no matter where it is, the links will automatically be maintained and the high-quality graphics will be included in the PDF document.

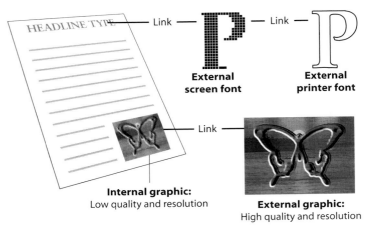

Internal graphic:
Low quality and resolution

External graphic:
High quality and resolution

Figure 2.7 A page layout document, with linked fonts and graphics

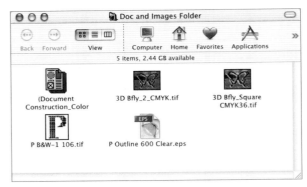

Figure 2.8 Document and images together in one folder

Choosing and Assigning Fonts Appropriately

Like graphics, font files need to be properly linked to document pages. But unlike graphics, there are no internal proxy font files to maintain the active links with the external font files. Each time a document is closed and then reopened, new links need to be established with the font files, and because of a myriad of naming and font-recognition problems (which are too lengthy to get into in this book), relinking with the same font files used the last time the document was opened often does not occur. Following are some tried and true, and hard won, font management guidelines to help you make sure you select, use, and maintain the font and typesetting integrity of your documents.

Separating Operating System Fonts from Document Construction Fonts

Every version of every operating system, whether it's Windows, Macintosh, or something else, requires a minimum set of fonts, known as operating system (OS) fonts, that are used by the OS to provide basic OS features such as window titles, menu choices, and dialog box text. These OS font files are specifically designed to work on screen and are therefore usually not appropriate for document construction. In addition, many OS fonts are copyrighted and should not be used to create documents. And in fact, copyrighted OS fonts often cause problems during the distilling process.

For these reasons it is generally best to avoid using operating system fonts when creating documents. One of the first things I do when I set up a new computer, besides partitioning my drive, is to separate the OS fonts from the document construction fonts. I place all the document construction fonts outside the default operating system folder(s). Creating this external fonts folder not only separates my OS fonts from my document construction fonts but also—critically—allows me to control access to my document construction fonts. Figure 2.9 shows how in Mac OS 9, you need only Chicago, Geneva, and Monaco in the system's fonts folder; all other fonts are in external folders and are available for document construction. You will need to determine which fonts are required by your operating system, leave those in the default system fonts folder, and organize and place the remainder of the fonts that you intend to use for document construction in a folder external to the operating system.

Creating and Using Font Sets

Once you have moved your document construction fonts to a folder external to your operating system, you will need to use a font management utility to access and control these fonts. There are a number of good font management utilities that work in both Mac and Windows environments; Figure 2.10 shows one called Suitcase by Extensis. (See the resource guide in the appendix for a list of recommended font management utilities.)

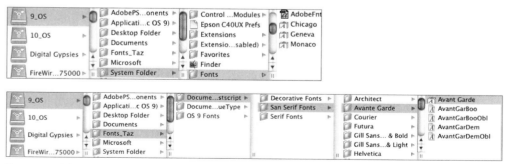

Figure 2.9 A default system fonts folder (top) and a document fonts folder outside the system (bottom)

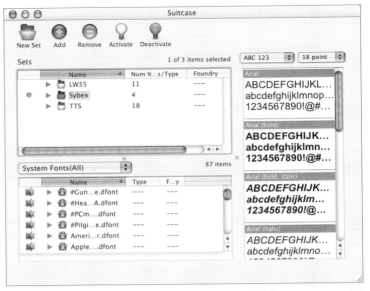

Figure 2.10 A font set, activated in Suitcase, one of several available font management utilities

One of the key aspects of using a font management utility successfully is to create and use sets of fonts. It is a good idea to collect font sets for each project. By creating and using separate font sets for each project, you can help guarantee that the same fonts will be used whenever you launch your document and that these same fonts will be available for embedding in the PostScript and PDF documents when you create those.

Matching Font Architecture Choice with End Usage

Font architecture refers to the basic type of font structure used to create a set of font files. There are a wide variety of font architectures available on most computers today, including the two most common PostScript Type 1 and TrueType fonts. Most current font technologies are OS specific and therefore not cross-platform compatible. For this and typesetting integrity reasons, make sure that the fonts you use to create your document are included in the final PDF file. For onscreen viewing, the Web, and low-end non-PostScript printing, TrueType fonts will work okay. But if you intend to output your final PDF document at a commercial printing company or other high-end PostScript-able output device, you will be better off using PostScript Type 1 fonts (most people simply refer to these as PostScript fonts since the earlier Type 3 variety is now out of use) because of the unpredictability of TrueType fonts on PostScript devices. Some publications (such as *Time Magazine*) and vendors are standardizing on PDF/X compatible files (a refined version of PDF) for their high-end printing workflows. While PDF/X files are made the same way as regular PDF files, one prerequisite for compatibility is that they contain only Type 1 fonts.

Acrobat uses another font architecture, known as Multiple Master fonts (a changeable version of PostScript Type 1), to create proxy or substitute fonts for PDF files that lack embedded fonts—more on this in the next section. Another font architecture to be aware of is called OpenType, which has been designed by Apple Computer with the intent of replacing the less-compatible OS-specific current versions of Post-Script and TrueType fonts. Table 2.7 provides an overview of font technologies and their recommended uses.

▶ **Table 2.7** Font Architectures and Recommended Usage

Font Technology	Recommended Uses	Uses to Avoid
Bitmapped fonts	Early version. Operating system fonts (Mac and Windows)	All printing
TrueType fonts	Monitor, web, non-PostScript printing	PostScript printing
dFonts (Apple TrueType)	Mac OS X system font use only	Anything other than OS X system
PostScript Type 1	PostScript Printing, PDFs, web	Non-PostScript printers
Multiple Master (Acrobat)	Acrobat font substitution	Any non-Acrobat function
Multiple Master (Standard)	PostScript printers*	Some RIPs don't like MM.
OpenType**	All and cross-platform	None known

* Multiple master (MM) fonts are special versions of PostScript Type 1 fonts that allow adjusting of its optical axes to create font style variations called iterations. MM fonts tend to be structurally more complex than standard Type 1 fonts and thus can be more problematic on output, particularly at high resolutions.

** It is hoped that OpenType will eventually replace the now platform-specific versions of TrueType and PostScript fonts. This will make font management, and in particular cross-platform font management, much easier. This transition may take some time due to the enormous investment many companies and individuals have made in purchasing their font libraries.

Avoiding Acrobat Font Substitution and Copyright Problems

One critical part of Acrobat font technology of which you need to be very aware is Acrobat's ability, even proclivity, to substitute fonts in PDF files. Adobe, being well aware of the font challenges we all face, built a font substitution capability into Acrobat. Whenever a PDF document is opened that does not have a complete set of embedded font files for all of the type characters used in that document, Acrobat or Reader will automatically attempt to simulate those type characters by using substitute character versions, which it creates using its Acrobat Multiple Master fonts.

Acrobat MM fonts are automatically installed on your computer whenever Acrobat or Reader is installed. And the dangerous part of all this font substitution is that it occurs transparently without warning or offering a choice. Unlike applications such as QuarkXPress or PageMaker, which will at least warn you when they attempt font substitutions and provide you with the chance to make substitution choices, Acrobat makes font substitutions on-the-fly, whether you like it or not. The good side of this slick font substitution is that it make Acrobat easier to use. The downside is that if you are not careful about including your font files in your PostScript files and PDF documents (covered later in Chapter 3, "Creating Quality PostScript Files," and Chapter 4, "Creating the PDF You Want"), the typesetting integrity of your PDFs may be violated each time the PDF is opened. Figure 2.11 shows the icons for the Serif and Sans Serif versions of the Acrobat MM fonts that are used to simulate font characters in PDF documents that have missing and/or incomplete font character sets.

Figure 2.11 Acrobat Multiple Master font files

One other key Acrobat-specific font point to make is that if you use operating system fonts, and particularly those from Microsoft, they may well be rejected or substituted during the PDF-creation process when distilling takes place. Many operating system fonts are copyright protected against document creation use. Acrobat Distiller is designed with the ability to recognize this type of copyright protection. When Distiller encounters a document using a copyright-protected font, it may either reject it, which will likely derail the distilling process, or substitute another font, usually an iteration of its Multiple Master variety. To avoid this potential problem, it is best to avoid using OS fonts in your documents.

One More Pitch for Style Sheets

Whenever you set type in a page layout document, you should use style sheets if possible to control the formatting of the type. Inside the style sheet dialogs, use your font menus to assign the typeface style. The Type Style field should always indicate Plain (see Figure 2.13). You will be able to use these style sheets to quickly and easily create and update an accurate table of contents. In addition, once you've constructed the PDF document, these same style sheet–based TOC elements will be used to create internal hyperlinks that will allow rapid navigation though the PDF document (this is covered in Part II of this book).

Selecting Typefaces and Styles

Besides using different fonts files in most documents, one of the most common problems to avoid is a phenomenon called false styling. Many body copy typefaces, such as Arial and Helvetica, have multiple styles commonly including roman, bold, italic, and bold italic. Other, typically display, typefaces, such as Copperplate, do not have any style variations; they have only one style (see Figure 2.12).

Figure 2.12 A multiple-style typeface (left, Arial) and a single style typeface (right, Copperplate)

A problem develops when you use a style menu or palette to assign a style to a typeface that does not exist. When this happens, the font characters appear on screen in their falsely styled appearance, and they may actually print with that false style on low-resolution printers. But when these falsely styled characters are included in a final PDF document, all sorts of font problems can arise. These fonts may be substituted, double printed, rejected, or just plain not recognized. You can easily avoid these false style–related problems by following one simple rule: Apply font styles from font menus only (Figure 2.13); don't assign font styles using style menus or style palettes (see Figure 2.14).

Preflighting

Preflighting is the preparation of a file for a specific use, such as for printing on the desktop, commercial printing, or use on the Web. In the case of PDF files, this could be any of these uses, so it is important to first identify the purpose for which your original and PDF files will be used. There are two types of preflight: content and technical.

Content preflight, where you check to make sure all the components are present, is the more critical of the two for the document creator to perform, because only the document creator can supply the proper pieces to the document.

In **technical preflight,** you check for items such as file format, resolutions, and color space conversions. You can change some technical items, such as file format, along the way in a workflow, although this can be time consuming and therefore costly.

You should note that once you've converted a native document file into a PDF, editing is often an even more costly and time-consuming process than working with native document files. So, it is in your best interest to perform complete content and technical preflight on your document prior to creating PDF files.

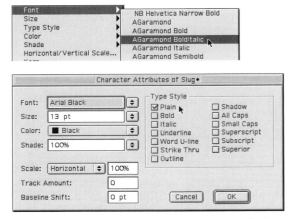

Figure 2.13 Proper application of typeface styles: Font menu (top), style sheet font menu (bottom, always check Plain)

Figure 2.14 Improper application of typeface styles: Style menu (left), palette style menu (right)

Content Preflight

As mentioned previously, content preflighting involves checking to make sure all the major components of a file are present. Table 2.7 is a checklist of items to look for and key concerns when performing a content preflight on a page layout document before generating the PostScript file used for creating a PDF.

▶ **Table 2.7** Content Preflight Items and Issues

Preflight Item	Issue
Page layout document	Most recent version
High-quality external graphics	Links established and updated
Font files	All used fonts currently active
Font style assignments	All styles should be set to Plain.
Color assignments	Colors should be properly assigned for the end use: RGB for the Web, CMYK for desktop printing, and spot and CMYK for commercial printing.
Bleeds	Any item that is to bleed off the page must be extended past the trim line of the document.
Composite proof	To check for accurate placement of document components and bleeds
Color-separated proof	Critical for commercial printing to check for proper spot and process color assignments

If any of these items are missing or incorrect, the final PDF will have missing pieces and/or be incorrect.

Note: Remember that you cannot tell by looking at your monitor if your graphics are properly linked or if your fonts are properly formatted.

Technical Preflight

In performing a technical preflight, you focus on the more technical aspects of your documents, such as file format and resolution, which initially may be less obvious but may ultimately have a large impact on the quality of your final PDF document. Table 2.8 is a checklist of some of the more important technical items to address and key concerns when performing a technical preflight on a page layout document prior to generating a PostScript file for creating a PDF.

▶ **Table 2.8** Technical Preflight Items and Issues

Item	Issue
Graphics file format	File format should be consistent with the end use: TIFF and EPS for prepress, GIF and JPEG for the Web.
Image resolutions	Image resolution should be appropriate for the end use: 200–400 ppi (depending upon the print lpi) for commercial printing, 200 ppi for desktop business printing, and 72–96 ppi for the Web.
Color gamut conversions	Match image color space with end use. Web = RGB and print = CMYK.
Font architecture	Use the font types that are most compatible with the output device. TrueType is fine for most low-resolution, non-PostScript business uses. PostScript fonts are preferred for commercial print and especially PDF/X compliant workflow uses.

Preflight Tools

While you can perform preflighting manually, using preflighting tools allows you to be more consistent, work faster, and make fewer mistakes. There are typically two categories of preflight tools: those built into page layout applications and dedicated preflight tools.

Built-in Preflight Tools

QuarkXPress, InDesign, and other page layout applications usually supply some level of preflight support. Table 2.9 shows some of the common page layout applications and their preflight tools.

▶ **Table 2.9** Page Layout Applications and Their Preflight Tools

Applications	Tool	Use
QuarkXPress	Font Usage	Check for font activity and formatting.
QuarkXPress	Graphic Usage	Check for graphic links and formats.
QuarkXPress	Collect For Output	Gather document components: document, fonts, and graphics.
InDesign	Preflight Utility	Check for font and graphics usage as well as links and formats.
InDesign	Package Utility	Collect and package document, fonts, and graphics.
PageMaker	Save For Service Provider	Check for font and graphic usage as well as collect these items.
Publisher	Pack & Go	Gather fonts and graphics into a custom package.

These application-based tools provide varying levels of sophistication and reliability. I would rank InDesign to be the king of the hill (see Figure 2.15), with Quark and Microsoft Publisher tied for second, and PageMaker a distant fourth. At a minimum you should use the tools provided by your page layout application to help you perform your preflight chores. However, if you create and therefore preflight a great many documents, you will likely find that using a dedicated preflight utility will be well worth the time it takes to learn and the expense of the purchase.

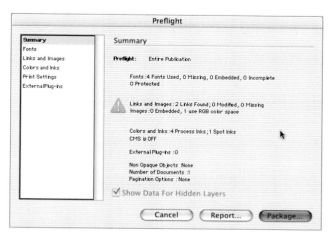

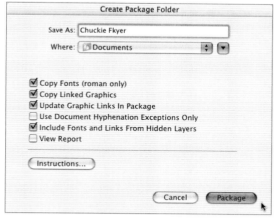

Figure 2.15 InDesign preflight tools: The Preflight utility provides for basic preflighting; the Package tool provides a collection of document components.

Dedicated Preflight Tools

I have discussed at some length using the right tool for the right job. The same rule applies to preflighting. If you want consistent high-quality, fast, and full-featured preflight, get a dedicated preflight tool. The top of the line when it comes to preflighting is Markzware. Markzware has a variety of single-station, network, and even web-based preflight tools and options. Their main tool, called FlightCheck, comes in two flavors—Collect and Classic (Figure 2.16)—and their network/web tool is called MarkzScout. Extensis also offers a competent set of preflight tools called Collect, Preflight Pro, and Print Ready.

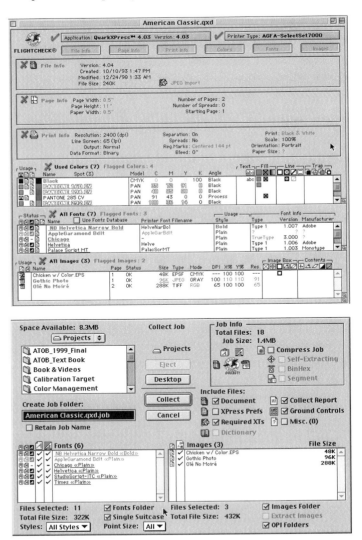

Figure 2.16 Markzware FlightCheck Classic and Collect provide professional preflighting and file organization and collection capabilities.

The various tools provide increasingly sophisticated capabilities, with the top-drawer products such as Markzware's Classic and Extensis Print Ready providing not only professional-quality preflight but interactive tools that provide solutions and aids to fixing problems, as well as tools for batching files and streamlining preflight workflow. These tools will inspect and report on all aspects of your document, including file type info; page geometry and setup; print settings; font usage, types, and problems; color space and assignment evaluation; and complete graphics evaluation. Not only are the preflighting capabilities of a tool such as FlightCheck better than those included in the page layout applications, but the collection components of the tools are far faster and easier and do a more consistent job. I have used FlightCheck for years and wouldn't let my documents leave home without it!

If you send your document and/or PDF files out to a printing company, they will perform their own preflight analysis of your file. So you might as well perform your own as well, saving you the time, expense, and embarrassment of having someone else finding the problems, or worse, risking the possibility that no one will find the problems and your file contains errors.

Note: Part III of this book covers preflighting and editing the PDF files themselves. I want to emphasize here, however, that you will save yourself much time, energy, effort, and money if you perform the preflighting of your document before creating your PDF files.

If you follow the recommendations in this chapter about document construction, font use, and file preparation and preflighting, you will have a complete document, which will be ready for you to convert into a PostScript file and then into a PDF. In the next two chapters we will tackle these next steps.

For a peek at Taz's "Document Construction Guidelines" and "Taz's Top Ten File Prep Tips," visit www.tazseminars.com.

Creating Quality PostScript Files

After you have created graphics, set type, combined all your document components properly in a good page layout program, and performed a competent preflight, you're ready to proceed to the next step in making a PDF document. At this point there are many ways (too many to cover here) to convert your page layout document into a PDF document. Here I will focus on creating a PostScript file and using Distiller, because this is the method that provides you with the most controls, is the most flexible, and will typically yield the highest-quality PDF document.

3

Chapter Contents

PDF creation methods

Selecting a PostScript printer driver

Understanding page and output settings

Choosing job-specific PostScript settings

Assigning PostScript settings

Streamlining the PostScript creation process

The final step: saving your PostScript file

So, the next step in your PDF workflow is making the PostScript file. This file, if properly made, will contain all the document components necessary to create a high-quality PDF. Once I discuss how to properly create a PostScript file, you will learn how to streamline the process through the use of print styles.

PDF Creation Methods

As I mentioned in this chapter's introduction, there are many methods of creating a PDF document. It can be as simple as the one-button method using an application called PDFMaker from within a Microsoft application such as Word, Excel, or Publisher (covered in Chapter 4): this provides a quick and easy method of creating a PDF document but little in the way of options. An increasing number of applications such as QuarkXPress 6, InDesign, and Illustrator have built-in PDF creation functions that often work through Save As or Export functions.

You can utilize PDF-specific printer drivers to create PDF documents from within any number of applications. Some manufacturers even have their own use-specific Distiller-like applications (such as Agfa's prepress-specific Normalizer), which can be used to create PDFs. Each of these methods has its uses, and we will cover several of them in this chapter and in Chapter 4. However, I am focusing on the PostScript file + Distiller method, because this is the standard, classic method of creating a PDF. The PostScript file + Distiller method offers the most control and provides you with the greatest flexibility, allowing you to fine-tune the creation of your PDFs for specific uses. For instance, the PDF/X options provided by Distiller are fast becoming prepress standards adopted by many companies, including such publishing luminaries as Time Magazine. The PostScript file + Distiller method also uses Adobe standard/specific tools, which provide a certain level of consistency and reliability that other methods might lack. The PostScript + Distiller method is really the method by which other PDF creation methods are measured. And if you understand and master this PostScript file + Distiller method, you will have the foundation from which to evaluate and possibly use other current and future PDF creation methods and PDF document standards.

Selecting a PostScript Printer Driver

As I discussed in Chapter 1, the printer driver you select is crucial because that's what creates the actual PostScript code that describes your document and its components. And it is worth emphasizing that you should select the proper PostScript printer driver *before* you construct your document, because the driver feeds information back into the document as well as into the PostScript file.

Note: If you are not sure of the final use of the document prior to constructing it, at the very least assign a generic PostScript printer driver before beginning your document construction, as changing from a non-PostScript to a PostScript printer driver is likely to have the greatest feedback effect on your document layout.

The first part of this chapter illustrates how to install and assign a PostScript printer driver, and the rest of this chapter shows you how it is used to provide various choices in the Page Setup and Print dialog boxes, to create the PDF you want.

Finding and Installing Printer Drivers

Nearly all printers are shipped with printer drivers, although they may not be the most recent or appropriate drivers to use for creating PDF documents. If your printer shipped with a PostScript printer driver, try to use that PostScript printer driver first. Then if that one does not provide you with the PostScript code you want and/or a service bureau manager recommends a different driver, you can always acquire and use another printer driver.

Printer drivers are free and can be freely distributed legally. Many manufacturers typically develop drivers for their output devices. Printer drivers are constantly being updated and improved to keep up with changes in software and hardware capabilities and to correct code problems that may appear after many people start using a particular driver. And while it is true that some "updated" printer drivers create more problems than they solve, it is generally a good idea to stay up-to-date and use the latest drivers available. Don't be shy about asking for printer driver suggestions from those who are knowledgeable about specific output devices, such as service bureau or website managers.

Selecting a PDF Creation Method

The PDF creation method you choose will likely depend upon the application you are starting in and how you intend to use your PDF. If you are working in Microsoft Word and want to create a PDF of your document to send to a coworker, then the built-in one-button method (introduced in Chapter 4) would be appropriate. If, on the other hand, you are working in InDesign or QuarkXPress and want to create a PDF that will print successfully at a commercial print facility, then you will likely want to use the PostScript file + Distiller option detailed here and in Chapter 4. Be sure to read the discussion in this chapter and in Chapter 4 of the use of print styles and watched folders as important workflow enhancement tools.

If you are preparing a PDF file to go to a commercial printing company or other professional output service bureau, ask their recommendation on which PostScript printer driver to download and use. You may be able to get their preferred PostScript printer driver directly from them.

Since PostScript was created and is owned and controlled by Adobe, you can acquire PostScript printer drivers that can be used on most PostScript printers through the Adobe website. You can go to the main Adobe website (www.adobe.com) and navigate through the downloads page, but try going directly to printer drivers here:

http://www.adobe.com/support/downloads/main.html#Printer

From that page, click to see a page of either Macintosh or Windows drivers, and then select the version you would like and proceed with the download. If you do not know which printer driver you want, select the most recent version of the PostScript printer driver available.

If you are working in Windows, you will notice that some versions of printer drivers are Windows version–specific; for example, some drivers work specifically in Windows 95 and 98. Others may be universal. On the Mac, prior to OS X, most printer drivers were *not* OS version–specific. When you migrate to OS X, new printer drivers will be required.

Once you have downloaded your printer driver, follow the installation instructions that accompany the download. As you will see in Chapter 4, "Creating the PDF You Want," you can select an Adobe PDF printer driver at this time to print directly to a PDF, but in either case the setup will be similar.

Once you have a driver installed—from your printer manufacturer, your print company, or Adobe—the next step is to assign it for use. The next three sections tell you how to do that in Mac OS X, older Mac OSs, and Windows.

Note: I recommend that you label the various printer drivers with their version numbers or uses (look back to Figure 1.3 for an example). This will make it easy to identify and select the printer driver you want when you have several to choose from.

Assigning Printer Drivers in Mac OS X

In OS X, printer drivers and printing are controlled through a utility known as the Print Center. Follow these steps to assure that you select the proper PostScript printer driver in OS X:

1. Activate the Print Center: boot drive > Applications > Utilities > Print Center. (I place the Print Center in the OS X dock to make it easy to access and launch.)

A Printer List window (Figure 3.1) should appear (if it doesn't, select Printers > Show Printer List). If the printer you want is in this list, skip to Step 2.

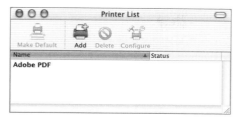

Figure 3.1 OS X Print Center Printer List window

Note: If you have already installed Acrobat 6, you will see a PDF printer listed. A little later I will discuss selecting this PDF driver. Here you will be using a standard PostScript printer driver to create a PostScript file, which you will then convert into a PDF file through Distiller.

1a. If no PostScript printer appears in the list, you need to add one. To do so, click the Add icon at the top of the Printer List window.

1b. An unlabeled "add printer" window appears (Figure 3.2). Click the top pull-down menu in this window, and select the network location of the printer whose driver you would like to use (here, AppleTalk is selected). If you have more than one zone to choose from, you can select it in the second pull-down menu (here, Local AppleTalk Zone).

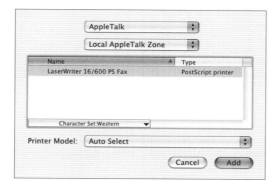

Figure 3.2 Adding a printer to the Print Center Printer List window

1c. Once you have located your printer and its associated driver, it will appear in the interior window (here, LaserWriter 16/600 PS Fax). Select this printer by clicking its name.

1d. Click the Add button in the lower-right corner. This printer and driver will then be added to the Printer List window (Figure 3.3).

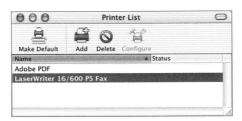

Figure 3.3 The Printer List updated

2. Select the printer and driver of your choice (here, LaserWriter 16/600 PS Fax).

3. To make this the default printer driver used, click the Make Default icon in the upper-left corner.

You have now selected a PostScript printer driver that can be used to create your PostScript file. You can add other printer and driver choices in a similar fashion.

Assigning Printer Drivers on Older Macs

On a pre–OS X Macintosh, you use the Chooser to assign printer drivers. Take the following steps to assure that you select the proper PostScript printer driver:

1. Under the Apple menu, select the Chooser.

2. On the left, click the PostScript printer driver you would like to use. Typically one or more printers will then appear in the Select A PostScript Printer pane on the right side of the Chooser.

3. On the right, click the PostScript printer. (If you are not on a network and a printer does not appear here, don't worry about selecting a printer.)

4. Close the Chooser.

Assigning Printer Drivers in Windows

PostScript printer drivers are standard fare on Macs but not always on Windows computers (particularly those set up for business use). But most Windows XP computers come with at least a generic PostScript printer driver. If you install a Windows printer driver but you don't have a specific PostScript printer to connect your driver to, have the installer install a generic PostScript printer driver. You can name it whatever you like, but I like to name it with the version of the PostScript driver, such as Generic_PostScript_Printer_5.

> **Note:** Again, I think it's useful to name the driver with a logical name that helps you identify the driver.

Once the driver is installed, initial control of the printer driver is though a utility called Printers And Faxes. Here is how to access and assign a printer driver:

1. Click Start > Control Panel > Printers And Faxes. The Printer And Faxes window (Figure 3.4) will appear.

Figure 3.4 Windows Printers And Faxes utility

2. Select View or Add the PostScript printer driver you would like to use. This will make this printer driver accessible to all of your applications.

> **Note:** If you intend to use this printer driver often, you might want to make it the default driver; just select File > Set As Default Printer.

3. You can use other printer controls, such as Add Printer if a printer driver does not appear in this window, here as well.

> **Note:** Windows users should know that there are default Adobe PDF Settings that are editable within the Properties of Printer Drivers. The default Job Option (Settings) can be specified here and how some fonts (particularly TrueType) are converted can be affected. These would only be used, however, if you were to print the PDF document directly from the application, rather than going through the PostScript file and Distiller as we are here.

Once you are in an application, you can and should check to see that the PostScript printer driver that you want to use is selected in the Print window. Here's how to do this:

1. Inside any application, select the Print command from the File menu; a dialog like the one in Figure 3.5 will appear.

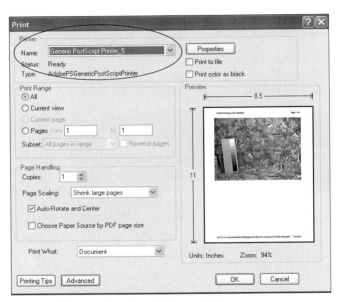

Figure 3.5 Selecting a printer from within an application

2. Click the Name drop-down list.
3. If the printer driver you want is not already selected, choose the driver you would like to use. Here I've selected Generic PostScript Printer_5.

Understanding Page and Output Settings

After you have assigned a PostScript printer driver, it is time to set up the page and print setup dialog boxes in preparation for creating your PostScript file. Depending upon your operating system version, application and version, and the printer driver you have selected, the distribution and organization of the page and print setup fields will vary. However, the key settings to which you need to pay attention are common to all applications, even if they are organized differently. Here I will go through and discuss the most common settings using QuarkXPress on the Macintosh, where most of the important print settings are accessible through one window, the Print dialog. You should be able to easily adapt this discussion to your specific OS, applications, and printer drivers. These output settings will typically be found under the File menu, in either the Page Setup or Print choices.

Later in this chapter, the section "Choosing Job-Specific PostScript Settings" contains tables that suggest how to select these various settings for various types of output.

Document Settings

In a window or tab of layout options like the one in Figure 3.6, you will typically determine which document pages you would like to print and how those pages will be organized. Here are some descriptions of the various layout settings:

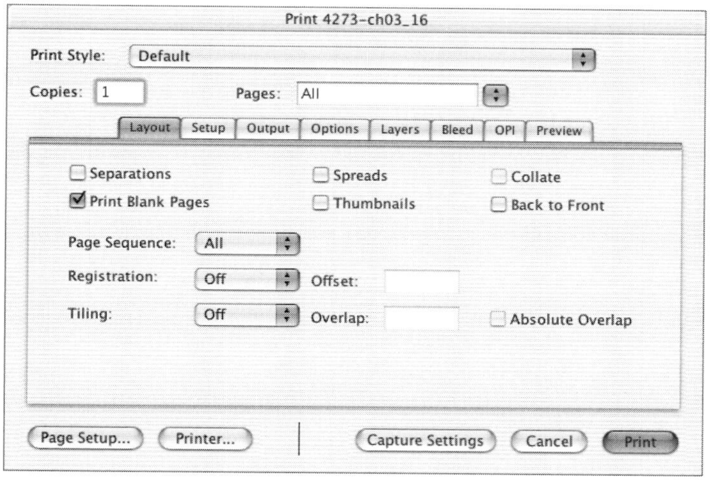

Figure 3.6 Quark's Layout tab

Separations You must define whether you want your color to print all together (unchecked) or as separate pages (checked). You should select the Separations check box when creating color-separated proofs and for final output for commercial color printing. Registration marks (see the third setting following) are often used whenever the Separations box is checked. The default is off/unchecked.

Print Blank Pages If you do not want blank pages in your document to output, leave this box unchecked. For instance, if you intend to output a facing page document, which may have some blank pages, into a single-page PDF file, the blank pages would be unnecessary. The default is usually on/checked.

Page Sequence In this drop-down list you can define whether the Even, Odd, or All pages will print. If you are hand-collating the pages, you may want to just print out either Odd or Even pages. The default is off/unchecked.

Registration Documents to be output with registration marks will have their colors separated and therefore will need to be aligned with the registration marks during the printing process. You would normally turn on this option for high-quality color-separated proofs and certainly for final output for commercial printing. Registration marks are often used when separations are printed. The default is off/unchecked.

Tiling Select Tiling whenever you want to print a document that is larger than the sheet size of your printing device and you do not want to scale down the document to fit on one page. You typically have the choice of selecting Automatic, which will allow you to define the amount of overlap, or Manual, if you intend to tile (and set the overlap) manually. The default is off/unchecked.

Spreads If you wanted to print facing pages side-by-side on the same piece of paper, such as two 8.5″×11″ pages on a single 11″×17″ sheet, select this check box. You should be careful *not* to check this box when sending in files for commercial printing, because each document page should be a separate element for imposition (print orientation) purposes. The default is off/unchecked.

Thumbnails Check this box to print small thumbnail views of document pages on single sheets. This option is useful for viewing the layout of a long document on just a few sheets of paper. The default is off/unchecked.

Collate Choose Collate when printing multiple copies of the same multipage document and you would like those pages to be printed sequentially rather than printing all copies of page 1, then all copies of page 2, etc. Collating during printing can prevent your having to collate all the pages after printing, but collation will significantly increase printing time and should be attempted only with fast printing devices. The default is off/unchecked.

Back To Front Some printers print the pages right side up. When this happens, the first page of the document ends up on the bottom of the final printed stack. In this case, it may be best to print them Back To Front so that they occur in the right order in the print tray, thereby preventing the need for manually resorting the pages. The default is off/unchecked.

Setup Settings

In a window or tab of setup options, like the one in Figure 3.7, you will typically define document print geometry such as height, width, any scaling that might occur, and placement on the output page. This window also contains a menu where you will select a Printer Description file, which may be located in a different place in your setup windows. Here are some tips on how you might use the settings in this window:

Printer Description Assigning the proper Post-Script Printer Description files, commonly known as PPDs, is an important, if unexciting, part of the output process. The PPD contains specific information, such as page geometry and margins, about the output device you will be using. When you have printed directly to a specific device, not going through Distiller and PDF, you historically have chosen the PPD that

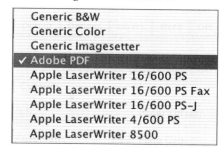

matches the specific printer. But in PDF workflow it is normally best to choose the Distiller or Adobe PDF PPD. The Distiller and Acrobat PPDs are more generic PPDs that provide for flexible formatting and use of the document on output. Some custom PDF workflows may prefer that you use a more device- or process-specific PPD. If you will output your PDF to a commercial printing company or other professional output service bureau, it won't hurt to ask them if they have a specific PPD that they prefer you to use.

Orientation For setting the page orientation you will typically click an icon that indicates either Portrait/Tall or Landscape/Long. I have gotten into the habit of assigning my page orientation immediately after selecting my Distiller/Acrobat PPD. I do this because it is critical to have the orientation of my document—Portrait or Landscape—match my final output. And if I don't check for the match right away, I find that I forget to do it, with unpleasant results (only part of my document page may image).

Figure 3.7 Quark's Setup tab

Note: In some PDF workflows in commercial printing, you may receive a request to always output your pages as Portrait pages, but this will be the exception rather than the rule.

Paper Size In this menu you can select a specific page size such as Letter. If you input a custom value such as 9.5″ in the width (which you would do if wanted to output an 8.5″×11″ document at 100 percent while still keeping registration and/or crop marks or create a custom page size with a border for display on the Web), Custom will automatically appear here. You may also want to create a custom page size for placing your PDF on the Web. Most of these page geometry settings are related to and often affect one another. (Please see the sidebar on paper size, width, and positioning.)

| ISO B1 |
| C5 |
| JIS B4 |
| JIS B3 |
| JIS B2 |
| JIS B1 |
| JIS B0 |
| 92 x 92 |
| ✓ Custom |

Paper Width and Paper Height Here again, as with the Paper Size setting, you will likely have either a standard size (for normal viewing or printing) or a custom size (such as printing with registration marks or adding a border to your document).

Note: One of the nifty characteristics of outputting a document to a PDF file is that you have the ability to change the final page size without affecting the size of the original document. This capability is very handy when you want to add extra page elements such as crop, trim, or fold and/or registration marks and borders, while keeping the original document size at 100 percent.

Paper Size, Paper Width, and Page Positioning

The paper size, width, and height and page positioning are all tied together and are affected by the settings you assigned in the Document tab, as well as the intended use of the PDF. For example, if you have activated the Registration check box, then you will need to assign a larger page size (typically at least an inch) than if you left it unchecked. In addition, page positioning typically differs for desktop and web use (Left Edge) than for commercial print use (Center). And while it is common to scale a document or use Fit To Print on the desktop and in a web environment, this is considered heretical in commercial printing.

To clearly illustrate the difference between a standard print setup and a commercial print setup, I will show two side-by-side setups, one for desktop and web use and one for commercial printing. This will allow you to clearly see the differences between the two. I will include varying setups in the Document tab as well as the current Setup tab and show how both of these settings will affect what you see in the View tab.

Reduce or Enlarge Here you control any scaling that might occur during output. An 85% reduction is commonly assigned to show registration marks and bleeds when printing an 8.5"×11" document on a standard letter-sized laser printer. You would set this field at 100% for commercial proofing and printing (along with increasing the PDF document size to accommodate any crop, trim, fold, or separation marks.) Or this field may contain a reduction percentage to reduce the size of the page for use on the Web. You can choose Fit In Print Area to automatically size the page to fit a specific imaging area on a specific output size of paper.

Page Positioning This setting will determine where your document page will be placed on the PDF page. If your document and PDF pages are the same size, there will be no visual difference between the document and PDF page sizes. However, for creating PDFs destined for commercial printing and for documents on which you want to create a PDF border, select Center Horizontal. For unbordered PDF documents destined for the display on the Web, a Left Edge selection is typical.

Note: At any time you can visually (as well as numerically) check the page positioning by activating the Preview tab.

Paper Offset and Page Gap Unless you are instructed to do so by your printing company, you typically will not need to make any adjustments to the Paper Offset and Page Gap field values, as these are nearly always set at the printing company.

Color Conversion

For the most predictable and dependable results, you should output your document elements in the same color spaces in which they were placed in the document. For instance, if you have RGB images in your page layout document, then your most predictable results will come from choosing RGB for your output colors. However, you will note that you could choose grayscale or CMYK and, if you have color gamut conversion capabilities built into your application, your application will make a conversion to grayscale or CMYK on-the-fly during output. The same applies to converting assigned spot colors to process colors during output. While this option is convenient, you are leaving the gamut conversion choices up to the application, so your results may not be what you like. If you want the most predictable RGB to grayscale or CMYK and spot to process results, you must convert your RGB images to grayscale or CMYK in an application such as Photoshop prior to placing them in the page layout application and then assign process colors in your page layout program.

Output Settings

A window or tab of output options, similar to the one in Figure 3.8, controls which colors will print and some technical details, such as line screen and angles that will be used to print those colors. Following are some insights into controlling color output:

Print Colors When you output a file you will typically be able to tell your page layout application which color space you would like to use for output. Most applications will conveniently allow you to make mode conversions, such as from RGB to grayscale or CMYK, on-the-fly during output. This is very convenient, but there is some uncertainty as well (please see the sidebar on color conversion). At the very least you will want to choose the color space that is consistent with the output device to which you are printing, such as RGB for web use and CMYK (or DeviceN for multitonal images) for commercial printing.

| Black & White |
| Grayscale |
| ✓ Composite CMYK |
| Composite RGB |
| As Is |
| DeviceN |

Note: Many desktop color printers prefer to perform their own RGB to CMYK conversion, so find out which color set (RGB or CMYK) your color device prefers to receive.

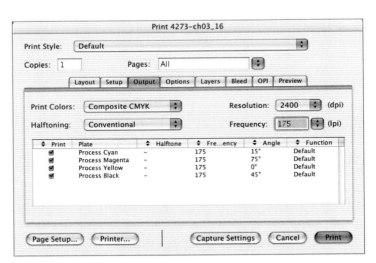

Figure 3.8 Quark's Output settings

Halftoning Printed images are typically reproduced as a pattern of dots, known as halftone dots. There are many different ways to create the halftone dots that are used to re-create your halftone images. The choices you have here will be largely dependent upon the printer driver and the PPD you selected earlier (see the "Setup Settings" section on assigning printer drivers and PPDs earlier in this chapter). Shown here are two typical choices, Conventional and Printer. When in doubt select Printer, which will allow the final output device to control the halftoning (which will likely occur anyway).

Resolution Next you will assign the output resolution of the final output device. Resolution here refers to the output resolution in dots (or spots actually) per inch of the output device for which you are preparing your document to print. Here you see values ranging from 72 to 4000. Web devices require low-resolution values of 72–96 ppi (for viewing on a monitor); desktop printing intermediate values of 300–1200 dpi; and commercial printing the highest of 2400–4000 dpi.

✔ Conventional
Printer

Frequency Frequency refers to the density or resolution of the halftone pattern, commonly called the line screen, which is measured in lpi (lines per inch). Values range from 50–60 lpi for 300 dpi laser printers to 175–200 lpi for commercial printing presses. If you intend to send out your PDF to be printed, you will want to call your service bureau or printing company to find out the line screen at which they intend to print your images.

72
144
300
600
1200
✔ 2400
3600
4000

Resolution, Line Screen or Frequency, and Halftoning

Resolution, frequency, and halftoning refer to the screen frequency (aka line screen or lines per inch or lpi) at which your contone images will be printed. This is a measure of how many halftone dots will be printed in each inch. Resolution and (screen) frequency are linked to each other because the dots (spots) are combined to create the halftoned dots that are used in the printing of contone images. The specific output characteristics—or resolution, frequency, and halftoning—are typically controlled directly at the specific RIP (RIP = Raster Image Processor, the print processor that converts your document components into printed spots and dots) that drives a particular printing device. However, it is a good idea to set values here for the highest-quality device on which you intend to output your final PDF document.

Resolution and screen frequency are directly linked to each other; often when you select the resolution, your application will recommend a typical line screen, such as the 2400/175 lpi pair shown in Figure 3.8.

Options Settings

The Options settings, like those in Figure 3.9, include a number of special output capabilities. Below is an overview of some of the common choices:

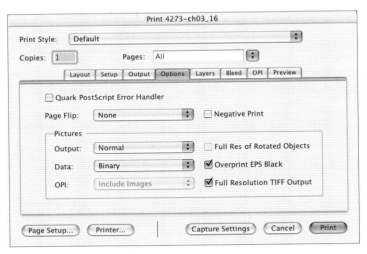

Figure 3.9 Quark's Options settings

Quark PostScript Error Handler If you are experiencing output problems, you can turn on an error handler, which will provide you with feedback as to possible problems that are occurring during output. Various output problems are assigned specific PostScript codes. Some of these messages are more useful than others.

Page Flip If you want pages to be flipped (you can accomplish this for some pages but not others by printing those pages you want flipped separately), then choose one of the flip choices from this drop-down list.

Output (quality) This handy function allows you to control the quality of output. I commonly select Low Resolution, which prints images at screen resolution, when I want to print low-resolution content proofs to my laser printer and image quality is not important (rough com-

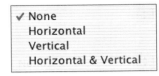

pletely suppresses printout of graphics and boxes). This dramatically reduces processing times both during initial output to a PostScript file (or printing) and during distilling if you want to make a low-resolution PDF content proof.

Data (type) This option determines the format of the PostScript code, with Binary being a smaller simpler "shorthand" version, while ASCII is fully written out PostScript code. Most

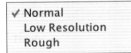

CHAPTER 3: CREATING QUALITY POSTSCRIPT FILES ∎

PostScript printing devices handle Binary well, so try this setting first, as it will result in significantly smaller PostScript and PDF files. If, on the other hand, you ever receive binary file error messages from your network servers or print devices, which is somewhat common in the Windows world, then start using ASCII and these problems will abate. The third choice, Clean 8-bit, is a portable combo file that combines ASCII and Binary. This setting is useful if you intend to send the data file itself rather than print it or convert it to a PDF.

OPI Open Prepress Interface (OPI) is used when you want to place only the low-resolution proxy/placeholder/FPO (for position only) images rather than link them to their high-resolution link files. This is sometimes used when creating large documents such as catalogs, containing hundreds or thousands of images, where the links to the high-resolution files typically occur only during final output. This keeps the page layout document small and easy to manage. This option will not be available unless you are using an OPI image swap system (see instructions on OPI below as well).

Note: Since you will likely be using OPI only in a commercial print setting, it's a good idea to consult your prepress manager for specific instructions on how they would like the OPI settings handled.

Full Res of Rotated Objects This setting ensures that rotated images will be printed if they are sent to non-Postscript printers. It will be inactive unless a non-PostScript printer driver is selected.

Overprint EPS Black This is a commercial printing object trapping setting that, if checked, will force all black inks in imported EPS graphics to be overprinted (typically a good idea).

Full Resolution TIFF Output When you check this option, no subsampling of graphics will occur during output (typically a good idea if you are sure that your graphics resolution is set the way you want it). If you do not check this option, any graphics that exceed a 2xLPI resolution value will be subsampled to 2xLPI.

Layers Controls

Many page layout applications allow you to construct documents with text and graphics elements on various layers. A layers output setting window like that seen in Figure 3.10 will allow you to deselect any layers you do not want to output.

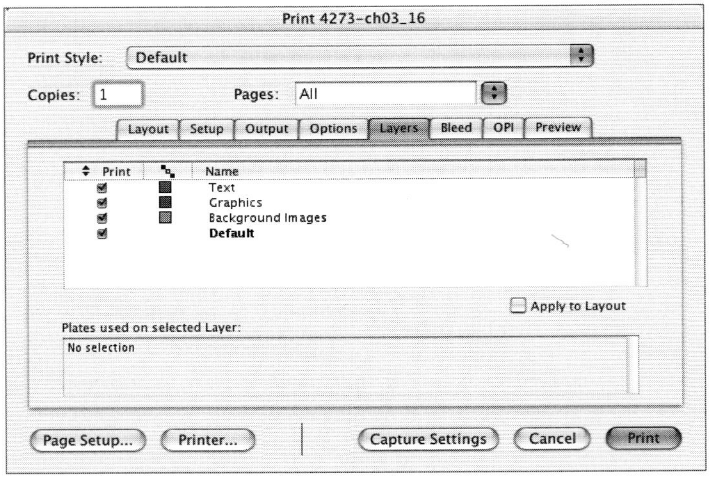

Figure 3.10 Quark's Layers settings

Bleed Controls

Bleed is a setting (see Figure 3.11) used in offset printing that will control how far any page elements that you want to extend ("bleed") past the edge of the printable page (print box) will overlap this print box. You use this option to make sure that slight variations in trimming accuracy do not create unbled images.

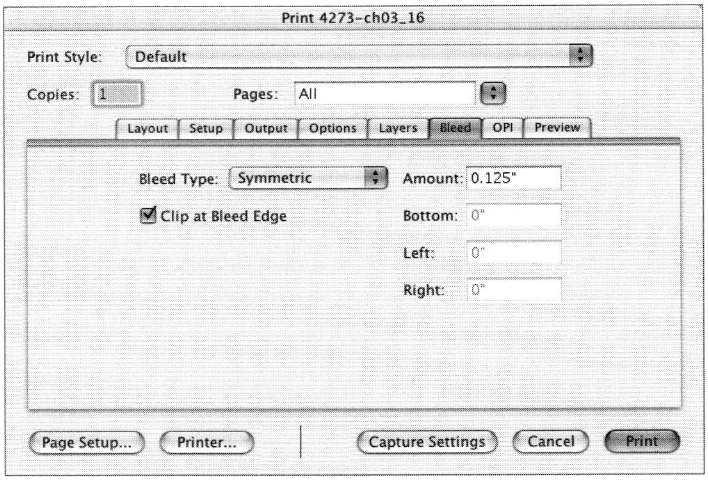

Figure 3.11 Quark's Bleed settings

A common value used here is 1/8″ or 0.125″. You can also assign the bleed to be symmetrical (the most common choice, with an equal bleed on all four sides), asymmetrical (you assign settings for each side of the document), or by page element (where the actual placement of each bleeding page element will control its bleed). Once again, a short consultation with your prepress manager will provide the specifics you need here.

OPI Settings

Sometimes, and this is one of those times, settings that should be all together are separated into different areas. Quark has an additional OPI control tab (Figure 3.12) that, if you are using OPI (see the previous discussion of OPI under the Options tab), you would need to activate and set as follows:

OPI Active Check this box if you will be using OPI.

TIFF Include Images Check this setting if you want to include your TIFF formatted images (typically this will be turned on).

TIFF Low Resolution Check this box if you want to include only the low-resolution versions of your images.

EPS Include Images Check this option if you want to include your placed EPS format images (typically this will be turned on).

> **Note:** Remember that when working in the world of PostScript you will have the best and most predictable output results if you stick to using TIFF and EPS file format graphics.

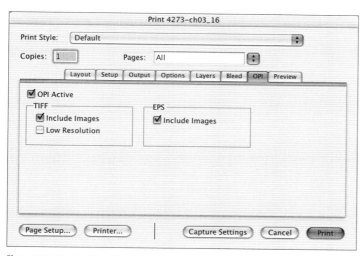

Figure 3.12 Quark's OPI settings

Preview Setting

Nearly all page layout applications provide some sort of preview similar to what the Preview tab shows in Figure 3.13. Using these previews is a good way to make sure that the output looks right. You can see major and minor mistakes at a glance, prior to output, preventing time-consuming and costly mistakes.

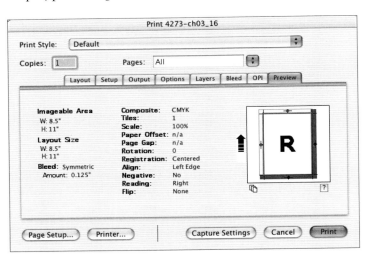

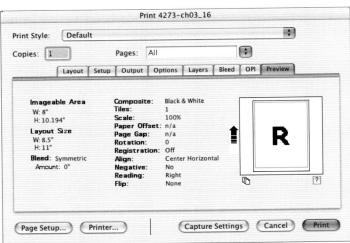

Figure 3.13 Quark's Preview settings: a problem preview (above) and with page size fixed (below)

Checking Page Size and Position

One common problem is the mismatch between input document size and output page size. This problem often occurs when creating PDF files that use custom page size settings, such as documents with registration marks. Registration marks typically add a full inch (with a 6 pt (1/2") offset) to the dimension on a document. It is easy to forget this increase in page size, as we do not think about registration marks on a regular basis. These previews often use colors—red for problems, green for okay—to highlight major problems or signal that all is well. Figure 3.13 shows an obvious problem preview (left) where the output page size (8.5"×11") is too small for the input document size, which should be at least 9.5" wide to accommodate the registration marks. The lack of space is shown as a red margin on the right side.

A subtler potential problem seen here is that the placement of this document is on the left margin, rather than in the center, where it should be for imposition purposes if this document is destined for prepress use (discussed earlier in this chapter). A centered document would show smaller red warning margins on both sides rather than one large red margin on the right side. You might also note that no bleeds have been set, which may or may not be a problem depending upon whether there are any bleed elements in the document. The second preview in Figure 3.13 shows green all around, with the page size fixed, the alignment changed to Center Horizontal, and the bleed set. Take time to review the list of document characteristics as well as the color visuals to make sure your settings are accurate before making your final PostScript file preparations.

> **Note:** Remember that an incorrect setting will not be visible in the PostScript file because it is nothing but code. Mistakes will not be apparent until you create and sometimes even output the PDF. This is why good preflighting and checking your output settings can prevent so many mistakes and save so much time.

Choosing Job-Specific PostScript Settings

The previous section covers the meaning and uses of a wide variety of print settings. This section offers some setting suggestions for specific types of output. Most of this section contains tables with recommended settings as well as a brief discussion of some of the key or unique settings for that particular use.

Print Settings for Commercial Printing

Key concerns for commercial print output with PDF documents are using registration marks; making your PDF document size large enough to accommodate any crop, trim, fold, and registration marks; having everything print at 100 percent; having CMYK ± spot colors rather than RGB colors; and setting bleeds properly. Table 3.1 shows an overview of settings for creating PDF files for commercial printing.

▶ **Table 3.1** Commercial Print Setup

Key Variables	Setting Value	Notes
Separations	Off	You will typically send in composite color files that will be separated at the printing company.
Registration Marks	On	The addition of registration marks creates a large page.
Spreads, Collate, Tiling, Back To Front	Off	None of these should be used.
PPD	Distiller or Acrobat	No difference unless custom request.
Page Size	Custom	Controlled by registration marks.
Page Width	9.5 minimum for 8.5″×11″ document	Controlled by registration marks.
Page Height	Automatic	Controlled by registration marks.
Page Positioning	Center Horizontal	Center preferred for imposition.
Reduce or Enlarge	Always 100%	No scaling, no Fit In Print Area.
Print Colors	Composite CMYK ± spot colors	No RGB colors.
Resolution/lpi	150–175 lpi / 2400, 200 lpi / 3600	Graphics resolution should equal $2 \times$ lpi.
Bleeds	Set bleeds (0.125″ standard).	Check with prepress manager for specific guidance.
OPI	Set OPI settings if using hi-res/low-res swap-outs, and keep TIFFS at full res.	Check with prepress manager for specific guidance.
Preview	PDF page includes all elements.	Note difference in imageable area.

Print Settings for Color-Separated Proofs

If you are using PDFs to create color-separated proofs (which, by the way, is a great idea since it saves so much time and paper and you can proof all pages at 100 percent), you will use the same settings as for commercial printing above, with two exceptions, separations and print colors. Table 3.2 shows the key variables that will differ from a standard commercial print setup.

Note: As we will see in Chapter 13, "Outputting PDF Documents and Their Contents," Acrobat 6 Pro version features a Tool/Separation Preview that enables the user to preview the color separation contained within the PDF, including spot colors.

▶ **Table 3.2** Color Separated Proofs Print Setup

Key Variables	Setting Value	Notes
Separations	On	You will typically print these separations to a laser printer to make sure your colors are properly assigned.
Print Colors	Use Process and Spot or Convert All Colors To Process	Each color will print to its own plate, which you should check carefully for accuracy.

Print Settings for Composite Grayscale Proofs

If you are using PDF to composite grayscale proofs, you will use the same settings as for commercial printing above, with the exceptions that all colors will print in grayscale and at a lower resolution. Table 3.3 shows the key variables that differ from a standard commercial print setup.

▶ **Table 3.3** Composite Grayscale Proof Print Setup

Key Variables	Setting Value	Notes
Resolution/LPI	300 dpi/60 lpi to 600 dpi/85 lpi, 1200 dpi/110 lpi	Graphics resolution should equal $2 \times$ lpi for final, not proof output.
Print Colors	Grayscale	All colors will be converted to grayscale.

Print Settings for Composite Color Proofs

If you are using PDF to composite color proofs, then you will use the same settings as for commercial printing above, with the exceptions that all colors will print in composite CMYK, no spot colors will print (which is why it is important to print color-separated proofs to check color assignments), and they will print at a lower resolution. Table 3.4 shows the key variables that differ from a standard commercial print setup.

Key Variables	Setting Value	Notes
Resolution/LPI	300 dpi/60 lpi to 600 dpi/85 lpi, 1200 dpi/110 lpi	Graphics resolution should equal $2 \times$ lpi for final, not proof output.
Print Colors	Composite CMYK	All colors will be converted to CMYK. Spot colors will likely not be very accurate.

Print Settings for Desktop Color Printing

Desktop printing for final output will always be a composite print, with no separations or spot colors involved. Desktop printing is also typically performed at a lower resolution than commercial printing but at a higher resolution than for the Web. Spot colors are not printed but are converted to process colors. Note that printers that offer an expanded process gamut with more than the four standard CMYK process inks will still print colors as process colors, but they will often be a better simulation of the original spot colors. Table 3.5 shows the key settings involved in a typical desktop color print setup.

► **Table 3.5** Desktop Color Print Setup

Key Variables	Setting Value	Notes
Separations	Off	You will typically send in composite color files that will be separated at the printing company.
Registration Marks	Off	No registration marks are necessary with composite printing.
Spreads, Collate, Tiling, Back To Front	On or Off depending upon your needs	Select the capability you need given the document, print size, number of copies, and printing path.
PPD	Distiller or Acrobat	No difference unless a custom request.
Page Size	Often Letter or Tabloid or Custom	Controlled by document size and media dimensions.
Page Width	Often Letter or Tabloid or Custom	Controlled by document size and media dimensions.
Page Height	Often Letter or Tabloid or Custom	Controlled by document size and media dimensions.
Page Positioning	Usually Left Edge, sometimes Center Horizontal	Most desktop print devices measure from the left edge.

Key Variables	Setting Value	Notes
Reduce or Enlarge	Various	Scaling and Fit In Print Area often used.
Print Colors	Usually Composite CMYK; some devices prefer to receive RGB images to convert.	Higher-quality devices usually recommend using CMYK.
Resolution/LPI	300 dpi/60 lpi to 600 dpi/85 lpi, 1200 dpi/110 lpi	Graphics resolution should equal $2 \times$ lpi for final, not proof output.
Bleeds	Set Bleeds (0.25″ standard)	Make sure any bleeding elements are at least 1/4″ past the edge of the print box.
OPI	Not used	Usually not an issue.
Preview	PDF page includes all elements.	Note difference in imageable area.

Print Setting for Web and E-books

Output settings for the Web and for e-books and onscreen viewing are similar in many ways to the desktop color printing settings but vary mostly with the choice of print colors and resolutions and some options that are not necessary, such as collating, tiling, and OPI. Table 3.6 shows some typical print setups for the Web and e-books.

► **Table 3.6** Web and E-book Print Setup

Key Variables	Setting Value	Notes
Separations	Off	You will typically send in composite color files that will be separated at the printing company.
Registration Marks	Off	No registration marks necessary with composite printing.
Spreads, Collate, Tiling, Back To Front	Off	Not necessary.
PPD	Distiller or Acrobat	No difference unless custom request.
Page Size	Typically + document size, but whatever you like	Controlled by document size and your display requirements.
Page Width	Typically + document size, but whatever you like	Controlled by document size and your display requirements.
Page Height	Typically + document size, but whatever you like	Controlled by document size and your display requirements.

Key Variables	Setting Value	Notes
Page Positioning	Usually Center Horizontal	Not of critical importance in most cases.
Reduce or Enlarge	Various	Scaling down is commonly used to fit in websites, but be careful with the type appearing too small.
Print colors	RGB (unless you are printing colors separations for display purposes)	Nearly all display devices prefer the RGB color space.
Resolution/LPI	No LPI involved. 72 ppi is original standard; 96 ppi is current standard.	Only low resolution is required for visual display, but remember if these files are ever printed, image quality may suffer.
Bleeds	Set bleeds (0.25″ standard)	Make sure any bleeding elements are at least 1/4″ past the edge of the print box.
OPI	Not used	Usually not an issue.
Preview	PDF page includes all elements.	Note difference in imageable area.

Assigning PostScript Settings

Once you have finished configuring the print settings, there is one final task to make sure that your PostScript files, and therefore your PDFs, contain all the required elements and are properly configured. This involves configuring the PostScript file settings. Sometimes these settings are obvious and sometimes they are buried in some submenu or dialog box. Here I will go through my process of locating and configuring my PostScript settings. You will go through a similar but somewhat different specific process depending upon the OS, application, and printer driver you are using. Windows users, please see the following Note.

Note: In the Windows OS, the main difference is that the Printer Driver is on the Print dialog window instead of in the Setup tab and the user has to click Properties to access specific setup and PDF conversion settings.

Creating the PostScript File

Now to complete the final steps for creating a PostScript file (remember that your windows may look somewhat different, but the process will be similar):

1. From the Print or Print Preview dialog (Figure 3.14), click the Printer button to bring up a window like the one shown in Figure 3.15.

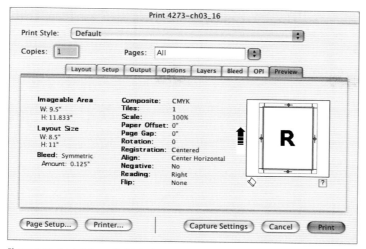

Figure 3.14 Print dialog with Printer button

Print

Printer: Adobe PDF

Presets: Standard

Output Options

☑ Save as File   Format PostScript

(?)   (Preview)   (Save As PDF...)   (Cancel)   (Save...)

Figure 3.15 Print to PostScript file setup

2.   Configure this window as follows:

2a.   Select the Adobe PDF or other PostScript printer.

2b.   Select Output Options.

2c.   Click the Save As File option.

2d.   Select Format: PostScript.

2e.   Click the Save button.

Note: In some Print dialog boxes this will be called Print To Disk or Print To File or Save To Disk. (It is *not* my fault that no one can agree on these names.) All of these choices will direct the PostScript code to write to a file rather than be sent to a printer. And remember that your windows and dialog boxes will likely be a bit different depending upon your OS and selected driver, but dig around and you'll find all these settings.

3.   In some cases you will also have the opportunity to control the specifics of the PostScript file settings as well, which you should do now before moving on to Step 4. See the details on controlling the PostScript file in the next section, "Configuring the PostScript Settings." After you have configured the PostScript settings, continue with Step 4.

4.   Locate where you would like to have the PostScript file saved, and click the Save button (Figure 3.16).

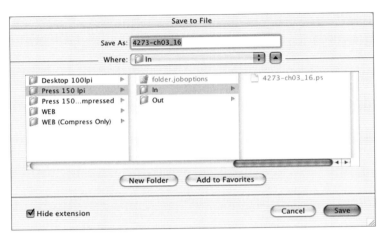

Figure 3.16 PostScript file location

 Note: Here I show printing the PostScript file to a Distiller watched folder (something I usually do), which will automatically take care of the conversion to PDF process. I describe watched folders in Chapter 4.

5.   You may be presented with yet another Print window, similar to the one seen back in Figure 3.14; if so, simply click the Save button again.

Your file will be printed to the location you designated in Step 3 and will be labeled with either a .ps (Macintosh) or .prn (Windows) extension.

Configuring the PostScript Settings

Once you have designated that you want to create a PostScript file (Step 2 above) you may need to configure the PostScript (or Save File) settings. There are typically four PostScript settings to which you need to pay close attention:

Format Choose the best file format for your use: You will often find a variety of settings here, including PostScript, EPS, and even PDF. You will typically choose Post-Script because you intend to create your PDF file through Distiller.

PostScript Level There are currently three levels of PostScript, from 1 through 3, each having progressively more capabilities. The key here is to choose the level of PostScript for the final output device you will be using. The higher levels of PostScript are most important for high-quality PostScript environments such as commercial printing companies that try to maximize the output of levels of gray and use color management. For most desktop equipment and the Web, level 1 is typically sufficient. Avoid selecting a level of PostScript greater than the level of the device where the PDF will be output, because incompatible PostScript levels may result in the file not printing. To reap maximum benefit from the highest levels of PostScript that your output devices can process, check the PostScript level of your RIP. If you are unsure of how your file will be used, or if you intend to create a general-purpose PDF, then choose a level that will be compatible with all level devices, as shown in Figure 3.17.

Data Format There are typically two choices here—Binary and ASCII. This setting determines the format of the PostScript code, with Binary being a smaller, simpler "shorthand" version, while ASCII is fully written out PostScript code. Most PostScript printing devices handle Binary well, so try this first, because it will result in significantly smaller PostScript and PDF files. If, on the other hand, you ever receive binary file error messages from your network servers or print devices, which is somewhat common in the Windows world, then start using ASCII and these problems will abate.

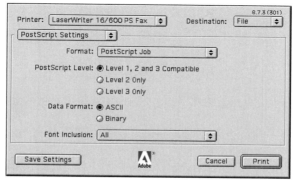

Figure 3.17 Choose a PostScript level no higher than what your devices can use, and select either a Binary or ASCII data format.

Font Inclusion Make sure the fonts are included. This may be the most important menu you ever overlook, so don't overlook it! As I said in Chapter 2, "Creating Pre-PDF Documents," fonts have always been the number one bugaboo, particularly when you want to take them cross-platform. So here is some more bad news: Even if you select and handle your fonts correctly throughout your document construction and pre-flight process, you can get tripped up here. "How?" you ask. Believe it or not—and again, this is *not my fault*—the default setting in many printer drivers is for fonts to *not* be included when all your document data is transferred to your PostScript file. The result of this unfortunate default would be that your PDF file would end up with substituted fonts. So, be sure to select Font Inclusion: All.

Streamlining the PostScript Creation Process

Now that you see how complex the whole PostScript creation process is, it's a wonder that anyone ever gets it right! But have heart. I have a nifty solution for you that will simplify your PostScript life considerably.

Using Print Styles

The entire process covered under "Understanding Page and Output Settings," with multiple tabs with dozens of choices, can be simplified to just one menu choice—yes, that's right, one menu choice. The magic one-button solution is *print styles*. All advanced page layout applications, including QuarkXPress, InDesign, FrameMaker, and PageMaker, offer print styles. The details differ from application to application, but in general here's how the process works:

1. Create a print style for every type of document you may want to print. (Figure 3.18). These styles will then show up in your Print windows, usually under a Print Styles menu.

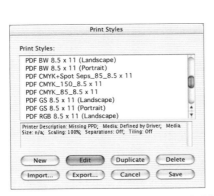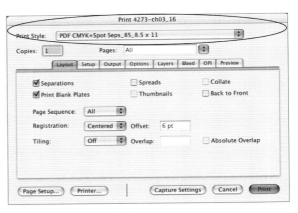

Figure 3.18 Create Print Styles (left) and then look for them in your Print window (right)

2. When you activate the Print dialog, choose the print style that covers the kind of document and output you want (Figure 3.19). Presto, you are finished—the entire Print dialog box and all its included tabs are preconfigured.

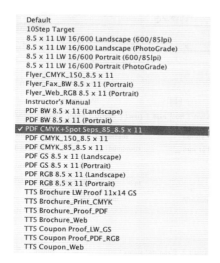

Default
10Step Target
8.5 x 11 LW 16/600 Landscape (600/85lpi)
8.5 x 11 LW 16/600 Landscape (PhotoGrade)
8.5 x 11 LW 16/600 Portrait (600/85lpi)
8.5 x 11 LW 16/600 Portrait (PhotoGrade)
Flyer_CMYK_150_8.5 x 11
Flyer_Fax_BW 8.5 x 11 (Portrait)
Flyer_Web_RGB 8.5 x 11 (Portrait)
Instructor's Manual
PDF BW 8.5 x 11 (Landscape)
PDF BW 8.5 x 11 (Portrait)
✓ PDF CMYK+Spot Seps_85_8.5 x 11
PDF CMYK_150_8.5 x 11
PDF CMYK_85_8.5 x 11
PDF GS 8.5 x 11 (Landscape)
PDF GS 8.5 x 11 (Portrait)
PDF RGB 8.5 x 11 (Landscape)
PDF RGB 8.5 x 11 (Portrait)
TTS Brochure LW Proof 11x14 GS
TTS Brochure_Print_CMYK
TTS Brochure_Proof_PDF
TTS Brochure_Web
TTS Coupon Proof_LW_GS
TTS Coupon Proof_PDF_RGB
TTS Coupon_Web

Figure 3.19 Select a print style in the Print dialog, and all your options configure themselves.

> **Note:** Print styles are very versatile. They can be copied, edited, duplicated, and transferred. I create over 2000 PDF documents every year, with over 95 percent being right the first time, and print styles are one of the three main reasons why. The other two reasons are saving PostScript settings (covered in the following section) and using watched folders (covered in the next chapter).

Saving PostScript and Other Settings

The other timesaving feat you can employ to reduce the assignment of PostScript files and other settings that you reuse is to capture them. Many Print dialog boxes and windows have a Save Settings or Capture Settings button, which can be used to secure a set of settings for reuse.

Using the Save Settings or Capture Settings feature will save the current PostScript setup, and it will remain saved and will be used every time you create a PostScript file until you either change the settings or switch your PostScript printer driver. Now, whenever you print a PostScript file, you can bypass the PostScript Settings window, saving lots of time.

The combined use of print styles and saving/capturing settings will save you considerable time and frustration.

The Final Step: Saving Your PostScript File

The final step in the whole process is creating a PostScript file:

1. When you changed the Destination in the unnamed printer window from Printer to File, the Print button probably changed from Print to Save. Click that button, and a Save or Save File window will appear (Figure 3.20).

2. Locate the folder where you would like to save your PostScript file.

3. Name your PostScript file. It should have either a .ps (Macintosh) or .prn (Windows) filename extension.

4. Click the Save button once again to create the PostScript file.

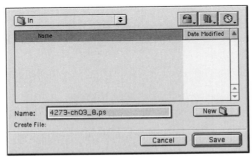

Figure 3.20 Browse to where you want your PostScript file saved.

In the next chapter you will see how to control the conversion of this PostScript file into a PDF using Distiller to suit any final output. In addition, we will explore a few alternative methods of creating PDF files.

Creating the PDF You Want

After you have combined your text and graphics in a page layout document and done a preflight on it, you are ready to create a PDF document. There are numerous ways to make a PDF. If you have created a PostScript file, you can go directly through Distiller. There are also methods for creating a PDF directly through other applications.

Chapter Contents

Creating PDFs directly through Distiller

Fine-tuning Distiller settings for your PDF purpose

Managing Distiller settings files

Setting PDF document security through Distiller

Controlling Distiller PDF file location and logging

Improving Distiller's efficiency with watched folders

Creating PDFs from within non-Acrobat applications

Creating PDFs Directly through Distiller

If you have created a PostScript file, you will likely proceed directly through Distiller to create a PDF document. Distiller provides a series of preset or default settings from which to choose, or you can create your own customized Distiller settings. For most PDF creations, selecting one of the default settings will be all you need to do, so let's cover those first (⌒ Bonus chapter "Complete Distiller Settings" on the CD).

 Note: Old hands at Acrobat and Distiller will note that with the release of Acrobat 6, Adobe has changed the name of Distiller Job Options to Distiller Settings.

Distiller settings control what will happen to your PostScript document information when it is converted into a PDF file. When selecting a Distiller setting, you are controlling the quality and characteristics of your final PDF document by adjusting document characteristics such as image resolution and compression and whether or not font files are included.

When creating a PDF, there is always a trade-off between the size of the PDF and its quality. Smaller PDF files typically have lower resolution and more highly compressed images. The Web tends to be a more forgiving environment for viewing PDFs, whereas as printing PDFs requires higher-quality images.

Distiller is installed with six basic settings designed to create PDF documents intended for various uses, such as commercial printing or on the World Wide Web. You can modify these six basic settings to suit your specific needs. You may also create your own Distiller settings from scratch or even load settings that someone else has created. First I will show you how to access Distiller's Default Settings; then I will discuss the details of customizing a Distiller setting. Once selected, a Distiller setting can be saved and moved around for others to use.

Choosing a Distiller Default Setting

When creating a PDF file in Distiller, selecting one of the default settings, which arrive preset in Distiller, may be all you will ever need to do. The key to effectively using Distiller Default Settings is to select the one that most closely matches how you intend to use your PDF document.

To create a PDF file for a specific use using Distiller Default Settings, perform the following simple process:

1. Launch Distiller 6. A window labeled Acrobat Distiller will appear (Figure 4.1).

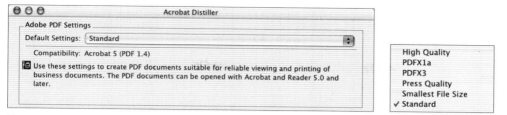

Figure 4.1 The Acrobat Distiller dialog with the Default Settings menu choices

2. Near the top of the window is a pull-down menu labeled Default Settings; click this menu. A list of six settings will appear—High Quality, PDFX1a, PDF/X3, Press Quality, Smallest File Size, and Standard (the initial default).

3. Select the Default Setting that most closely matches your PDF document's use. The following list is an overview of PDF uses and settings. At the end of this section, Table 4.1 provides an overview of the major characteristic differences between the various Distiller Default Settings. Later in this chapter I will show how you can fine-tune these settings for your particular PDF purposes.

Medium quality, for regular business viewing and printing: Standard This is the initial Default Setting that appears when Distiller is launched. This Standard setting is intended for creating medium-quality documents for typical office or business uses, including for viewing on a monitor as well as printing on a desktop inkjet or laser printer.

Web and/or screen viewing only: Smallest File Size Choose this Default Setting for PDFs that will be used primarily for viewing and distribution over the Web and for when you want to make the smallest possible PDF file. However, be aware that choosing this setting will result in some pretty severe image and typography compromises (⌖ "Creating Small PDFs for the Web with Font Integrity Preserved" later in this chapter, especially the sidebar "Font Substitution").

High-quality desktop printing: High Quality Choose this setting if you are creating a PDF to print on a high-quality printer such as a photo-quality printer or high-resolution proofing or final print device. If you have already converted your graphic images to CMYK and are printing to a CMYK printing device, in other than a commercial printing environment, this would be a good choice for you because the colors are untouched by the distilling process. Likewise, if you are printing to a high-quality printing device that prefers high-quality RGB color space files, and you have already applied the RGB color space of your choice, this High Quality setting will be a good choice. Image quality and typesetting integrity are maximized over reducing the file size.

Commercial printing not requiring PDF/X compliance: Press Quality This Distiller setting is intended to be used when you are creating a PDF document to be printed on a commercial printing press, and you are not using one of the PDF/X standards or have not received any specific Custom Distilling setting instructions from the printing company (☞ "Fine-Tuning Distiller Settings for Your PDF Purpose" later in this chapter).

Commercial printing requiring PDF/X compliance: PDF/X1a or PDF/X3 Select either PDFX1a or PDFX3 if you intend to create a PDF document to be printed in a commercial printing process that requires PDF/X-compliant files. PDF/X-1a compliance includes files that contain CMYK and spot colors only, while PDF/X-3 also accepts alternative device-independent color spaces such as Lab. As with the Press setting, image quality is maximized over file size and the original character of the document is well maintained.

4. Once you have selected your Default Setting, it is time to find and open a PostScript file that you have created for the purpose of distilling (see Chapter 3, "Creating Quality PostScript Files"). Select File > Open, and a file navigation dialog box will appear to allow you to locate and open your PostScript file. Navigate to and open the PostScript file you would like to distill (Figure 4.2).

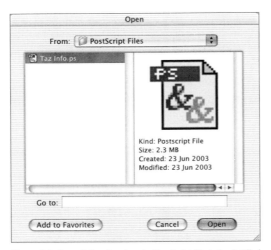

Figure 4.2 Open dialog showing the PostScript file to be distilled

5. Once you have opened your selected PostScript file, Distiller will, by default, automatically start to process (distill) this file into a PDF document. You can follow the progress of the distilling process by viewing the Acrobat Distiller main window (Figure 4.3).

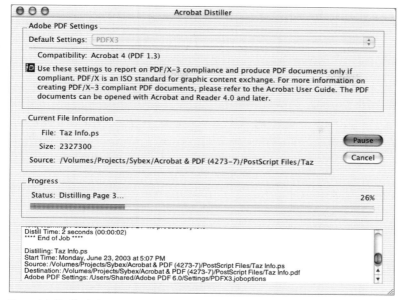

Figure 4.3 Distiller dialog showing the progress bar

Note: You can also view information about the distilling process, including file locations, final results, and any error messages, in the unlabeled pane at the bottom of this same Acrobat Distiller window.

6. The new PDF file will, again by default, be placed in the same folder as the original PostScript file (Figure 4.4). Open your new PDF document to see the results of the distilling process.

Figure 4.4 Original PostScript file and finished PDF

Later in this chapter, when I cover configuring Distiller Preferences and using watched folders, I will discuss how and why to direct Distiller to locate the final PDF documents in places other than the folder containing the original PostScript file.

PDF/X Standard

PDF/X (which stands for Portable Document Format Exchange) is an international printing industry standard set of specifications, created by the ISO, for preparing and testing PDF files for commercial printing. There are several PDF/X file specifications, but the two most commonly used PDF/X standards, PDF/X-1a and PDF/X-3, are supported in Acrobat 6. PDF/X standards have been created and adopted to help streamline the creation and use of PDF files in commercial printing workflows. Later in this book I will discuss how to use Acrobat 6 to check for PDF/X compliance in PDF documents.

Table 4.1 compares the major characteristic differences between the six Distiller Default Settings.

Fine-Tuning Distiller Settings for Your PDF Purpose

In some circumstances the Distiller Default Settings give you *almost* what you want. Distiller Default Settings are completely customizable through editing some 72 Distiller setting values. Here we will discuss two of the more common fine-tuning adjustments you may want to make to your Distiller settings. Learning how to adjust these two Distiller settings will provide you with a good introduction into customizing Distiller settings.

▶ **Table 4.1** Distiller Default Settings Key Characteristics

Feature	Standard	Smallest File Size	High Quality	Press Quality	PDFX1a	PDFX3
Version Compatibility	5.0/6.0	5.0/6.0	5.0/6.0	5.0/6.0	4.0	4.0
Image Resolution	150ppi	100ppi	300ppi	300ppi	300ppi	300ppi
Image Quality	Medium	Low	Maximum	Maximum	Maximum	Maximum
Font Handling	Embedded	Not Embedded	Embedded	Embedded	Embedded or Job cancelled	Embedded or Job cancelled
Color Handling	Convert All to sRGB	Convert All to sRGB	Leave Alone	Leave Alone	Leave Alone CMYK, SPOT	Leave Alone CMYK, SPOT + Lab
Other key features			Auto Rotate Page ON	Auto Rotate Page OFF	Auto Rotate Page OFF	Auto Rotate Page OFF

Creating Small PDFs for the Web with Font Integrity Preserved

The Smallest File Size Distiller Default Setting produces a small PDF that will travel nicely across the Web. The only disadvantage of this choice is that the font files used to create the original document are not included in the PDF, so your typesetting integrity may not be preserved. This is because Acrobat Multiple Master font files may be used to create substitute font characters whenever your PDF is opened. This is particularly true if you use nonstandard fonts. So if you want to create a PDF that is small but will always use your font files, here is how to create a Distiller setting to do just that:

1. Launch Distiller 6.

2. Open the Default Settings menu (shown back in Figure 4.1) and choose Smallest File Size. This will define the basic set of Distiller values, which we will now fine-tune.

3. Click the Settings menu and choose Edit Adobe PDF Settings (or use the keyboard shortcut ⌘/Ctrl+E). The Adobe PDF Settings: Smallest File Size dialog will appear.

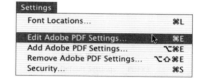

4. Click the Fonts tab (Figure 4.5).

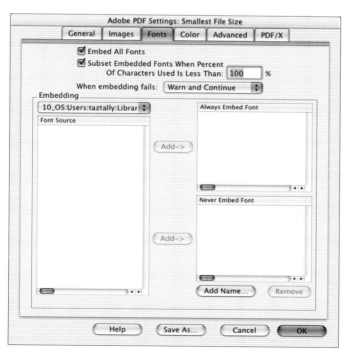

Figure 4.5 Opening the Distiller Smallest File Size setting Fonts tab

5. The Embed All Fonts check box near the top of the window is, by default, unchecked. Check this box to ensure that Distiller will embed all the font files that were used in the creation of this document, which will, in turn, prevent any font file substitution later on.

6. Click the Save As button at the bottom of the Fonts tab. A Save As dialog will appear with the Distiller Settings folder automatically located (Figure 4.6).

Figure 4.6 Distiller Save As Settings dialog

7. Type in a name for the new/edited setting you have just created. Create a logical name that will clearly inform you later what the setting contains. Here I have labeled the setting "Smallest File Size with Fonts."

8. Click Save. This will save your new setting in the Distiller Settings folder, thereby making it available as a choice in the Distiller Default Settings menu.

9. Now return to the main Distiller window. Open the Distiller Default Settings menu. It will contain your newly created Distiller setting (Figure 4.7).

Figure 4.7 Updated Distiller Settings menu

Font Substitution

Documents in which standard fonts such as Arial or Helvetica and/or Times or Times New Roman are used in the original document will likely look similar in the font-substituted PDF. This is because the Acrobat Multiple Master fonts (see Chapter 2, "Document Construction and Preflighting," for more information on these), which are used for PDF substitution, simulate these font typefaces fairly well. If you use typefaces that are significantly different from the Arial, Helvetica, Times, Times New Roman pair, the final PDF font characters will likely look quite different from the originals.

Creating PDFs that Prevent Alteration of the Graphics

The Press Quality, High Quality, and the two PDFX Distiller Default Settings all are set up to produce high-quality PDFs. But even these higher-quality settings are set up to downsample the resolution of images that are greater than 450 ppi, and they will apply minimal compression to your images. There may be times when you want to make sure that no alteration of your images occurs during distilling. This might be for use in prepress or when you have already sampled and compressed your images with specific characteristics to control their appearance on the Web. If you want to make sure that Distiller does not alter the resolution or apply any compression to your images, here's how to do it:

1. Launch Distiller 6.

2. Click the Default Settings menu (shown back in Figure 4.1) and choose one of the higher-quality settings (Press Quality, High Quality, or one of the two PDFX menu choices). We will start with the Press Quality Default Setting here. This will define the basic set of Distiller values that we will now fine-tune.

3. Click the Settings menu and choose Edit Adobe PDF Settings (or use the keyboard shortcut ⌘/Ctrl+E). The Adobe PDF Settings: Press Quality window will appear.

4. Click the Images tab (Figure 4.8). You will notice the following default resolution and compression settings:

Image Type	Resolution Downsampling	Compression
Color images	Downsample to 300 if above 450	JPEG (Auto) Maximum Quality
Grayscale images	Downsample to 300 if above 450	JPEG (Auto) Maximum Quality
Monochrome images	Downsample to 1200 if above 1800	CCITT

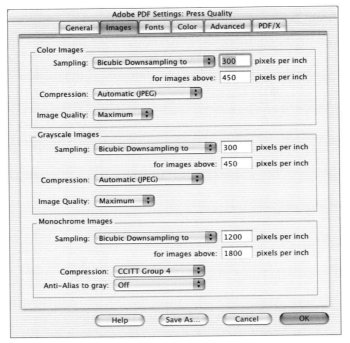

Figure 4.8 The original Distiller Press Quality setting Images tab

5. To disable any sampling or compression of any of the images, select Off from each of the six Sampling and Compression menus, as shown in Figure 4.9. After completing Step 5, all of the Sampling and Compression menus should register Off. This will prevent Distiller from altering the resolution of, or applying any compression to, your images.

Disabling Image Sampling and Compression

Disabling image sampling and compression will preserve the original quality of your graphics, but it will also substantially increase the size of your final PDF files. Be extra careful when creating your graphics and preflighting your documents to make sure that you have controlled the size of your images by assigning just enough resolution to your images to output at their best quality but not much more. Few output devices will require more than 300 ppi for contone images or 1200 ppi for detailed line art. And remember that you should scale your images to 100 percent for final placement in your page layout documents prior to making your PDFs, for best results and fastest RIPping.

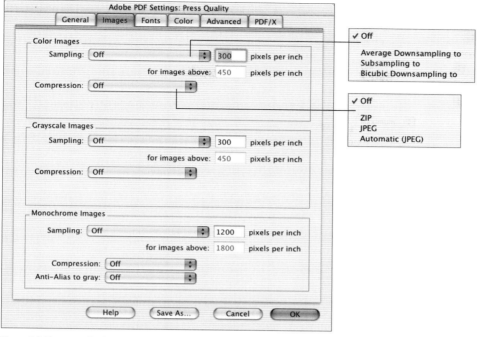

Figure 4.9 The customized Press Quality setting Images tab

6. Click Save As; a dialog will appear with the Distiller Settings folder automatically located.

7. Type in a name for the new/edited setting you have just created. Create a logical name that will clearly inform you later what the setting contains. Here I have labeled the setting "Press Quality NO Image Change."

8. Click Save. This will save your new setting in the Distiller Settings folder, thereby making it available as a choice in the Distiller Default Settings menu.

9. Now return to the main Distiller window. Open the Distiller Default Settings menu. It will contain your newly created Distiller setting (Figure 4.10).

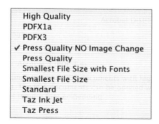

Figure 4.10 Updated Distiller Default Settings menu

Note: When I scale my computer monitor/screen grabs/shots, I allow the resolution to vary without constraint so that no interpolation-based degradation of my screen shots occurs. Turning off sampling in Distiller, as we have done here, will maintain that resolution, which will in turn guarantee the best-quality screen shots.

We have covered two of the most common customized settings in Distiller, font embedding and control of resolution and compression of included images. As I mentioned, there are over 70 customizable Distiller settings in the six Distiller Default Setting tabs.

PDF for Special Uses

PDFs can be created for just about any special use. If you are preparing PDFs for a specific or specialized use, the key to success is to ask yourself what the main characteristics of that use are and then be sure to create your PDFs to cater to those needs. Below are a few specialized PDFs with discussion of key PDF creation considerations.

PDFs for Archiving

Paper documents can be converted into PDFs for archiving and access through Acrobat with the use of a special paper capture application known as Adobe Capture. Additionally, a companion series of four plug-in utilities, known as Capture Agent Pack, provides batch control compression, forms, tagging, and security for long and/or multiple documents. Adobe Capture and its companion Capture Agent Pack Utilities can be purchased through the Adobe website: www.adobe.com/PDF.

PDFs for Engineering

Some engineering documents, with all of their multiple layers of drawings, can be saved from some native applications, such as AutoCAD and Visio, with their layers intact. These layers can be opened and viewed in Acrobat. Check your drawing application for instructions on saving your drawing documents as PDF with the layer included. (See the section "Using Layers in Acrobat" in Chapter 7 for more information on working with these layers in Acrobat. One of the key considerations when saving CAD-type drawing documents is preserving the variable and thin line weights that are often created in CAD-type drawings. These variable and thin-weight lines are often altered and/or lost when converting to PostScript-based file formats such as EPS, so special care should be taken to make sure these line characteristics are preserved. Going directly to PDF rather than through an intermediate stop in EPS format often does the trick. Test and check your PDFs to be sure CAD lines are not altered.

PDFs for Multimedia and Online PDFs

Multimedia-oriented PDFs usually involve the linking of several PDFs. Publishing or distributing these PDFs with cross-document indexes will make these PDFs more accessible and useful. In addition, if your multimedia PDFs are to be distributed online, you will want to make sure that you consider the total size of your multiple files, because sound and video clips, as well as the combined size of the multiple-host PDFs, can grow quickly. Compression and subsampling of sound and video clips, as well as the reduction of the size of your PDF documents, is definitely in order. (See the section "Creating a Searchable Index" in Chapter 7 for information on index creation and "Reducing and Simplifying PDFs" in Chapter 12 for more on reducing the size of PDF documents.)

Managing Distiller Settings Files

Once assigned (default) or created (custom), Distiller settings can be saved, added, deleted, or shared. This functionality makes it much easier to use and reuse Distiller settings.

For all of these actions, you need to know where Distiller stores its settings. They're found in the program's Settings folder, located as follows:

Windows:

    C:/Program Files/Adobe/Acrobat 6.0/Distiller/Settings

Mac OSX:

    ~/Users/Shared/Adobe PDF 6.0/Settings

Saving Distiller Settings

To save a Distiller setting, follow these steps:

1. Choose Settings > Edit Adobe PDF Settings (or use the keyboard shortcut ⌘/Ctrl+E).

2. Click the Save As button.

3. Name the Setting; here, I've used "Taz Press."

4. Locate the Distiller Settings folder (Figure 4.11) and place your new Distiller setting there. You will see the other settings already there, and this will make your setting available for use in Distiller.

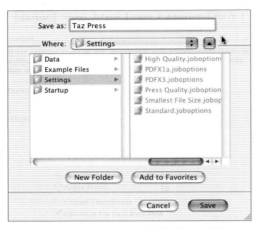

Figure 4.11 Saving a setting to the Distiller *Settings* folder

Adding Distiller Settings

You may have created a Distiller setting in a location Distiller doesn't automatically recognize, using Save As (as described in the previous section) or by receiving a file from someone else. To add such a Distiller setting to the Default Settings menu, do *one* of the following:

- Choose Settings > Add Adobe PDF Settings (Ctrl+Alt+E/⌘+Option+E). Then navigate to where a Distiller settings file has been saved on your disk (Figure 4.12), select it, and click Open.

- Or, as an alternative, you can copy the desired Distiller settings file directly into the Distiller Settings folder.

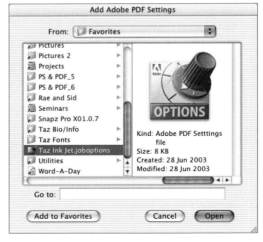

Figure 4.12 Opening a Distiller setting to add it

Either of these methods will add the new setting to those already there (Figure 4.13), and this will make your setting available for use in Distiller.

Figure 4.13 The setting added to the Default Settings menu

Deleting Distiller Settings

To delete a Distiller setting from the list of Default Distiller Settings menu list, do *one* of the following:

- Choose Settings > Add Adobe PDF Settings (Shift+Ctrl+Alt+E/Shift+⌘+Option+E). Then navigate to where a Distiller settings file has been saved on your disk (Figure 4.14), highlight it, and click Open. You can, using the Shift and ⌘ (Mac) or Ctrl (Win) keys, click to highlight more than one settings file at a time.
- Again, instead of using the menu command, you can just delete the desired Distiller settings file directly from the Distiller Settings folder.

Either of these methods will delete the selected Distiller setting from the Default Settings menu.

Sharing Distiller Settings

Once created, a Distiller settings file can be shared with other users by moving the file to another computer. After it has been moved, this file can be added to another Default Settings menu using the methods described in the preceding sections.

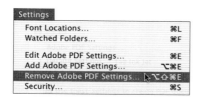

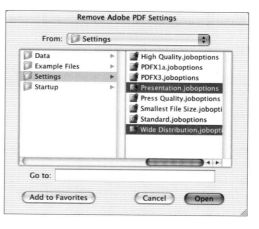

Figure 4.14 The Remove Adobe PDF Settings command takes you to a dialog where you click the Open button, but what you're really doing is deleting!

Setting PDF Document Security through Distiller

One of the nifty features of PDF files is that you can control who has access to them and what can be done with them. You do this by setting PDF security options. There are two ways to assign and control the security of a PDF document: through Distiller when creating the PDF and in Acrobat after the PDF has been created. Here I cover controlling security during distilling.

To access the dialog where you assign security functions to a PDF file, *first* set the other options in your Distiller setting, especially the Compatibility setting in the General tab.

 Note: The level of security offered will depend upon the Compatibility selected in the General tab: Acrobat 3 and 4 use 30-bit RC4; Acrobat 5 and 6 use 128-bit RC4.

Once your Distiller setting is arranged the way you want it, select Security from Distiller's Settings menu (or use the shortcut ⌘/Ctrl+S). A Security dialog will appear (Figure 4.15).

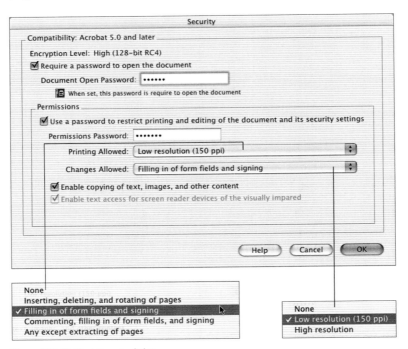

Figure 4.15 Distiller's Security dialog

Password Support System

If you are going to use passwords to control access to your PDF documents, it is important to set up at least a minimal password support system. You need to:

1. Remember the passwords.

2. Set up a secure means of providing passwords to those who need to receive and use them.

3. Develop a system to protect those passwords.

If you create lots of passwords for many documents, then you will probably want to create a database or spreadsheet with documents, passwords, and people's names so that you can keep track of them and recall them at a later time. Then, of course, you will want to protect your database with a password...and a safe place to store that...hmmm. Also, don't go password-crazy and start assigning passwords to documents that really do not need them. Security is important for protecting sensitive information, but it can also inhibit free-flowing communication.

You control access to a PDF file by assigning a password, which will allow access to the document, and then determining what functions that password will allow the viewer to perform. Here is how to set up the security:

Require A Password To Open The Document Click this check box to activate the basic access security to the document.

Document Open Password Assign a password. The most secure passwords contain both alphabetic and numeric characters. You will need to decide how secure you need the document to be.

Use A Password To Restrict Printing And Editing Of The Document And Its Security Settings Check this box if you want to control what viewers can do with the PDF document once they open it.

Permissions Password Create a password for the control of the document. This password should generally be different from the one assigned in the Document Open Password field.

Printing Allowed Choose what kind of printing you will allow from this PDF: None, Low Resolution, or High Resolution.

Changes Allowed Select the level of editing you want to allow. Here are some examples of how I use these various choices:

> **None** I use this level when I send out samples of my books and/or seminar manuals to show the contents, which will allow the viewers to see everything in the PDF but will not allow them to copy, edit, or print the document.

Filling In Forms And Signing I use this level when I create a PDF form that I want folks to be able to only fill out or sign. However, I often wait until I have created the form in Acrobat before I assign this choice, and then I assign this through Acrobat instead of in Distiller. (See Chapter 7, "PDF Document Management," for more information on creating and using PDF forms, and Chapter 5, "Controlling Acrobat and Access to Your PDFs," for assigning security in Acrobat.)

Commenting, Filling In Forms, And Signing This level adds commenting to the preceding setting and allows for feedback other than what is provided in a form.

Inserting, Deleting And Rotating Pages This is a good selection if you want to limit editing to pages only but not the content of these pages.

Any Except Extracting Pages This is the most liberal editing choice with the exception of turning off the password protection altogether, and it is the one I use most commonly when engaged in collaborative publishing where editing passwords are required.

Enabling There are two choices here: Deselect Enable Copying Of Text, Images And Content to protect your PDF contents. Check Enable Text Access For Screen Reader Devices For The Visually Impaired if you wish to allow this access. The screen reader option can be chosen without checking the first box, but if you activate "Enable Copying," the screen reader option is automatically activated.

Controlling Distiller PDF File Location and Logging

By default, Distiller will automatically create and save a log of the distilled job and place the distilled PDF in the same folder as the PostScript file. You will probably want to change these default processes, which are controlled through Distiller Preferences. Here's how:

Select Distiller Preferences (Figure 4.16): in Windows choose File > Preferences (Ctrl+K) or on a Mac choose Distiller > Preferences (⌘+K). You will notice that the Windows and Mac versions of this dialog have slightly different options. I recommend that you set the options in the Preferences panel as follows:

- Select the Ask For PDF File Destination radio button. Setting this preference will allow you to redirect the destination of your finished PDF file to a folder other than the one that contains the original PostScript file.

- Check Delete Log Files For Successful Jobs to remove the files that you will likely never pay attention to or need.

- Check Notify When Watched Folders Are Unavailable. This will let you know when a watched folder is deactivated, moved, or otherwise unusable. (See the next section for more information on watched folders.)

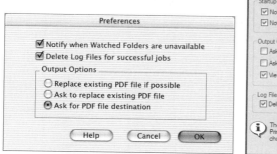

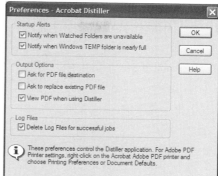

Figure 4.16 Distiller Preferences: (left) Macintosh and (right) Windows

- In Windows, check Notify When Windows TEMP Folders Are Available (this option isn't available in Mac OS). Distiller will let you know if you are running out of room in the TEMP folder on your disk, which when full will prevent you from creating PDF documents through Distiller.

- Check View PDF When Using Distiller (another Windows-only option) if you want to view the PDF file once it is created.

Improving Distiller's Efficiency with Watched Folders

Earlier in this chapter you learned how to properly configure Distiller to create just the type of PDF you want. As you now know, there are six tabs and some 72 different Distiller settings that can be configured—so it's easy to make a mistake in all this. You also learned how to use default Distiller settings and to save sets of custom Distiller settings for easy access to help simplify the use of Distiller settings.

But there is an even faster method for applying Distiller settings: watched folders. Watched folders are "hot" folders that have Distiller settings files assigned to them. All that is required to create the PDF file of your choice is to print a PostScript file to the watched folder, and Distiller takes care of the rest. Here's how to make it all happen.

Creating and Configuring a Watched Folder

To create and configure a watched folder,

1. Create a folder on your hard drive; label it Press 150 lpi. This will be the folder you set up as your first hot folder.

> **Note:** Create this folder on a partition with plenty of free space so that you will not run out of room when printing PostScript files and distilling them into PDFs.

2. Launch Distiller if you have not already done so.

3. Choose Settings > Watched Folders (⌘/Ctrl+F). A Watched Folders dialog will appear (Figure 4.17).

4. Click the Add Folder button.

5. Browse to and select the folder you created in Step 1 (Press 150 lpi), and then click Open. This will add the selected folder to the Path window, which is how Distiller locates its watched folders.

6. Now you must assign a set of Distiller settings to the newly identified watched folder. To pick the settings that will be applied to the files you distill in this folder, do *one* of the following:

   • Click Load Settings to locate and assign a set of Distiller settings to this watched folder. You can use any of the default or previously created custom Distiller settings in the Acrobat Settings folder.

   • Click Edit Settings to create a set of Distiller settings from scratch or to edit a previously loaded set. If you choose this button, refer to the "Fine-Tuning Distiller Settings for Your PDF Purpose" section of this chapter for instructions on configuring custom Distiller settings.

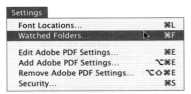

Figure 4.17 Identifying and configuring a watched folder

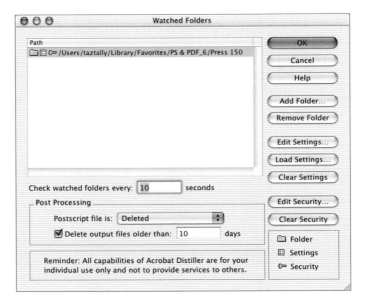

You will notice that when you finish assigning a set of Distiller settings to the watched folder, a Settings icon will be added to the folder in the Path window.

7. The Watched Folders dialog contains a few more options on how Distiller should use and manage the folder. Set these up as needed for the jobs you're going to process in the watched folder:

Check Watched Folder Every Assign a time period for how often Distiller will check the watched folder for incoming PostScript files; 10 seconds is the default, which I use.

PostScript File Is Choose either Deleted or Moved To "Out" Folder. If you choose the "Moved To" option, you will be asked to locate and select a folder into which any processed PostScript file will be moved. I suggest that you take advantage of Distiller's offer to eliminate the PostScript file by selecting Deleted. You don't need them and they just take up valuable disk space.

Delete Output Files Older Than If you want Distiller to delete any PDF still in the watched folder after a certain period of time, place a number of days value in here. I really like this feature, because I create lots of intermediate PDF documents that I do not want to keep. If I haven't moved them to another location in 10 days, I don't intend to keep them anyway, so I just have Distiller take them to the trash for me.

Edit Security If you would like to place any security controls on the PDF file created through this watched folder, click this button and configure the security to suit your needs (see the section on setting Distiller security earlier in this chapter). If you do assign any security setting to your watched folder, an icon will appear next to the folder's icon in the Paths window.

8. Once you have completed assigning and configuring your watched folder, click OK.

Now take a look inside your watched folder. You will see that Distiller has added In and Out subfolders and a Distiller settings file (Figure 4.18).

You have now completed your first watched folder. You can create as many watched folders as you like for any kind of PDF you would like to create. Figure 4.19 show a list of watched folders that I regularly use to create various kinds of PDF files for commercial printing, desktop printing, and the Web.

Figure 4.18 Distiller adds contents to a watched folder

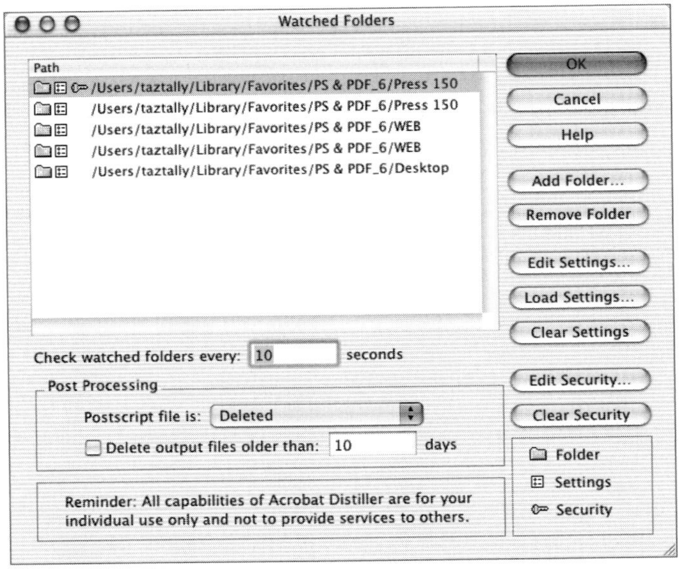

Figure 4.19 Taz's watched folders

Using a Watched Folder

Using a watched folder is the easy part:

1. Launch Distiller.
2. Print a properly configured PostScript file from your page layout application to the In subfolder of the watched folder that contains the Distiller settings of your choice. (☞ See Chapter 3 for information on creating PostScript files.)

Note: Although you will normally create/print your PostScript file from within your page layout application, as specified in Step 2, you can also generate a PostScript file from a PDF document by saving a PostScript file from Acrobat. This is a handy way of reconstructing a PDF if you do not like the manner in which it was originally distilled and you do not have the original page layout document file. (☞ See Chapter 13, "Outputting PDFs and Their Contents," for more information on exporting as a PostScript file.)

That's all! Distiller will automatically begin distilling the PostScript file into a PDF document, deleting the no-longer-needed PostScript file, and relocating the newly created PDF document into the Out folder. This is the fastest and most dependable way I know of creating a PDF document though Distiller. It eliminates the need to configure or even select a Distiller setting, and you don't even have to open the PostScript file—just print it to the In folder. Creating a PDF becomes a one-step, difficult-to-mess-up process. About all that you can do wrong is print the PostScript file to the wrong watched In folder. And if you do that, just print it again to the correct folder.

Putting It All Together: Preflight, Print Styles, and Watched Folder

In Chapters 2 and 3, I discussed preflighting to make sure your documents were properly constructed and using print styles to streamline and improve the consistency of creating PostScript files. Now that I have discussed the use and creation of watched folders, you have a complete set of tools to quickly and accurately create the PDF document of your choice. Here are the three keys tools and steps:

1. Preflight your page layout documents with a professional preflighting tool, such as Markzware's Flight Check, to make sure your documents have all the right linked and prepared components such as fonts and graphics.

2. Create and use print styles (including saved PostScript settings) to create a properly configured PostScript file.

3. Use watched folders to control the creation of your PDF documents.

This three-part workflow and tool set will dramatically improve the speed, ease of creation, accuracy, and consistency of your PDF documents. Using this set of tools and processes is the core reason why I can create thousands of PDF documents each year and have more than 95 percent accuracy the first time out.

Creating PDFs from within Non-Acrobat Applications

The first section of this chapter dealt with creating PDF files working directly with Distiller. As I said, this is often the preferred method of creating PDF files because it gives you immediate access to Distiller and its settings. Alternatively, you can create PDF files from within other applications such as your page layout program. While it is not possible to cover all the PDF creation methods, I'll talk about some of the more common applications, which will not only provide you with specific instructions for these applications but also provide you with a good background for dealing with similar applications and PDF creation circumstances.

Alternative PDF Creation Methods

When creating PDF documents in applications other than Distiller, it is good to know whether your application has its own built-in Distiller-like functionality or if Distiller is being used indirectly (such as with PageMaker 4.5 and QuarkXPress 5) to create the PDF. PDF creation problems, and particularly with PDFs being created for prepress, can often be traced to non-standard/non-Distiller PDF creation programs. Some PDF creation applications, such as Agfa's Normalizer, are designed to create PDFs for very specific purposes, such as a particular PDF prepress workflow, and they actually work better than standard Distiller PDFs. In any case, it's always good to know which tools are being used to create your PDF documents.

Creating PDFs through QuarkXPress 5

Any document created in QuarkXPress 5 can be exported—kinda-sorta—as a PDF file. QuarkXPress 5 really just creates a PostScript file that you then process through Distiller. Here's how:

1. Create the final version of your document (preflighted, of course!) and perform a Save As to sweep your document clean of unnecessary stuff.

2. Select a PostScript printer driver. (I recommend a printer driver of version 8.7.3 or above on the Mac and PostScript5 or above for Windows XP and 2000.)

3. Choose File > Export > Document As PDF. The Export As PDF window will appear (Figure 4.20), looking very much like an ordinary Save dialog.

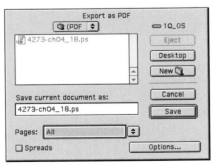

Figure 4.20 QuarkXPress 5 Export As PDF

At this point you have two choices: You can create a PostScript file that will be processed through Distiller using a predefined Distiller setting, or you can augment and/or override some of the predefined Distiller settings. If you intend to use an established set of Distiller settings (either a default set or one you have customized), continue with the following steps. To customize and override Distiller settings for this particular job, skip ahead to "Overriding Distiller Settings in a Quark Job."

1. In the Pages field, type in the page numbers you would like to save in the Post-Script file.

2. Click Spreads if you want facing pages to be saved as a double-page spread. (Typically you would ignore this and especially for prepress.)

3. Type in the filename for the PostScript file, making sure that it ends with the proper PostScript file extension: .ps (Mac) or .prn (Windows).

4. Locate the folder where you want QuarkXPress to place the PostScript file. (This could be a watched folder if you want Distiller to process the PDF automatically; ⌒ the section on watched folders earlier in this chapter.)

5. Click Save. QuarkXPress will use the PostScript printer driver you assigned in Step 1 to create a PostScript file in the location you designated.

6. If you have printed the PostScript file to a watched folder, Distiller will automatically convert it to a PDF file. If not, your next step is to launch Distiller, assign Distiller settings as discussed earlier in this chapter, and create the PDF there.

Overriding Distiller Settings in a Quark Job

Once you're ready to PDF your Quark document and you choose File > Export > Document As PDF, you may want to override or customize some of your Distiller settings. If so, click the Options button in the Export As PDF window (shown back in Figure 4.20; a new dialog titled PDF Export Options For *Document Name* will appear (Figure 4.21).

Document Info tab Type in the title, subject(s), author(s), and keyword(s) you want to associate with this PDF. These data can be used to help identify the creator of the PDF and can be used in search functions later on.

> **Note:** These Document Info data fields can also be assigned or edited later in the Acrobat application (see Chapter 5).

Hyperlinks tab Select the portions of your QuarkXPress document you would like to have exported as internal hyperlinks, such as lists and indexes. You can also have any (or all) lists appear as bookmarks when your PDF is opened in Acrobat. You can control the appearance of the hyperlinks in the Appearance area and set the initial display of the PDF document when it is opened in the Display menu.

Job Options and Output tabs These final two tabs can be used to override any of the Distiller settings offered here, such as font inclusion, graphics sampling and compression, or color output.

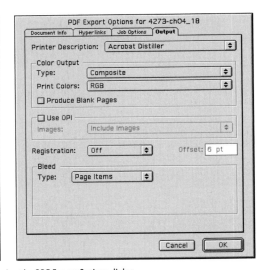

Figure 4.21 In QuarkXPress, customize your distilling process using the PDF Export Options dialog.

Creating PDFs through QuarkXPress 6 and OS X

QuarkXPress 6 for Mac OS X is created specifically for OS X and does not work in earlier versions of the Mac OS. Therefore all printing will employ OS X–based tools (which do not include a Chooser!) and techniques. QuarkXPress 6 provides the ability to create a standard PostScript file, print to a PDF, or export directly to a PDF. Here is how these methods work.

Overriding a Distiller Setting

When you override a Distiller setting, such as can be done here in the QuarkXPress PDF Export Options dialog, a series of instructions, known as prologue instructions, is embedded in the PostScript file. These embedded instructions will override any Distiller settings. However, this deserves a few words of caution.

- Remember that you can control these setting functions in Distiller, and if you constantly alter where you control them, it may result in a confusing and inconsistent PDF workflow.

- By controlling these functions outside of Distiller, you are adding another layer of complexity, and therefore possible error, to your PDF workflow.

My preference, in PDF control windows such as this Quark PDF Export Options window, is to use the controls that apply uniquely to that application—in this case, the Hyperlinks tab, which Distiller would not control—but leave the basic Distiller controls such as those in Quark's Job Options and Output tabs to Distiller.

Printing PostScript Files

The Mac OS X utilizes a printer utility, called the Print Center, similar to the printing utility in Windows. Here's how it works.

1. Create the final version of your document (preflighted, of course!), and perform a Save As to sweep your document clean of unnecessary stuff.

2. Launch the Print Center: Applications > Utilities > Printer Center.

Note: I dragged the icon of the Print Center into both the Dock and the top of the Finder window so that it will always be just a click away.

3. From the list of printers, select the PostScript printer driver you would like to use to create your PDF document. (Here I selected the driver for the LaserWriter 16/600 PS Fax.) You can make this the default printer if you intend to use this printer driver frequently.

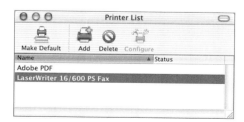

4. Using the Print dialog boxes and tabs, create a PostScript file as outlined in Chapter 3. One difference you will encounter in OS X is that in the Setup tab you will likely see and select a printer description file (PPD) for Adobe PDF rather than Distiller.

5. Process your PostScript file through Distiller to create your PDF. (I like to use Distiller watched folders for this process.)

Printing PDF Files

Printing PDF files involves selecting a specifically labeled PDF printer driver rather than a general PostScript printer driver. Please ↩ see the section later in this chapter titled "Creating PDFs through PDF Printer Drivers."

Exporting PDFs

QuarkXPress 6 includes the ability to export documents as PDFs while controlling distilling options in the process. Here's how:

1. After creating and preflighting your page layout document, choose File > Export > Layout As PDF.

2. An Export PDF window appears. Click the Options button to set the distilling options.

3. The PDF Export Options window appears. Click the Layout Info tab and configure the document information fields. Any data you enter here will become part of the PDF metadata.

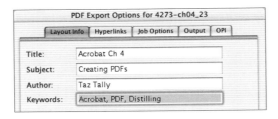

4. Click the Hyperlinks tab (Figure 4.22). This tab allows you to determine which document elements, including lists and indexes, will become internally

hyperlinked to their corresponding information in the document. Configure this as follows:

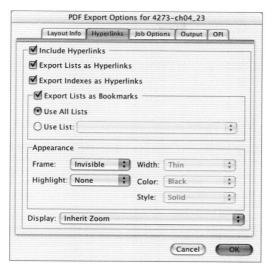

Figure 4.22 Decide which Quark elements will become PDF hyperlinks and how they will appear.

Include Hyperlinks Check this option to activate the hyperlinking capabilities.

Export Lists As Hyperlinks Check this option if your document contains any lists (commonly a Table of Contents list created from style sheets) that you want to be hyperlinked to their internal sections.

Export Indexes As Hyperlinks Check this box if you have created an index in QuarkXPress and would like those index entries to be hyperlinked to their corresponding text.

Export Lists As Bookmarks Any list you have created in your document, such as chapter and section lists based upon style sheets, or lists of graphics, can also be bookmarked in your PDF document for easy access by checking this box. You can select the lists you want bookmarked, while leaving others unlinked.

Appearance You can control the appearance of the hyperlinks by making Frame and Highlight selections.

5. Click the Job Options tab and configure the Compression and Resolution fields as you would in an Images tab in Distiller (Figure 4.23). (↩ See "Creating PDFs Directly through Distiller" earlier in this chapter for more information on compression and resolution settings.)

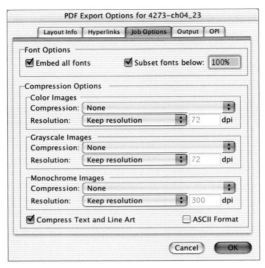

Figure 4.23 The Job Options tab

6. Click the Output tab (Figure 4.24) and configure this section as you would any normal Print dialog box that allows you to designate the colors, registration, and bleed information you would like to include in your final PDF. (☞ See Chapter 3 on printing PostScript files for more information on output and Open Prepress Interface (OPI) topics.)

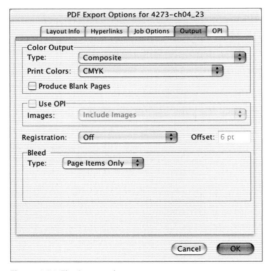

Figure 4.24 The Output tab

7. Click the OPI tab and configure it to suit your needs.

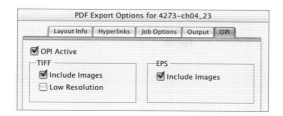

8. When you have finished configuring the PDF Export Options window, click OK. An Export As PDF window appears.

9. Locate the folder where you would like your PDF file to be placed and click Save.

> **Note:** The QuarkXPress 6 Export function does *not* use Acrobat Distiller to effect the distillation of the PDF. QuarkXPress 6 comes with a licensed Jaws PDF Library from Global Graphics. The PDFs export quickly but are often much larger than those created using Distiller and may require Reduction or PDF Optimization (available only in Acrobat 6 Pro). For this reason, I typically do not use the QuarkXPress Export function, but prefer to use the more traditional method of printing a PostScript files to a Watched folder.

Creating PDFs through InDesign

Adobe InDesign is fully integrated with Acrobat technology, and in fact it has its own built-in version of Distiller so that PDF files can be created directly though Distiller. InDesign allows you to access a default set of Distiller settings (similar to the ones in Distiller), and as with Distiller you can edit or create your own settings called setting styles. Here is how you can control the creation of PDF documents through InDesign.

Style Sheets, TOCs, and Hyperlinks

Back in Chapter 2 we discussed the importance of constructing page layout using style sheets, and here we see another one of the benefits. TOC lists created from style sheets can automatically be converted into PDF hyperlinks and bookmarks, dramatically enhancing the functionality, and particularly the accessibility, of the final PDF document.

InDesign Styles vs. Distiller Settings

InDesign's PDF Styles list will be similar to, but may not be identical to, the Settings list in Distiller. For instance, in the Styles list in Figure 4.25 you do not see any PDF/X styles, but you do see an eBook style. This set of InDesign PDF styles is consistent with Acrobat 5 rather than Acrobat 6. So if you intend to use InDesign to create your PDF files, be sure to update InDesign to the most recent version of its built-in Distiller and styles.

Choosing, Creating, and Editing PDF Styles

In InDesign, Distiller settings are called PDF styles. You can access and modify InDesign PDF styles with the following steps:

1. Choose File > PDF Styles; the PDF Styles dialog will appear (Figure 4.25).

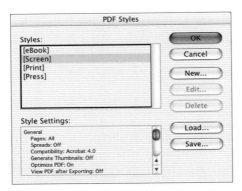

Figure 4.25 InDesign PDF Styles dialog

2. Select one of the PDF styles from the Styles list. This selection will become the default style used to create PDF files.

3. To create a new PDF style or edit a previously customized one, click the New or Edit button in the Style dialog. A window labeled New PDF Style will appear with a list of five categories of options on the left side (Figure 4.26).

4. Click the General category. Fill out this window to meet your specifications. You may notice, depending upon the version of InDesign you have, that the choices here may not match those in Distiller. For instance, here you will note that there is no Acrobat version 3.0 compatibility, which Distiller 6.0 has. You will also have non-Distiller choices for including hyperlinks and bookmarked items marked in your InDesign document.

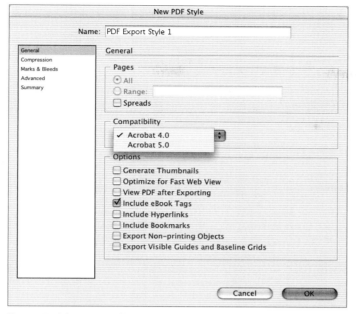

Figure 4.26 InDesign New/Edit PDF Style dialog

5. Click the Compression category (Figure 4.27). Assign the resolution sampling and compression type you prefer.

6. Click the Marks & Bleeds category (Figure 4.27). Fill these out to suit your output. Once again you may see a difference between some of the setting choices from Distiller, such as the Color Bars option, which is available here but may not be available in Distiller.

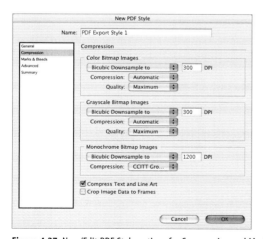
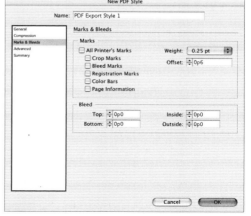

Figure 4.27 New/Edit PDF Style options for Compression and Marks & Bleeds

7. Click the Advanced category (Figure 4.28) and select the font and color handling choices you would like. You will note that this window has a setting not found in standard Distiller, and specific to InDesign document elements that have transparency, labeled Transparency Flattener.

8. Click the Summary item (Figure 4.28) to view a complete summary of all the PDF setting choices you have made. When the setup is what you want, click OK to save the style.

9. Once you've chosen or created a PDF style and edited it as you wish, then back in the PDF Styles dialog click OK to lock in your choices.

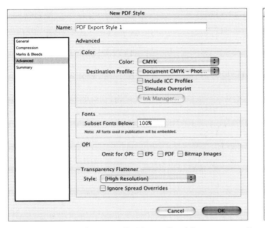
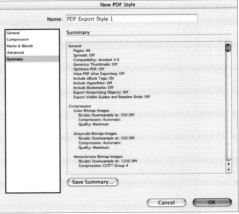

Figure 4.28 New/Edit PDF Style Advanced and Summary panels

Exporting PDFs from InDesign

Once you have created the PDF styles you would like to use, you can then use those styles to export PDF documents. Here's how:

1. Create and preflight your InDesign document, and perform a Save As to create a separate print copy of your document. (This is a precaution in case anything happens to your document during printing or PDF creation.)

2. Choose File > Export (⌘/Ctrl+E); an Export dialog will appear (Figure 4.29).

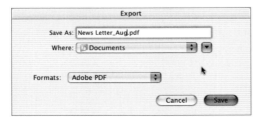

Figure 4.29 InDesign Export dialog

3. Select Adobe PDF from the Formats menu.

4. Name the file (here, I've used News Letter_Aug.pdf). Use a filename of eight characters or less if you intend to send this file across the Internet, and be sure the extension is .pdf.

> **Note:** If you (like me) hate having to use only eight characters to name a file, here is a tip: Name the file whatever you want, and then to send the file across the Internet, compress the file as a .zip (a format produced by programs such as WinZip or ZipIt) or .sit (usually produced with StuffIt) archive (.zip is probably the most universal) with an eight-character name. Whoever receives the file can then decompress the file and see its full name. This archiving has the extra benefits of making your file smaller and adding a "protective coating" around it as well.

5. Select a location for where you want the PDF to be placed.

6. Click the Save button; the Export PDF dialog will appear (Figure 4.30).

7. Select the PDF style you would like to use to create your PDF document.

8. If necessary, edit any of the PDF settings.

9. Click the Export button.

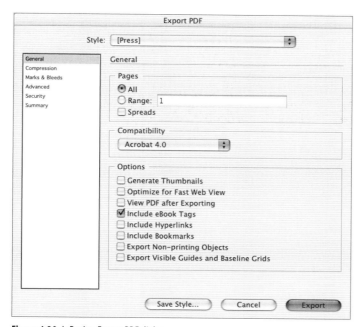

Figure 4.30 InDesign Export PDF dialog

More Techniques

Many other applications have PDF export functions similar to those I've discussed within QuarkXPress and InDesign. Some, like InDesign, have built-in PDF creation capabilities. Others, like QuarkXPress 5, ultimately use Distiller as the PDF creation tool. While their specifics may vary somewhat from what I have covered here, the general processes, procedures, and settings will be similar. Refer to the manuals that come with your specific applications and versions for any application-specific detail you may need.

That said, here are some notes about alternate methods of creating PDFs: directly through a PDF printer driver or through Adobe's PDFMaker plug-in for Microsoft applications.

Creating PDFs through PDF Printer Drivers

In Chapter 3 we discussed in detail how to create a proper PostScript file, which will be used to create a PDF. This is still the preferred method for many, but there is also another approach. Instead of creating an intermediate PostScript file using a PostScript printer driver, you can select a printer driver that will print directly to a PDF. Doing this incorporates the creation of the PostScript file and the PDF file into one step. Here, we will use InDesign as the original page layout document creation application, but these steps will apply to any application, such as QuarkXPress, which will allow you to use a PDF printer driver. Here's how (but also see my note at the end of this section):

1. When you select your printer/printer driver, select one that is labeled Adobe PDF (Figure 4.31). (If you are creating many PDFs, you may want to consider making this your default driver.)

Figure 4.31 Printer/printer driver selection

2. Inside your page layout application (InDesign here), select the Print command (usually from your File menu). A Print window will appear, similar to the one in Figure 4.32.

3. Configure this dialog box to suit your output purposes. Confirm that the printer driver is set to Adobe PDF (near the top here). In this Print window you will see six different sets of settings to configure, from General down to Advanced. Your dialog will vary depending upon your application and version.

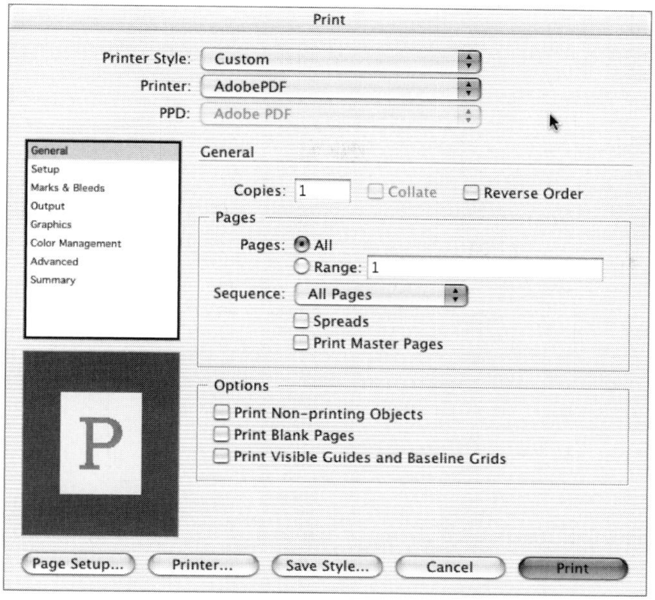

Figure 4.32 Setting up the Print dialog to print to PDF

4. At this point you can just hit the Print button (in the lower-right corner here), and a PDF will be printed to the last folder into which you saved or printed a file.

5. If you want to rename or redirect the location of the PDF file you will be creating, click the Printer button (lower left here). Another dialog will appear, possibly named Print or Printer.

6. Click the Save As PDF button. Another dialog will appear, probably named Save To File or Save As PDF.

Note: This same Save As PDF button may be available if you select either a standard PostScript or a specific PDF printer driver.

7. Assign a name and location for the PDF file, and click Save. Often the original Print window will reappear.

8. Click Print, and the PDF file will be created with the name and in the location you specified.

The actual number and appearance of the dialog boxes will vary depending upon your application and version. But any application that allows you to use an Adobe PDF printer driver will allow you to create a PDF in this manner. It is worth noting that you will not have the level of control over the distilling PDF file that you have when you go through Distiller.

Note: I would be remiss if I did not mention that I personally never use this Save As PDF method to create PDF documents from QuarkXPress, because the result is often large and/or unreadable PDF documents. I have included the method here for those who would like to try it in their applications, with the hopes that this method might work better with other applications or will become less stricken with problems in the future. As I have said before, I prefer printing standard PostScript files to watched folders.

Creating One-Button PDFs with PDFMaker

Acrobat technology, or at least the PDF document portion of Acrobat technology, has become so much a part of computer-based communications that the ability to create at least some kind of a PDF documents increasingly is being incorporated in many types of applications. Acrobat 6 includes the ability to quickly create PDF documents from a wide variety of Microsoft Office applications, including Word, Excel, PowerPoint, and even Outlook.

When Acrobat 6 is installed, an application called PDFMaker is automatically installed and linked to all currently installed Microsoft applications. After installing PDFMaker, whenever you launch a Microsoft application, two Acrobat technology icons will be available in your floating tool palette in your document window: one to create a PDF and one to create and e-mail a PDF file.

These are called "one-button" PDFs, although there are still two or three steps involved.

Note: If you install a Microsoft application after you install Acrobat, you may need to reinstall Acrobat in order to have PDFMaker available in that new application.

I'll use Microsoft Word as the example. Here's how to quickly create a PDF using PDFMaker:

1. Create and edit a document in Microsoft Word. Save the document when you have finished.

2. Click the Convert To Adobe PDF button in the floating tool palette of the document window.

3. Assign a name to the PDF file and select a location to save it in. (By default it will use the last location where you saved this document.)

4. Click Save. A progress window will appear.

5. Wait for this progress window to complete; when it's done, you can either click the View button to view the PDF or click Done to complete the process. (I always view the PDF to make sure everything looks okay and that I didn't do something silly like having a Landscape orientation when I should have had Portrait!)

Creating and e-mailing a one-button PDF is just as easy. Follow all the preceding steps. Then, after the progress window is done and you click the Done button, your default e-mail program will be automatically launched, with a new blank message begun and the PDF included as an attachment. That's it, you've finished!

Choosing a PDF-Making Method

The decision of how to create a PDF file used to be easy: Distiller was the only choice. But now we have many ways to create PDF files. In this chapter I covered four major methods:

- Using a PostScript file and Distiller
- Using an Export function
- Printing directly to a PDF using an Adobe PDF printer driver
- Using a Save As PDF button with a PostScript or PDF printer driver
- Using the "one-button" PDFMaker through Microsoft applications

Any of these methods may work for you. You have probably noticed that the PostScript and Distiller method provides you with the most control and PDFMaker the least. Also note that some methods (such as Save As PDF) might have well-documented problems.

The more demanding your output, the more control you will want to have. I typically create PDF files for high-quality output, so I normally choose the PostScript file and Distiller route. But if all you need to do is just share a quick letter with someone viewing your PDF over the Internet, and you have no images or image quality is not a key concern, then a one-button PDFMaker PDF may be all you need. Indeed, PDFMaker has been optimized for creating PDFs with the associated Microsoft applications.

I suggest that you use a method that will work for all of your PDF creation needs and stick with it. This way you become very familiar with all the settings and dialog boxes, and they will be second nature to use and you will make few mistakes. For those of you who want the ultimate in control, speed, and consistency, be sure to become familiar with the earlier section on "Putting It All Together."

Fundamentals of Acrobat

II

In Part I, I discussed that fact that PDF documents are page-based rather than document-based. The benefits of this become clear in Part II, as I demonstrate how PDF documents can be manipulated. PDFs can be viewed, printed, and published or transferred electronically; they can be used collaboratively, as presentations, as forms, or as full-featured e-books. And for those with security needs, Acrobat provides a full set of security features, including encrypted digital signatures.

Controlling Acrobat and Access to Your PDFs

5

Acrobat provides two levels of control over how the Acrobat application and PDF files look and behave: through setting Acrobat application preferences and through setting individual PDF document properties. Document Properties settings take precedent over Acrobat Preferences settings, which allow you, the creator of a PDF file, to define how that PDF file will look and behave when you send it elsewhere. I'll cover Acrobat Preferences first and then show you how to control individual document properties.

Chapter Contents

Controlling how Acrobat behaves
Controlling the look of individual PDFs
Controlling who has access and what they
   can do to your PDF

Controlling How Acrobat Behaves

Your Acrobat application can be made to behave in any number of ways through control of its preferences. To access Acrobat Preferences, choose Preferences from the File menu (Windows) or the Acrobat menu (Mac), or type ⌘/Ctrl+K. The Preferences window will appear. As you can see, there are quite a few preferences. Here we will cover a few of the most important fundamental preferences to get you started using Acrobat. We will set other preferences later as they affect other specific tools, skills, and capabilities.

From the list of preferences categories on the left side of the window, click the General preferences (you can also type the first character of the preference name—G here—or use your Up and Down arrow keys to navigate the list of categories). The General preferences (Figure 5.1) will appear in the right side of the window. Here are tips on setting some of the important fundamental preference options:

Allowing the Hand tool to select If you like to select text from PDF documents, check the box Enable Text Selection For The Hand Tool. This will allow your Hand tool to be used as a selection tool. This prevents you from having to change to the Text Selection tool. Next set the text and column margin sizes (which are in pixels) to the number of pixels away from the text the Hand tool will automatically turn into the Text Selection tool.

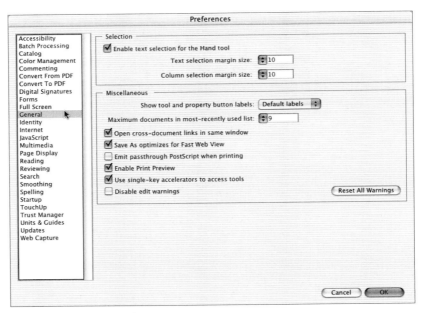

Figure 5.1 Acrobat General preferences

Controlling views of linked documents Check Open Cross-Document Links In Same Window if you want a hyperlinked document to open in the same window. This reduces the number of windows that are open. If you want to see both parent and linked document windows, then leave this option unchecked.

Making your PDFs more web-savvy To enable your multipage PDF document to be served up over the Web one page at a time (thereby delivering the PDF faster), check Save As Optimizes For Fast Web View. There is no downside to this, so do it!

Speeding up printing For the fastest printing of your PDF documents, *do not* check Emit Passthrough PostScript When Printing. Keeping this option unchecked allows recurring page objects (known as PostScript objects) such as Master Page elements to be downloaded to a printer's memory once. This requires more printer memory but will speed up printing of multipage PDFs.

Allowing print previewing of PDF pages If you want to be able to see print previews of your PDF pages prior to printing, check Enable Print Preview. This previewing process will slow down the printing process, however, so if you are confident of what you are printing, you may want to disable this feature.

Speeding up access to Acrobat tools Definitely check Use Single-Key Accelerators To Access Tools. This will enable you to use single keystrokes to access your Acrobat tools, thereby speeding up their use. See "Navigating in and through PDFs" in Chapter 6, and the keyboard shorts list in the appendix on the CD.

If warnings drive you crazy! Check Disable Edit Warnings if you do not want Acrobat to warn you each time you are about to change a PDF document.

Establishing Your PDF Identity

Whenever you share a PDF file in collaborative publishing, creating reviews, and using digital signatures, you want to have a complete PDF identity established. This information will be automatically included in the PDF document. Here is how you do it:

 Open the Preferences window by choosing Preferences from the File menu (Windows) or the Acrobat menu (Mac), or by typing ⌘/Ctrl+K. Then, from the list of categories on the left, click the Identity choice (or type I). The Identity preferences (Figure 5.2) will appear on the right.

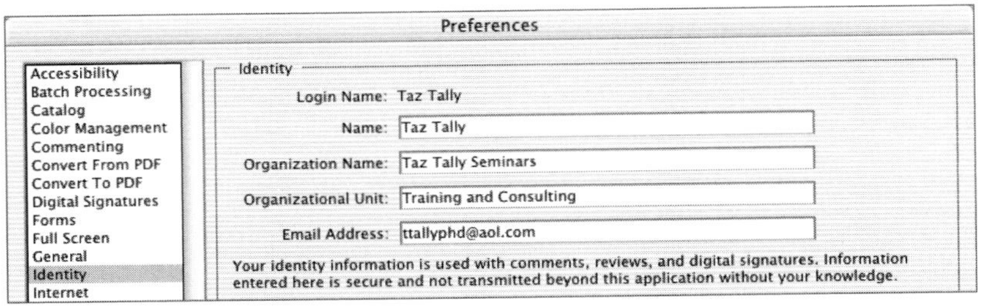

Figure 5.2 Acrobat Identity preferences

Type in your name, organization, level, and e-mail address. This information will now become an automatically included part of your PDF files that you use for collaborative publishing, reviews, and digital signatures.

Controlling How PDFs Look When They Open

Acrobat can be set up to make PDF files have various "looks" depending upon how they are used. You can set your PDFs to open in various page layout arrangements and magnifications, control which tools and features will be automatically visible, and choose how your text will be displayed. Here is how to control what you see when you open a PDF.

Open the Preferences window by choosing Preferences from the File menu (Windows) or the Acrobat menu (Mac), or by typing ⌘/Ctrl+K. Then, from the list of categories on the left, click the Page Display choice (or type **P**). The Page Display preferences (Figure 5.3) will appear on the right.

Choosing the opening document layout If you find yourself constantly changing the layout of PDFs when you open them, you may want to reset the default page layout. Select Continuous - Facing (my favorite choice) if you like to have facing-page documents appear side-by-side on screen.

Viewing prepress elements If you want to view all the page elements that are important for commercial printing, check Display Art, Trim, Bleed Boxes. I have this option disabled most of the time, since I do not want to see this information constantly.

Removing the white page border To remove the thin white border that often is created and printed around the border of a PDF page, check Display Page To Edge. This is a good default setting if you intend to print your PDFs and especially if they have page elements that bleed off the edges.

Showing a grid behind transparent objects Check Display Transparency Grid.

Activating alternate/customized page numbering To enable you to use Acrobat's ability to renumber pages, check Use Logical Page Numbers. (See Chapter 7, "PDF Document Management," for a complete treatment of this topic.)

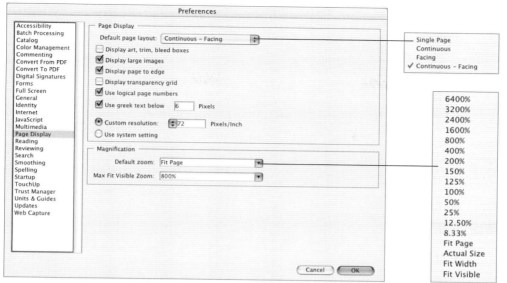

Figure 5.3 Acrobat Page Display preferences

Speeding up screen redraw of text When you zoom out and the text gets very small, Acrobat will still attempt to redraw all the text. This can takes a lot of time in a large or text-heavy document displayed on a small monitor. To prevent this extended redraw, check Use Greek Text Below. Use a value of 6 to 8 in the accompanying Pixels field to set the minimum text size that will be redrawn on screen.

Adjusting screen resolution Not all monitors are 72 ppi. If you are working on a monitor that has another resolution, you can click the Custom Resolution button and type in the resolution number you want. If you are unsure of the resolution, you can check Use System Setting instead.

Controlling page magnification on opening If you like to see the entire page when a PDF is opened (my favorite choice), then select Fit Page from the Default Zoom menu. Any other supported magnification can be chosen as well. If you want to set a limit on how much zooming will be allowed when one of the "Fit" choices is selected, you may do so with the Max Fit Visible Zoom menu.

Adjusting How Smooth Page Elements Look on Screen

This might seem like a no-brainer, as you think, "Well, of course I want everything to appear as smooth as possible on screen." But there may be a price to be paid for smoothness: redraw time. The more elements that need to be smoothed, the longer the draw takes. And if you are trying to rapidly navigate through a PDF, smoothing may slow you down a bit. Some systems have enough video RAM that the difference in redraw speed is negligible. Acrobat also provides you with the ability to fine-tune the smoothing to match your monitor's capabilities, which can be a big bonus for reducing eyestrain. Here is how you do it:

Open the Preferences window by choosing Preferences from the File menu (Windows) or the Acrobat menu (Mac), or by typing ⌘/Ctrl+K. Then, from the list of categories on the left, click the Smoothing choice (or type the letters **SM** in quick succession). The Smoothing preferences (Figure 5.4) will appear on the right.

Activating smoothing Check the Smooth Text, Smooth Line Art, and Smooth Images boxes. If you display your images on a laptop or LCD screen, try the Use Cool Type option to see if you like the effect.

Fine-tuning smoothing Look carefully at the sample displays of type and line graphics provided in the two sets of displays. Click the Next button to see the second set of display samples. Select the one that shows the best-looking type and line art. I focus on the diagonal lines (near horizontal and vertical) to make my choices. I use sample F for my laptop.

Controlling What Displays When Acrobat Launches and Opens Documents

You can control what will be automatically displayed when Acrobat launches. To do so, open the Preferences window by choosing Preferences from the File menu (Windows) or the Acrobat menu (Mac), or by typing ⌘/Ctrl+K. Then, from the list of categories on the left, click the Startup choice (or type the letters **ST** in quick succession). The Startup preferences (Figure 5.5) will appear on the right.

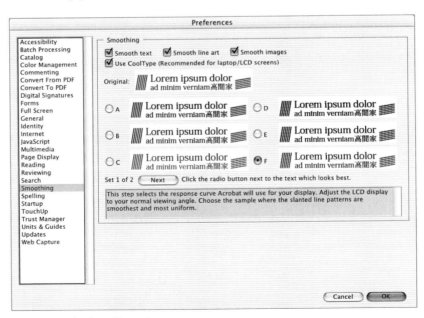

Figure 5.4 Acrobat Smoothing preferences

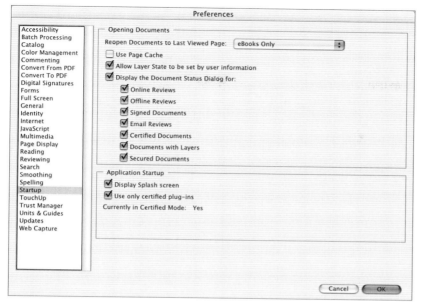

Figure 5.5 Acrobat Startup preferences

What shows up when you open a PDF From the list under Display The Document Status Dialog For, check the items about which you want information displayed. For instance, if you work a lot with digitally signed documents, you would want this information always displayed.

Faster navigation If you often work with long documents, you may want to check the Use Page Cache check box, because this will automatically load the second page of a document prior to displaying the first page, thereby making page 2 ready for viewing. I typically leave this option turned off, since I view lots of PDFs over the Web and I don't want to delay the appearance of the first page.

What gets loaded when Acrobat launches To minimize any potential problems from using Acrobat plug-ins that are not written to meet Adobe specifications, check Use Only Certified Plug-ins.

Determining Ruler and Grid Spacing and Viewing

If you use the rulers and guides available in Acrobat, you will want to define their units and spacing early on. Open the Preferences window by choosing Preferences from the File menu (Windows) or the Acrobat menu (Mac), or by typing ⌘/Ctrl+K. Then, from the list of categories on the left, click the Units & Guides choice (or type U). The Units & Guides preferences (Figure 5.6) will appear on the right.

- Select the units you want used for page measurements and the rulers from the Page & Ruler Units drop-down list.

- Assign the width, height, number of subdivisions, and color you would like your grid system to have.

- Assign a different color to the guides than you have to the grid system, to make them easy to distinguish on screen.

Controlling Acrobat Update Frequency and Behavior

Acrobat can automatically check for updates over the Web. This is a good thing, but I usually don't want the update alert dialog boxes appearing, and sometimes I just want to perform this task manually. Here's how to control both.

Open the Preferences window by choosing Preferences from the File menu (Windows) or the Acrobat menu (Mac), or by typing ⌘/Ctrl+K. Then, from the list of categories on the left, click the Updates choice (or type the letters **UP** in quick succession). The Updates preferences (Figure 5.7) will appear on the right.

- From the Check For Updates drop-down list, choose whether you want the updates to occur automatically Every Month or Manually.

- Check Show Auto-Update Confirmation Dialog if you want to be reminded that the update has occurred.

- Check Display Notification Dialog At Startup if you want to be reminded about updates at startup.

I typically have Acrobat check automatically for me monthly, but I disable the notifications because they make me crazy!

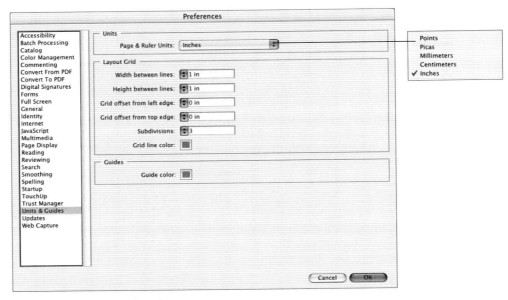

Figure 5.6 Acrobat Units & Guides preferences

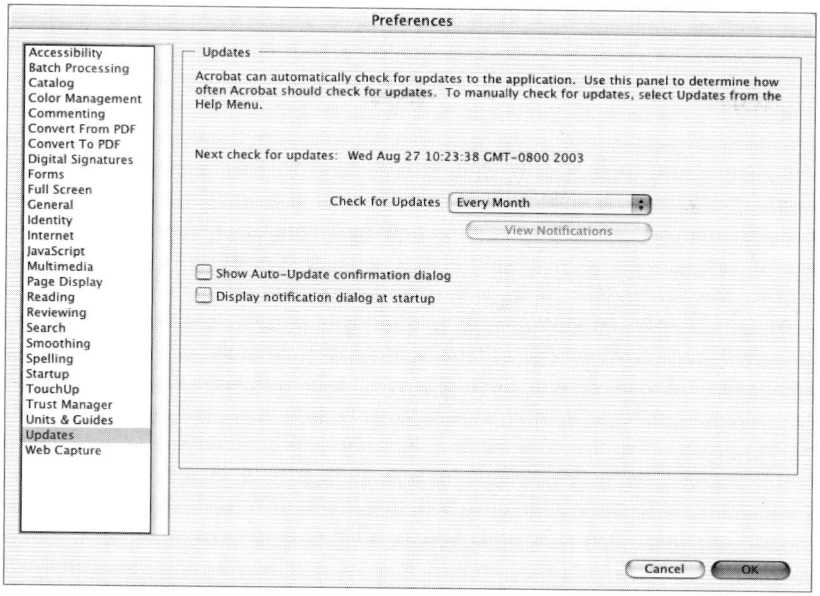

Figure 5.7 Acrobat Updates preferences

Controlling the Look of Individual PDFs

In addition to being able to control the Acrobat application, you can also define how individual PDF documents will look and behave when they are opened. You do this through the Document Properties menu option.

Getting Familiar with the Other Preferences

Here we have covered some of the more important initial preferences used to give you control over some of Acrobat's basic functions. As you can see, there are many more preferences to control. We will return to many of these as we cover new skills. But I suggest that it is a good idea for you to take a few minutes to peruse the various preferences offered here, so that you know what is available. Then when you start using other Acrobat tools and capabilities, you might remember that you saw some control for those features in the preferences. Just use the Up and Down arrow keys to navigate through the various preferences.

Note: Any characteristic controlled through the Document Properties will take precedent over the same setting configured in an Acrobat Preferences window. This allows you to control the behavior of your Acrobat documents when you send them elsewhere.

Here is how to preset the look of an individual PDF file:

1. Open the PDF document you would like to configure.

2. Choose File > Document Properties. The Document Properties window will appear.

3. Select the Initial View choice from the list of categories on the left side of the window (Figure 5.8).

4. Configure the Initial View window to control how *this* document will appear when opened.

Here are some guidelines for the various choices. If you select Default for any option, the choice made in the Acrobat Application preferences will be used for that option.

Show (Document Options) Use this menu to determine what will be visible upon opening: the page only, or the page plus the bookmarks, layers, or pages panel. Typically you may want to show just the pages. But if you were collaborating on a document and sending comments back and forth, you might want to show bookmarks as well.

Page Layout Your options here are Default, Single Page, Continuous, Facing, and Continuous - Facing. My favorite is Continuous - Facing so that both the left and right sides of my facing-page documents will automatically display on screen.

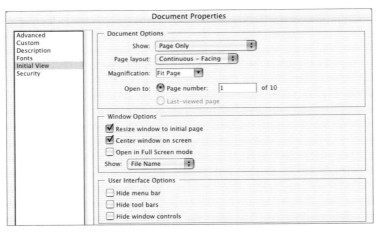

Figure 5.8 Document Initial View properties

Magnification Set the zoom level, or choose Fit Page, Fit Width, or Fit Visible. My favorite here is Fit Page so that initially the entire page will show on screen, regardless of the resolution of the monitor on which it is opened.

Open To If you want your PDF to open on a specific page, such as a part of a document of particular interest, set that page number here. You can also set the Last-Viewed Page; this is often useful for long documents, such as e-books, which will likely be viewed in multiple sessions.

Window Options Check these first two check boxes if you want the PDF window resized to the initial viewed page size and if you want it centered on screen.

Open In Full Screen Mode You would check this if you want your PDF to be displayed presentation-style with a solid background and without any of Acrobat's menus, palettes, or tabs. (Creating PDF presentations will be covered completely in Chapter 7.)

Show (Window Options) Select either the File Name or the Document Title to be displayed in the PDF header.

User Interface Check any of the interface controls—menu bar, toolbars, window controls—that you do not want to be displayed when the PDF is opened. Note that these will all be hidden automatically if you select Open In Full Screen Mode.

The Document Title is initially the same as the File Name, but you can change this in the Document Properties Description options. Select File > Document Properties and click the Description category (Figure 5.9).

Once you set these document properties, you control how this PDF document will look and behave initially wherever it is opened.

The Custom settings allow you to add custom property values that can be used in document searches (see Chapter 7). The Advanced settings allow you to control e-book and URL settings (see Chapter 10, "Acrobat E-mail, E-book, and Web Features").

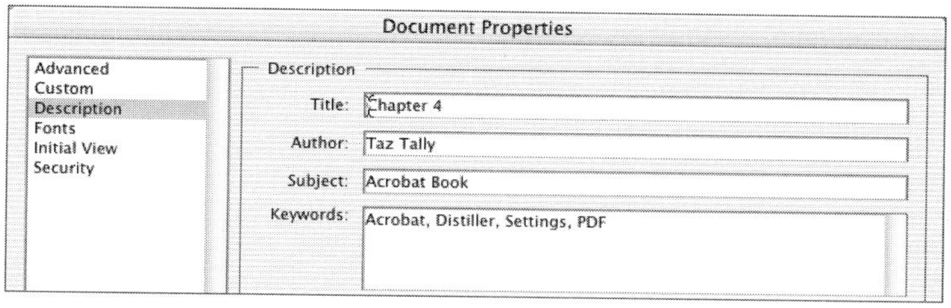

Figure 5.9 Document Description properties

Controlling Who Has Access and What They Can Do to Your PDF

Acrobat provides a complete set of access and use controls through its security functions. You can control who can open and view your PDFs as well as who can edit and output them with varying levels of permissions. PDFs also offer digital signature capabilities for document tracking and authorization. And this is easier to set up and use than you might think. Here is how it all works.

See What Access You Have to a PDF

If you can open a PDF, you already know that you have been allowed access. To check to see what restrictions might have been placed on its use, you once again consult the Document Properties. Here's how to open those properties and view the current settings:

 Note: The rest of this chapter describes how to *change* various security settings.

1. Open the Document Properties by choosing File > Document Properties or by typing ⌘/Ctrl+D. The Document Properties window appears.

2. Select Security from the list of Document Properties categories in the left side of the window. The Security preferences appear (Figure 5.10).

3. View the permissions associated with this PDF. Here you can see that there is a password set to allow access to perform certain functions such as Printing and Commenting, while other functions such as Changing The Document and Content Copying Or Extraction are not allowed.

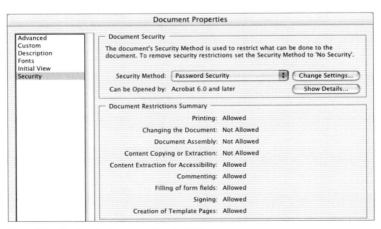

Figure 5.10 Viewing the document's Security Method

4. To get more specifics on the permissions, click the Show Details button. A window labeled Document Security appears (Figure 5.11). Here you see, for example, that while printing is allowed, it is allowed only at low resolution.

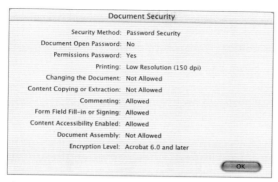

Figure 5.11 Viewing the document's security details

5. If you would like to change the Security settings and have access to do so, click the Change Settings button. Setting and changing Acrobat security is the subject of the following sections.

Controlling Access and Use of Your PDFs

In Chapter 4, "Creating the PDF You Want," you learned how to set PDF security when you create a PDF during the distilling process. Here you'll see how to control access after a PDF is created and learn how to use Acrobat's expanded security capabilities.

From the main menu bar, choose Document > Security > Restrict Opening And Editing. The Password Security - Settings window appears (Figure 5.12).

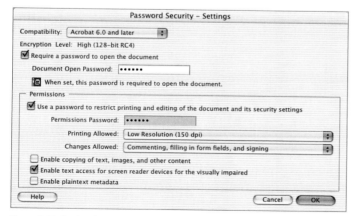

Figure 5.12 Setting document open and access security

Compatibility

The lower the version number, the greater the compatibility. Before you select Acrobat 6.0 And Later, be sure that the recipients of your PDFs are equipped with Acrobat 6 or Adobe Reader 6. Unless you need the Enable Plaintext Metadata feature provided exclusively in Acrobat 6, the Acrobat 5.0 And Later setting is a more compatible, and equally powerful, choice.

Version incompatibility is the most common reason why someone cannot read one of your PDF documents. Therefore, I save in the lowest possible version of Acrobat. I often save all the way back to version 3 for PDFs that I intend to distribute widely across the Internet. Even version 3 provides good basic document security features.

Configure the Security settings to match your needs. Following are a few guidelines and suggestions:

Compatibility Select an Acrobat version compatibility that will match the latest version of Acrobat the users of these PDF documents will have. Your choices are Acrobat 3.0 And Later, Acrobat 5.0 And Later, and Acrobat 6.0 And Later.

Document Open Password Check the Require A Password To Open The Document option and assign a password to restrict the opening of the document. Be sure to record this password and supply it to those who need it.

Permissions Password If you want to control what can be done with your PDF file once it is opened, then you should check the Use A Password To Restrict Printing And Editing Of This Document And Its Security Settings option and set a Permissions Password. This password should be different than the Document Open Password.

Note: Anyone who has the Permissions Password will automatically have Document Open access as well.

Printing Allowed Set the quality of printing, if any, that will be allowed: None, Low Resolution (150 dpi), or High Resolution. Using the Low Resolution setting is a good way to allow some printing access. But remember that most desktop printing devices can print very well with 150 ppi of resolution, so sometimes setting this Low Resolution restriction has little real impact.

Changes Allowed Read carefully through these choices to make sure you allow only what you want in terms of change to your document. The choice of Commenting, Filling In Form Fields, And Signing is a favorite of mine because it allows all kinds of feedback but prevents any fundamental changes to, or access to content from, the document.

```
None
Inserting, deleting, and rotating pages
Filling in form fields and signing
✓ Commenting, filling in form fields, and signing
Any except extracting pages
```

Enable Copying Of Text, Images, And Other Content Check this option if you want others to be able to access the data in your documents. Sales datasheets would be a good example. I typically leave this unchecked, since I usually do not want others to freely use my content.

Enable Text Access For Screen Reader Devices For The Visually Impaired I usually check this option to facilitate access.

Enable Plaintext Metadata This is an Acrobat 6–only feature. Turn this feature on to allow digital asset-management software to search the document metadata. If you need to store, search, and retrieve data from your PDFs, this is a good option to activate.

Once you've set these restrictions the way you want them, click the OK button. Acrobat will lead you through a sequence of windows asking you to type in and verify any passwords you have set.

To finish the process, save and close the document. The next time you or anyone else opens this document, Acrobat will prompt them to enter any assigned passwords and will restrict the usage to those allowed during this security assignment session.

That's all there is to it. After you have done this a couple of times, it will be easy.

Encrypting Documents

In addition to the document access security, you can also encrypt PDF documents and control access to encrypted documents through Digital IDs, Digital ID Certificates, and trusted lists of certificates.

Creating a Digital ID

The first step in using encrypted documents and trusted lists is to set up a certified Digital ID. Once established, this Digital ID can be used to create a Digital ID Certificate, which in turn can be used to encrypt documents and to control access to encrypted documents. Here's how to create an ID:

1. From the main menu bar, choose Document > Security > Encrypt For Certain Identities Using Certificates. The Document Security - Digital ID Selection window appears (Figure 5.13).

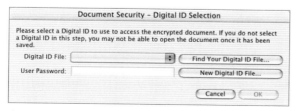

Figure 5.13 No Digital IDs have been created yet.

Click the New Digital ID File button. The Create Self-Signed Digital ID window (Figure 5.14) appears.

Figure 5.14 Creating a Digital ID

3. Fill in all the data fields in the Digital ID Details; the first few fields (Name, Organizational Unit, Organization Name, Email Address, and Country/Region) should be self-evident. Here are some details on the rest:

   Enable Unicode Support If you want to use UNICODE extended character sets, click this check box and fill in the ID info fields that appear to the right of the first set of ID fields.

   Key Algorithm Select either the 1024-bit or 2048-bit RSA encryption algorithm. The 2048 is more secure (that is, more difficult to hack) but is less compatible/widely used. 1024-bit is usually my choice since it is plenty secure and more universally used.

   Use Digital ID For Select one of the three uses for Digital IDs Digital Signature, Data Encryption or Digital Signature And Data Encryption (my standard selection).

   Digital ID File Security Enter a password and confirm it.

4. Click the Create button. A New Self-Sign Digital ID File Save As window will appear (Figure 5.15) with the Acrobat Security folder preselected.

5. Click the Save button. Macintosh Digital ID files will have a .p12 extension; Windows files will have a .pfx extension.

   Once any Digital ID has been created, it can be shared with other (trusted) individuals who can use this Digital ID to open your encrypted files.

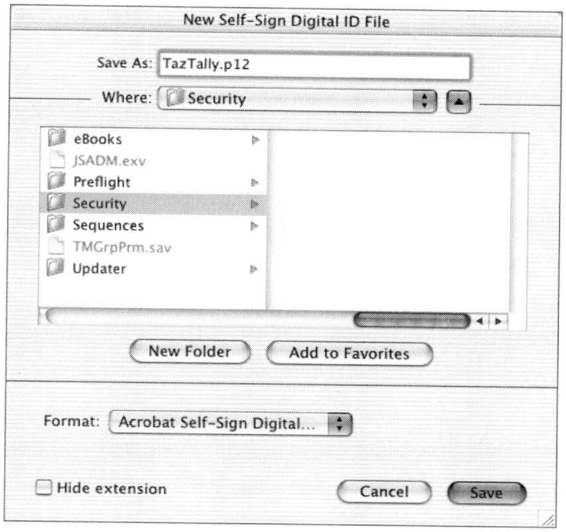

Figure 5.15 Save your Digital ID in the Acrobat *Security* folder.

Managing Digital IDs

Once you have created a Digital ID, you can create others and manage them using the Digital ID Manager. You access these features from a submenu; from the main menu bar, select Advanced > Manage Digital IDs > My Digital ID Files, and you will have the choice of three commands (Figure 5.16):

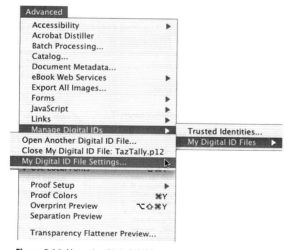

Figure 5.16 Managing Digital ID Files

Open Another Digital ID File Allows you to create new Digital ID files or open other already created ID files (Figure 5.17).

Figure 5.17 Open or create an ID.

Close My Digital ID File Allows you to close your current Digital ID file and access other IDs.

My Digital ID File Settings Allows you to manage Digital ID files: add, remove, view, export, change the password of, or change the setting of your ID (Figure 5.18). We'll use the Export function next to create a Digital ID Certificate, which can be used to create and control access to an encrypted PDF.

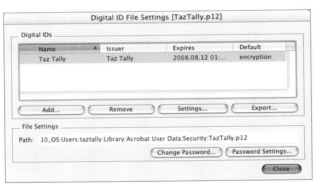

Figure 5.18 Manage existing IDs from this dialog.

Creating a Digital ID Certificate

Once you have created a Digital ID file, this can be used to create a certificate, which can be used for a number of purposes, including creating and opening encrypted files. Digital ID Certificates are password-protected portable files that contain the information you placed in your Digital ID file. Here's how to create one:

1. Choose Advanced > Manage Digital IDs > My Digital Files > My Digital File Settings (Figure 5.18).

2. Select the Digital ID file you would like to convert into a Digital ID Certificate.

3. Click the Export button. The Data Exchange File – Export Options window appears (Figure 5.19).

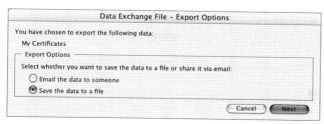

Figure 5.19 Export Digital ID data as a Certificate.

4. Select either the e-mail or save option. Digital ID Certificates can be e-mailed to those people (referred to as trusted recipients) to whom you would like to provide access to your encrypted and signed files.

5. Click Next. An Export Data As window appears.

6. Select a location to save your certificate file and click Save. Your new Digital ID Certificate file will be saved in this location.

The file extension of this Digital ID Certificate is .fdf, which is the standard data exchange format for PDF document data.

Creating an Encrypted Document

Once you have created a Digital ID Certificate, it can be used for several purposes, including creating and opening encrypted files. Here's how:

1. Using either the Document > Security submenu or the Secure icon in the Tool palette (Figure 5.20), select the command Encrypt For Certain Identities Using Certificates. A window appears labeled Restrict Opening And Editing To Certain Identities (Figure 5.21).

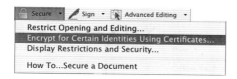

Figure 5.20 Begin the encryption process either from the Document > Security submenu or from this Secure icon.

2. To add a certificate to the list of trusted identities, click the Browse For Certificates button.

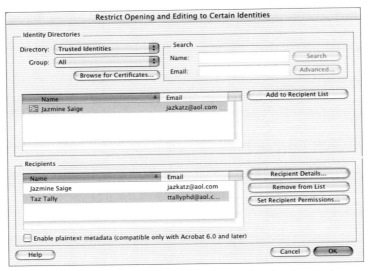

Figure 5.21 Set up identities for certificates you have and recipients for others who have your certificate.

3. In the Locate Certificate File dialog (Figure 5.22), locate the certificate (an FDF file) for the person you want to add to the list, and click Open. This certificate name (Jazmine Saige here) will be added to the list of names in the Identity Directories area.

Figure 5.22 Browse for the certificate to add.

4. Click this new name in the Identity Directories area to select it, then click the Add To Recipient List button. The new name (Jazmine Saige here) will be added to the list at the bottom.

5. Click the Set Recipient Permissions button.

6. Configure the Recipient Permission Settings window (Figure 5.23) to suit your wishes, and click OK.

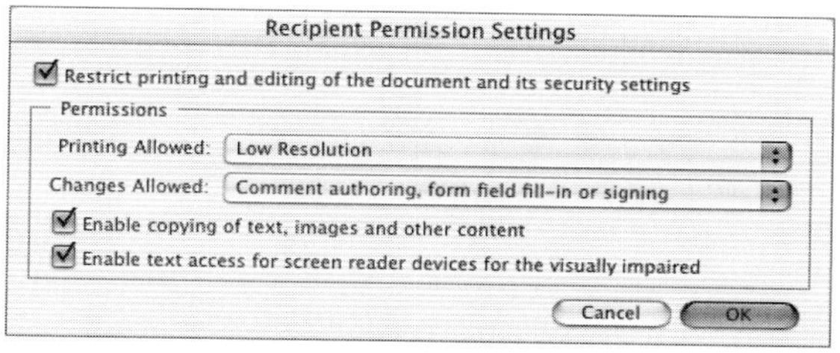

Figure 5.23 Set the permissions for this recipient.

7. Back in the Restrict Opening And Editing To Certain Identities window, click OK to finish the assignment process.

8. Save and close the document to apply the encryption. (Acrobat should present you with a reminder message to do this.)

Once you have mastered creating and editing Digital IDs and Digital ID Certificates you will be in good shape to use all of the variations of security offered by Acrobat. One security function you might find useful is the ability to use digital signatures to track documents, so we will cover this next.

Tracking Documents Using Self-Signed Security

In addition to the document access and encrypting security described in the previous sections, Acrobat provides document tracking and verification security through the use of digital signatures, both regular and certified. Digital signatures can be either text-based or customized graphics.

Creating a Certified Digital Signature

Creating a certified and signed PDF not only allows you to track who has opened a document, through the use of signatures, but also protects the integrity of the file through certification:

1. The first step in using encrypted documents and trusted lists is to set up a certified Digital ID. Once established, this Digital ID can be used to sign and track document use. Follow the instructions for creating a Digital ID in the previous section on encrypting.

Certification

Certification provides a way of tracking a document as it moves from one location to another. If a document is certified, it has not been altered, without permission, from its original form. If you want to make sure that a document's contents are not altered without you finding out about it, then certification is the way to go. If document integrity is not paramount, but you want to track a document's use, then you may want to use digital signature without going through the process of certification.

2. Open the PDF to which you would like to assign a digital signature.

3. Using either the Document > Digital Signatures submenu or the Sign icon in the Tool palette (Figure 5.24), select the Sign This Document command.

Figure 5.24 Certifying a PDF begins with the Sign > Sign This Document command.

4. If this is the first time this document has been signed, a window appears labeled Alert – Document Not Certified (Figure 5.25). (If the document has already been signed and certified, you will be led through the following signing steps without the Alert window.) This window gives you two choices, either to sign without certifying or to certify the document. Click the Certify Document button, because this will provide you with the most control over the document. This process will lead you through a series of dialog boxes; let's see where this journey takes you.

Figure 5.25 Yes, certify the document.

5. The Save As Certified Document window appears (Figure 5.26) and provides the option of using either your own Digital ID or one from an third-party Adobe partner. Using third-party IDs can be useful if you want to distribute your PDF

widely and want to use an ID that can be obtained elsewhere, thereby eliminating the need to distribute your own Digital ID Certificate to all whom you may want to see the file. You will use your own in this process, so click OK.

Figure 5.26 Click OK to continue saving your PDF as a certified document.

6. In the Choose Allowable Actions window (Figure 5.27), select the use capabilities you want to allow from the Allowable Actions drop-down list, and then click Next.

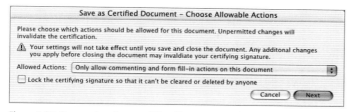

Figure 5.27 Choose what viewers will be able to do with your document.

7. In the Select Visibility window (Figure 5.28), choose whether you want the certification to be visible or not, and then click Next.

Figure 5.28 Make your certification visible or hide it.

If you decide to make the certification visible, the next window (Figure 5.29) instructs you to draw with your mouse an area where the certified signature will be placed. Note, that the larger you draw the area, the larger the signature will be. Click OK and draw the area.

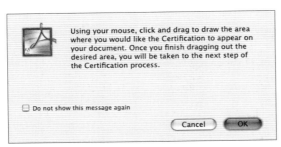

Figure 5.29 Drag out the area on the PDF page where your signature will appear.

8.   Once you have drawn the signature area (or chosen not to make the certification visible), the Sign window appears (Figure 5.30). You can specify a reason for the digital signature here before you continue. Type in your password; you must use the password for the currently active Digital ID. (To see the currently active Digital ID, click the View Digital ID button or choose Advanced > Manage Digital IDs > My Digital ID Files.) Click the Sign And Save As button or the Sign And Save button to complete this window. I recommend that you routinely use Sign And Save As so that a security-free copy of your document will still be available.

Figure 5.30 Sign your certified document and save it with a new filename.

 Note: We'll examine the Show Options button in the next section.

CHAPTER 5: CONTROLLING ACROBAT AND ACCESS TO YOUR PDFS ■

9. A standard Save As window will appear. Name and choose a location for your signed and certified PDF to be placed. I like to place a *C* at the end of the name of any PDF that I sign in this manner to indicate that it is certified. Click the Save button.

Your digital signature will appear where you drew the signature area during Step 7; an example is shown here. You will note that in the upper-right corner of the signature is a small certificate icon, indicating that it is a certified as well as a signed PDF. What you see here is the basic, default text-based signature. Your signature can be customized in many ways, and that's what we will do next!

Customizing a Graphic Digital Signature

If you want to customize your digital signature, Acrobat provides a variety of customizing capabilities, including using a graphic as a digital signature. To customize your signature, first follow Steps 1–7 in the preceding section to get to the window titled Save As Certified Document - Sign (illustrated back in Figure 5.30). From there, continue with these instructions:

1. Click the Show Options button. The window title changes to Apply Signature To Document, and the window expands to include an Options section (Figure 5.31).

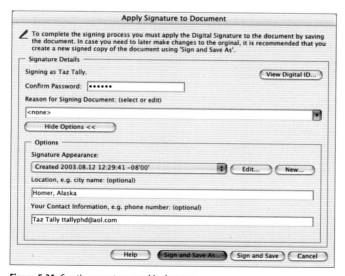

Figure 5.31 Creating a custom graphic signature

2. Click the Edit button if you want to edit a current signature or New if you want to create a new signature. The Configure Signature Appearance window appears (Figure 5.32).

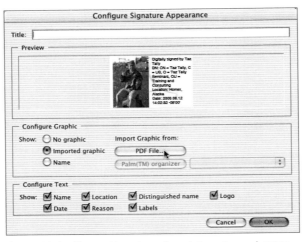

Figure 5.32 Combine graphics and text elements to create your signature.

3. To import a graphic, click the PDF File button under the heading Import Graphic From. A Select Picture window appears (Figure 5.33), where you browse to and open the PDF picture you would like to use as a signature icon. Click OK to return to the Configure Signature Appearance window.

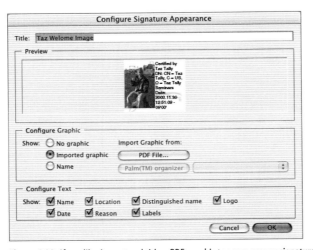

Figure 5.33 If you like, import and title a PDF graphic to serve as your signature.

4. Type in a name the Title Field a the top of the window, here Taz Welcome Image.

5. Under Configure Text, check each of the text items you would like included in your custom signature, and then click OK.

6. Continue the signature process as before (Step 9 from the preceding section), clicking the Sign And Save As button.

7. View your new graphic signature in all its glory!

Validating, Checking, Editing, and Deleting Digital Signatures

Once a digital signature has been created, there are numerous ways to check, validate, and modify the signature. Here are a few of the most common and useful ones:

- First, visually check the digital signature to see if it has a check mark next to it. If it does, it is probably in good shape.

- To receive more information about the signature, simply double-click it and a Signature Validation Status window will appear with information about the signature (Figure 5.34). You can also click the Signature Properties button to get even more data.

Figure 5.34 Double-click a signature to see details.

- The Document > Digital Signatures submenu (Figure 5.35) includes more digital signature and validation functions; some of these are also available by clicking the Sign icon in the Tool palette. You can find the most comprehensive overview and editing of digital signatures by selecting the Signatures tab on the left side of the PDF document page and then clicking the Options button.

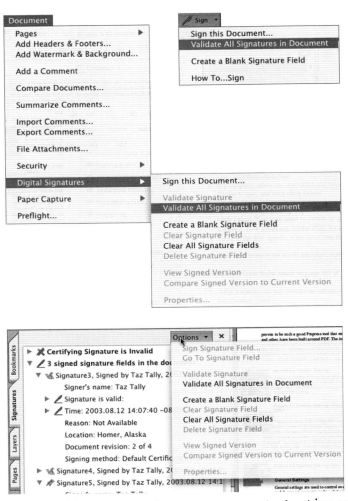

Figure 5.35 Validate signatures, sign documents, and compare versions from these menus.

Using Acrobat and Navigating PDFs

Acrobat 6 provides a wide variety of tools and methods for managing the program itself and for navigating your PDFs (although I favor keyboard shortcuts for speed). If you are visually or hearing impaired, Acrobat has tools to help you get around in PDF documents.

Chapter Contents

Customizing tools, palettes, menus, and tabs

Navigating in and through your PDFs

Making PDFs more accessible

Customizing Tools, Palettes, Menus, and Tabs

There are several ways to navigate around a PDF document and through multiple PDF files and the Acrobat tools.

For speed reasons, I usually prefer to use keyboard shortcut methods to navigate around and through Acrobat tools and PDF documents. However, there are some tools and controls that you can access only through the mouse. Some users prefer to mouse around, and in fact there are times when the manual controls are convenient, such as when your hand is already on the mouse and the pointer is near the page control. So, in this section I look at both the mouse-manual and keyboard-shortcut methods.

Customizing Acrobat Tools and Palettes

Let's start with the default Acrobat tools and see how we might use and modify them to good advantage.

The File, Task, Basic, Zoom, Rotate, and How To toolbars appear by default and are organized as they appear in Figure 6.1. Note that each tool set is separated from the other tool sets by a double-line divider. The Task toolbar contains common tasks, and they have menu choices associated with them.

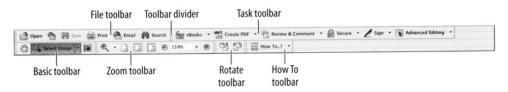

Figure 6.1 Default Acrobat toolbar

Using tools You can access any tool by simply clicking that tool.

Adding tools You can add other tools to the default tool set by using the View menu. Let's add the navigation tools to the toolbar: Choose View > Toolbars > Navigation (Figure 6.2). This addition expands the Acrobat tool set to include the navigation tools, which I recommend. You can add other tools on the tool list in a similar fashion.

Floating tools Any tool palette can be floated from the main tool palette (aka dock) by simply clicking that tool's side of the divider and dropping it down into the Document pane. This will allow the tool set to float freely in its own window (see Figure 6.3). Then you can move that tool palette anywhere on the screen you like.

Docking tools Any floating tool palette can be returned to the main dock by dragging the title portion of the floating tool palette. Or, if you have a whole slew of floating palettes and you want to clean up your mess, you can return them all by choosing View > Toolbars > Dock All Toolbars.

Locking tools On the other hand, if you would like to lock your tool palettes in place rather than dock them, select Lock Toolbars from the same menu: View > Toolbars > Lock Toolbars.

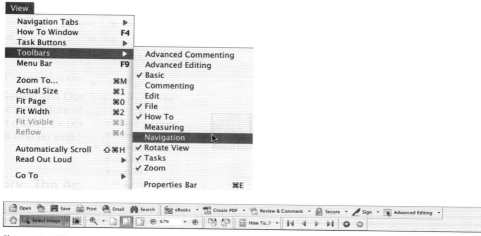

Figure 6.2 Adding navigation tools through the View menu

Figure 6.3 Drag a tool set to float it.

Customizing and Using Acrobat Menus and Tabs

Acrobat, like most applications, has a main set of menus at the top of the screen. But there are other menus as well, such as tab menus, which will allow you to access controls faster than main menus, and tool menus, which can be altered to appear as floating palettes. Here is how:

Quicker Access to Main Menu Controls

The controls for managing pages, which we will be doing later in this chapter, can be accessed in three main ways (Figure 6.4):

Slow Main menu: Choose Document > Pages > Control List.

Faster Tab menu: Click the Options menu in the Pages tab.

Fastest Keyboard/mouse shortcut: Right-click (Windows) or Control+click (Mac) in the Pages tab.

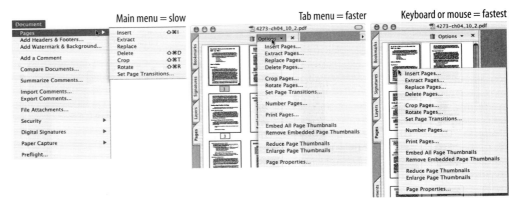

Figure 6.4 Quicker access to main menu controls

This same three-way access to information and controls—main menu, tool or tab menu, and keyboard shortcut access—is available throughout Acrobat. Whenever possible, I encourage you to use the keyboard shortcut access, because it will typically be faster.

Creating Floating Palettes from Menus

Many of the tools in the tool palette offer multiple options. If a tool, such as the Selection tool, has multiple options, a small down-arrow appears to the right of the tool. Click the down-arrow next to the Selection tool to see its options. If you want to have all these tool options visible, select the last menu choice, Show Selection Toolbar. This will create a floating palette, which can be placed anywhere on the screen with all the selection tool options visible (Figure 6.5).

Figure 6.5 Converting menus to tool palettes

Converting Floating Tabs to Stationary Tabs and Back

In addition to menus and palettes, Acrobat makes use of tabs, known as navigation tabs, to provide you access to document information and controls. The primary access to navigation tabs is through the main menu. Let's start there:

1. Activate the Articles navigation tab by choosing View > Navigation Tabs > Articles. The Articles and Destinations tabs will appear as a floating set (Figure 6.6).

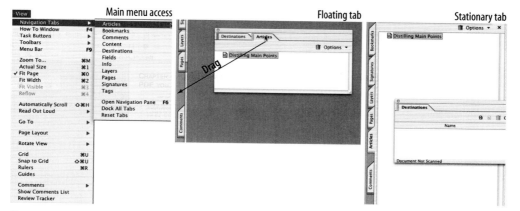

Figure 6.6 Converting floating tabs to stationary tabs

2. Click the Articles tab and drag the tab to the Tabs pane on the left side of the window. The Articles tab will now become a stationary tab, and the Destinations tab will remain floating by itself.

3. To float any of the navigation tabs, simply click the tabs and drag them into the Document pane.

Navigating In and Though PDF Documents

Acrobat provides several ways to navigate through your PDF documents. There are both mouse-oriented and keyboard shortcut–based techniques in Acrobat to help you navigate and access tools easier and faster. Here are some of the ones that I think will help you most:

Navigating by Mouse

There are several useful mouse-based tools in Acrobat, including the Navigation palette, the window controls, and the Navigation pane. Let's look at all three:

Using the Navigation Tool Palette to Navigate

First make sure that the Navigation tool palette is available. If you do not see it, choose View > Toolbars > Navigation. This toolbar can be either stationary or floating (☞ "Floating Tools" earlier in this chapter). Once visible, this Navigation palette will allow you to move forward and backward one page at a time, move to the beginning or the end of the document, or go to the previous or next view with a click of the mouse (Figure 6.7). The Previous View and Next View controls are perhaps the most interesting, because Acrobat keeps track of not only pages viewed but also your location and magnification of the page, and it allows you to visit previous views.

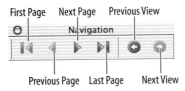

Figure 6.7 Navigational tool palette

Window Controls and Information

At the bottom of every default Acrobat document window is a window control area that provides all of the navigation controls of the Navigation palette, plus page layout controls and document page information (Figure 6.8). The page layout controls determine whether you will see single or facing pages and whether they can be displayed in a continuous scrolling fashion or a single page at a time. The document information area shows the total number of pages and the currently active page.

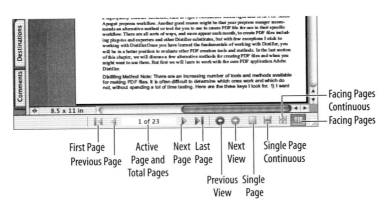

Figure 6.8 Window controls and document information

If the window controls are not visible at the bottom of a PDF document page, this indicates that they have been disabled in the Document Properties Initial View. To make the window controls visible, choose File > Document Properties > Initial View, and then deselect/uncheck the Hide Window Controls check box.

Complex Navigation and Reordering with the Navigation Pane

If you want to engage in extensive and/or complex navigation, such as moving through nonsequential pages, and even want to reorganize the page sequence, then the Navigation pane will be your tool of choice. To access the Navigation pane, do *one* of the following:

- Select View > Navigation Tabs > Open Navigation Pane.
- Type F6.
- Click the Pages tab on the left side of your PDF document page.

The Navigation pane will appear and will contain thumbnail views of all the document pages (Figure 6.9).

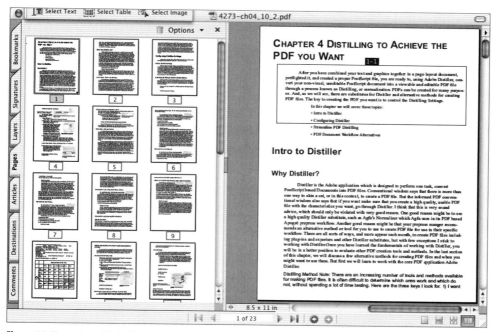

Figure 6.9 Navigating with the Navigation pane

- To control the width of the Navigation pane, and therefore the number of visible pages, drag the divider between the document page and the Navigation pane to the left or right.
- To change the document page that is visible in the Document pane, simply click the thumbnail of the page you would like to see.

Note: When you click a thumbnail page, two other things happen: The Navigation pane will activate if it is not already active, and the selected thumbnail page will highlight.

- You can quickly navigate through the entire document without changing the document page view by using the scrollbar between the Document pane and the Navigation pane. Then when you see the page you want to view, click it and it will appear in the Document pane (see the keyboard shortcuts following for an even faster method!).

- You can change the order of pages in a PDF document by clicking and dragging thumbnail pages around. I suggest that you make a copy of the original PDF before doing this!

Navigating by Keyboard

The fastest and easiest way to navigate through a PDF document when working in Acrobat is to use your keyboard. Adding keyboard shortcuts to the skills you learned above will make you a navigation ace. Here are some tips on how to do this:

 Note: The ⌘ icon represents the Command key on a Macintosh keyboard; this is usually the equivalent of the Ctrl key on a Windows keyboard.

Moving page to page Use the Right and Left arrow keys to move forward and backward, respectively.

Moving view to view (continuous single and facing layouts) Use the Page Up and Page Down keys to move up and down respectively. The amount of movement will depend upon the magnification and the size of the window. Higher magnifications and smaller windows will result in less movement.

Moving to the beginning and the end of a PDF document Use the Home and End keys to move to the first page and the last page of the document, respectively.

Reordering Pages

With document-based QuarkXPress or InDesign documents, the pages are linked together, and reordering pages can cause all kinds of document complexity nightmares, often resulting in corruption! PDF documents are page-based, which means that each document page is a separate entity. So reordering is not a problem in terms of document complexity, and there are no fears of corruption. It is a still a good idea to make a copy prior to reordering, so you can have a copy of the original page order in case you get confused.

Moving from page to page in the Navigation pane Select any thumbnail page and then use the Right, Left, Up, and Down arrow keys to jump from one page to another, often skipping many pages as you move between rows.

Jumping multiple pages in the Navigation pane Use the Page Up and Page Down keys to move multiple thumbnail pages in the Navigation pane. The number of thumbnail pages jumped will depend upon the size of the Navigation pane and the number of thumbnails visible. Larger Navigation panes (with more thumbnails showing) will result in more pages jumped.

Moving through views Just add the ⌘/Ctrl key to the Right and Left arrow keys to move forward and backward between views in any single or multiple PDFs you have open. Views include not only moves between pages but changes in magnification and locations. This is a handy way to move in and out of a magnified or whole page view.

Jumping from one PDF document to another Just add the Shift+⌘ (Mac) or Shift+Ctrl (Windows) keys to the Right and Left arrow keys to move forward and backward between any PDFs you have open in Acrobat.

To see an overview of all these page and view shortcuts, choose View > Go To.

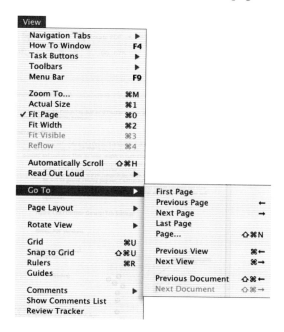

Zooming by Keyboard

Instead of typing numbers into the magnification field to obtain various views, here are some fast ways to zoom in and out, as shown in Table 6.1.

Key Combo	Effect
⌘/Ctrl++	Zoom in
⌘/Ctrl+−	Zoom out
⌘/Ctrl+0	View the entire document page
⌘/Ctrl+1	View the document page at 100%
Spacebar+drag	Activate the Hand tool and move locally
Spacebar+⌘/Ctrl+drag	Zoom into a specific view area (This is much faster and more intuitive than specifying a zoom percentage.)

Here is a sequence I often use to get around a PDF page quickly:

1. ⌘/Ctrl+0 to view the whole page.
2. Spacebar+⌘/Ctrl+drag to zoom in.
3. Spacebar+drag to move locally to a specific location.
4. ⌘/Ctrl+0 to zoom back out to full page view.
5. ⌘/Ctrl+Left arrow, then Right arrow to zoom in and out on the same area.

An overview of the zoom shortcuts can be found midway down the View menu. A complete list of navigation and other Acrobat shortcuts is shown in the Appendix.

Of Mice, Menus, and Keyboard Shortcuts

If you practice all the mouse and keyboard skills covered in this section, over time you will learn to use combinations of the mouse and the keyboard tools (while avoiding using actual menus whenever possible). This will allow you to have quick and complete control of your navigation, locations, and views and access to the menu controls as well.

Progressive and Continuous Zooming

The zooming techniques we have covered suffice for most of the zooming work you need to do. However, there are times when it would be nice to do some progressive zooming and/or keep track of where you are in a document while you are zooming, such as when you are making a presentation and you want to help keep your audience oriented. This is where some of Acrobat 6's specialty zoom tools—the Dynamic Zoom tool, the Loupe tool, and the Pan & Zoom window—come in handy. Here is how they can help you:

Progressive Zooming with the Dynamic Zoom Tool

Let's start with the Dynamic Zoom tool:

1. Open a document and navigate to the page(s) you would like to view with a progressive zoom.

2. Choose Tools > Zoom > Zoom Toolbar to activate the Zoom toolbar.

3. Select the Dynamic Zoom tool (Figure 6.10).

4. Drag the Dynamic Zoom tool from the *bottom* of the page to the top to progressively zoom *in* on the page(s) you have selected (Figure 6.11).

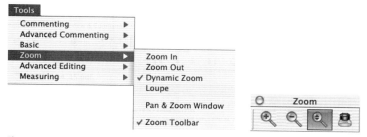

Figure 6.10 Activating the Zoom palette and the Dynamic Zoom tool

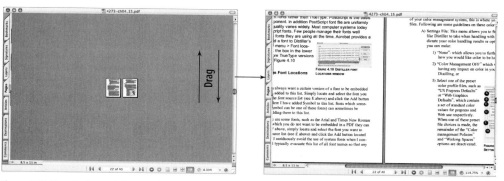

Figure 6.11 Drag the Dynamic Zoom tool up to zoom in, down to zoom out.

5. Drag the Dynamic Zoom tool from the *top* of the page to the bottom to progressively zoom *out* on the page(s) you have selected.

 Note: This zoom will function from 8.3 percent to 6400 percent. You can stop at any point and adjust the zoom location using the Hand tool (spacebar) or any of the other zoom and location techniques we discussed.

Location Zooming with the Loupe Tool

If you need to zoom in on a location and keep track of where the original location is, then the Loupe tool is a good solution. Here's how it works:

1. Select the Loupe zoom tool.

2. Click the center of the location you would like to zoom in to. A magnified view of that area will appear in a separate Loupe Tool window (Figure 6.12). The original zoom area will still be visible on screen in its original window.

3. Move the slider (C) at the bottom of the Loupe Tool window (B) back and forth to change the zoom magnification. A zoom area outline (A) will appear around the zoomed area in the original view.

4. Click and drag the zoom area outline in the original document to move the position of the zoomed area.

Figure 6.12 Loupe Tool window and zoom area outline

Move and Magnify with Pan & Zoom

If you would like to move around a document, keep track of where you are, and have a magnified view, then the Pan & Zoom tool is a dandy choice.

Choose Tools > Zoom > Pan & Zoom to activate the Pan & Zoom tool and window. The Pan & Zoom window appears (Figure 6.13) showing the reduced location view. The document itself will be magnified. (Note: This is just the opposite of the Loupe Tool window, which shows the magnified view in the dialog box.)

- Drag one of the four corner control points of the red zoomed-area outline in the Pan & Zoom window to adjust the magnification.
- Drag the center of the red outline to reposition the zoom area.
- Use the navigation arrows at the bottom to navigate through the document pages.

Figure 6.13 Pan & Zoom view

Split-Screen Viewing and Navigation

Another cool view and navigation feature that Acrobat has is the ability to split a document into two screens and view each one separately…and it's easy to do. Here's how:

1. Open a document.
2. View a whole document page (⌘/Ctrl+0).
3. Choose Window > Split. The window will split into two screens.

You can now navigate and change views in each screen separately using any of the view and navigation techniques you have learned in this chapter (Figure 6.14).

Scrolling

Acrobat provides the ability to scroll through a document when you are in any view, although I typically do this when I have zoomed in to some extent.

To scroll manually, zoom in on the entire width of a column of text, using the spacebar+⌘/Ctrl+drag. Then use the Up and Down arrow keys to scroll one line at a time.

 Note: For information on automatic scrolling, see the following section on making PDFs more accessible.

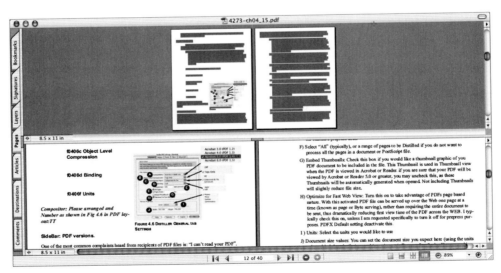

Figure 6.14 Split-screen view

160

CHAPTER 6: USING ACROBAT AND NAVIGATING PDFS

Making PDFs More Accessible

In addition to the view and navigation tools we previously covered, Acrobat offers some view and navigation tools designed specifically to help motion-impaired, visually impaired, and hearing-impaired people access Acrobat and PDF documents.

Preparing PDFs with Accessibility in Mind

PDF accessibility starts when the documents that are to become PDFs are created and then converted into PDF documents. Be sure to keep this in mind during both the construction of the original page layout document and when the page layout document is distilled into a PDF.

Structured and Tagged Document Construction

Making sure that PDF documents are properly structured and tagged when they are created is important to creating a flexible PDF. Here are some key tips:

- Choose a current PostScript printer driver when creating your PostScript files (☞ Chapter 3, "Creating Quality PostScript Files").

- If you are not going through the PostScript route to creating PDF files, then check to make sure that your PDF maker is recent enough to be creating DSC (Document Structuring Convention)-compliant PDFs. (See Note below.)

- Configure Distiller's General and Advanced Settings (Figure 6.15) or other PDF creation settings (such as the InDesign PDF Styles option named Include eBook Tags) so that they are properly tagged and that DSC information is retained when the PDFs are created.

Structured and Tagged PDFs

During the process of creating a PDF document, keep in mind that when you distribute your document electronically it will likely encounter a wide and ever-expanding variety of output devices supporting a range of page sizes and resolutions, including computer monitors, desktop printers, e-book readers, handheld devices, text-to-voice converters, and screen readers.

One of the keys to making sure your PDFs can be properly read and output with all these devices is to make sure that your PDFs are properly structured and tagged, so that these many different devices will be able to properly interpret and render *all* of your PDF document contents in the proper order. A structured PDF document has recognizable formatted text; in a tagged file, all the page elements—including tables, tables of contents, and formatted lists—are tagged so that they can be recognized, in their proper order, by reading devices.

Note: An easy way to check to see if a PostScript file has basic DSC compliance is to open the PostScript file in a word processor (a PostScript file is nothing more than a basic ASCII text file written in the language of PostScript) and check to see that the first line of the PostScript code text contains the characters % PS-Adobe, which indicates that this is indeed a basic DSC-compliant Adobe PostScript file.

Distiller General settings

Distiller Advanced settings

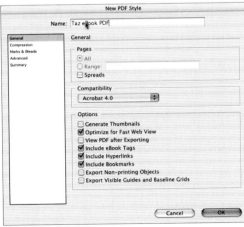

InDesign PDF Styles

Figure 6.15 Tag and DCS Settings in Distiller and InDesign

Adding Tags to PDFs

If you have PDFs that are not already tagged, you can add tags in Acrobat:

1. First run the Accessibility checker: Advanced > Accessibility > Full Check.

2. If the tags are missing, add the tags to the PDF by returning to the same menu: Advanced > Accessibility > Add Tags To Document.

3. If you have numerous PDFs to check for accessibility and add tags to, you can accomplish this with a "batch" function to help speed up the process and ensure consistency. (☞ Chapter 13, "Outputting PDFs and Their Contents," for instructions on executing batch functions.)

Adding tags to a PDF will dramatically improve its readability by a wide variety of devices.

Note: If you are unhappy with the way your PDF content flows, ☞ Chapter 12,"Editing PDFs," for instructions on how to reflow the contents of a PDF file.

Making Your PDFs More Visually Accessible

After you have created DSC-compliant and tagged PDFs, you can make several adjustments and use several tools to enhance your PDF access if you are visually challenged.

Setting Up a Document with More Visible Colors

To make a PDF more visually accessible, it's easy to modify the overall document colors to enhance visibility to meet specific needs. To do so, open the Acrobat Preferences: Acrobat > Preferences (Mac), or Edit > Preferences (Windows), or ⌘/Ctrl+K. Select the Accessibility Preferences (Figure 6.16), and adjust them to suit your needs.

Replace Document Colors Check this box. This will allow you to change background and text colors throughout the PDF.

Page Background and Document Text Change these options to colors that are more visible to a specific viewer. For instance, people with macular degeneration often find it easier to see white text on black backgrounds.

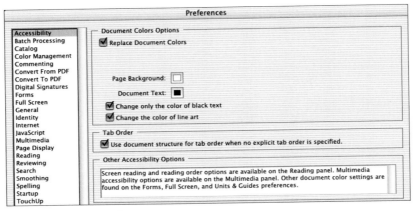

Figure 6.16 Accessibility Preferences

Change Only The Color Of Black Text If you change the Page Background or Document Text colors, and your documents have colored text as well as black text, you may want to change just the black text and let the colored text remain. If so, check this box.

Change The Color Of Line Art If you change the Page Background or Document Text colors to a dark color such as black, you may want to change the color of line art (which is often dark colored) to the same lighter color as the text. If so, check this box.

Use Document Structure For Tab Order When No Explicit Tab Order Is Specified Check this box to have Acrobat use the document structure to determine the order in which page elements will be viewed. If you are unhappy with the order in which your PDF file flows when it is read, ☞ Chapter 12 for instructions on how to reflow the contents of a PDF.

Making Forms More Visible

The colors in forms can be adjusted to make them easier to read if you are visually challenged:

1. Open the Acrobat Preferences: Acrobat > Preferences (Mac), or Edit > Preferences (Windows), or ⌘/Ctrl+K.

2. Select the Forms Preferences (Figure 6.17).

3. Check the option Show Background And Hover Color For Form Fields.

4. Select a background color that will be visible to a specific viewer. You may want to use the same background color you selected in the Accessibility Preferences if you made a background choice there.

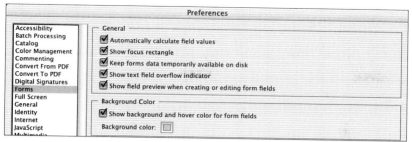

Figure 6.17 Adjusting forms accessibility

Making Multimedia Components More Accessible

In addition to text and graphic document components, Acrobat supports multimedia components such as sound and video. These too can be adjusted to be more accessible. Here's how:

1. Open the Acrobat Preferences: Acrobat > Preferences (Mac), or Edit > Preferences (Windows), or ⌘/Ctrl+K.

2. Select the Multimedia Preferences (Figure 6.18).

3. Check to select all the Accessibility Options that relate to the content of your documents. (When I want to enhance accessibility, I turn them all on just to make sure I cover all my bases.)

4. Select the language you would like under the Preferred Language For Content menu.

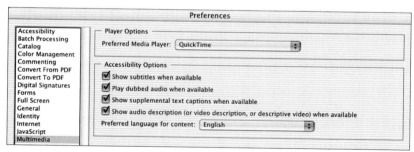

Figure 6.18 Adjusting multimedia accessibility

Text and Line Art Smoothing

The smoothness of text and line art can have a significant effect on how readable the text is and how recognizable the line art graphics are. Acrobat allows you to adjust how these elements will appear to a specific person on a specific viewing device. ᡩ Chapter 5, "Controlling Acrobat and Access to Your PDFs," for instructions on how to control on-screen text and line art smoothness.

Adjusting Bookmark Text Size

If you are using bookmarks to navigate through a PDF document, you can make the text in the bookmarks larger and therefore more visible. Click the Bookmarks tab to the left of the Document pane. Then click the Bookmarks tab's Options menu. To enlarge the size of the bookmark text, choose Options > Text Size > Large (Figure 6.19).

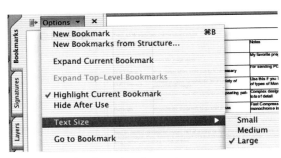

Figure 6.19 Bookmark text size adjustment

Using Acrobat if You Are Motion Challenged

We have already discussed the speed advantages of using keyboard controls, even if you can use a mouse, but if using a mouse is a challenge—if you can't or don't like to use a mouse to navigate PDFs and control Acrobat—then keyboard controls are your best bet. Here are some tips to using a keyboard to navigate PDFs and control Acrobat.

Note: Also see "Navigating In and Though PDF Documents" earlier in this chapter and the more complete listing of Acrobat keyboard controls in the Appendix.

Mac OS X Keyboard Access

If you are working on a Macintosh and using OS X, then you will first want to engage the full use of the keyboard through the System preferences. Here's how:

1. From the Apple menu, choose System Preferences. The System Preferences window appears.

2. Click the Keyboard icon. The Keyboard Preferences appear (Figure 6.20).

3. In the Keyboard Preferences window, check the Turn On Full Keyboard Access check box and select the Any Control radio button. This will allow non-operating system keyboard controls though other applications, such as Acrobat, to become active.

Windows Keyboard Explorer/Acrobat Keyboard Controls

If you are working in the Windows OS and are accessing a PDF though Explorer, any keyboard controls will initially apply to Explorer and not Acrobat. Here's how to activate the Acrobat keyboard controls:

1. Press the Tab key to switch the controls from Internet Explorer to Acrobat.

2. Press the Ctrl+Tab keys to switch the controls back from Acrobat to Internet Explorer.

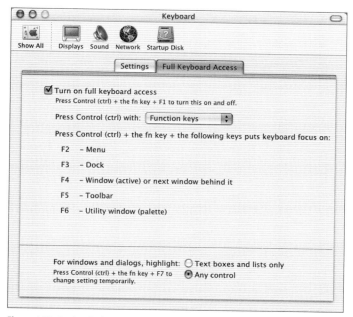

Figure 6.20 Setting Keyboard Preferences in Max OS X

Mac/Windows Keyboard Shortcuts

If you work in both the Mac and Windows operating systems, you know that the keyboards, and therefore the keyboard shortcuts, are not identical. Windows keyboards have Ctrl and Alt keys while Macs have Command and Option keys, all of which are used for primary keyboard control functions. If you switch back and forth from Windows to Mac, it can be confusing. Here is how I keep it straight: I keep the two "Cs" (Command (Mac) and Ctrl (Win)) together in my mind. If it is the "C" word on either system, it is the "C" word on the other. Command (Mac) = Ctrl (Window).

That leaves Option (Mac) = Alt (Win). And that's easy to remember too because Option means, roughly, Alt(ernative).

Rarely the Control key on the Mac is used, but when it is this usually equates to a right mouse button click on the Windows side.

Keyboard Controls of Acrobat

There is a complete list of keyboard controls in the Appendix, but here are a few of the most important ones to help you select and navigate:

Accessing tools Each tool has its own single alpha key shortcut. Many are obvious, such as H for the Hand tool. Others are less obvious, such as V for the Text tool. The keyboard shortcut key appears next to the name of the tool if you move your cursor over the tool and wait a second or two.

Navigating around windows and panes Press the Tab key to navigate through most windows, panes, and dialog boxes. Once you have reached the destination you can type in field values and then use the Enter or Return key to apply your settings.

Navigating through a document Use the Left and Right arrow keys to go from page to page. Use the Page Up and Page Down keys to move from screen view to screen view. Use the Home and End keys to take you to the beginning and end of the document.

Zooming Press ⌘ (Mac) or Ctrl (Windows) plus the + and – keys to zoom in and out.

Navigating between multiple open PDFs Press ⌘ (Mac) or Ctrl (Windows) plus the Left and Right arrow keys to move between PDF documents.

Automatic Scrolling

Acrobat can even be enticed to automatically scroll down a page. Here's how:

1. Zoom in to a full column of text.

2. Press Shift+⌘+H/Shift+Ctrl+H. The screen will begin to scroll down.

3. Use your numeric keypad keys 0 through 9 to control the scroll speed, with 9 being fastest. A reminder of this Automatically Scroll command can be found in the View menu.

4. Other controls for automatic scrolling are as follows:

- To reverse the direction of the scroll, press the minus sign (–).
- To jump to the previous or the next page, use the right and left arrows.
- To stop the scrolling, hit the Escape (Esc) key.

Note: Another useful way to set up easy-to-use navigation in a PDF is by creating articles that automatically lead a viewer around a PDF document with linked text columns. See the section on "Creating a PDF Article" in Chapter 9 for more info on creating and using articles.

Using Read Out Loud Capacities

Rather than you having to read a PDF on screen, Acrobat can read the document for you! And you can adjust how the document is read. Here's how to use and adjust Read Out Loud capabilities:

Activating the Read Out Loud function is easy. Simply choose View > Read Out Loud > Read This Page Only or Read To End Of Document, depending upon your preference (Figure 6.21).

Pausing and stopping Read Out Loud is also possible through this menu, but the keyboard controls are much more convenient. Here are the four Read Out Loud keyboard controls:

Command	Shortcut
Read This Page Only	Shift+Ctrl+V / Shift+⌘+V
Read To End Of Document	Shift+Ctrl+B / Shift+⌘+B
Pause	Shift+Ctrl+C / Shift+⌘+C
Stop	Shift+Ctrl+E / Shift+⌘+E

Figure 6.21 Read Out Loud menu

Modifying Read Out Loud

A set of default controls, such as voice type, reading speed, and pitch, is applied to the Read Out Loud function. You may want to adjust these to suit specific viewers. To do so, activate the Acrobat Preferences: Acrobat > Preferences (Mac), or Edit > Preferences (Windows), or ⌘/Ctrl+K. Select the Reading Preferences (Figure 6.22), and adjust these to suit your needs:

Volume The default volume is 7, which will have various output levels depending upon the sound system it is run through. Adjust to suit your listening level.

Note: Most computers have a sound level control button on the computer and/or a keyboard control through the operating system. You may want set the Acrobat sound higher than you normally like, to act as a maximum level, and then use your other sound control tools to adjust the final sound output level.

Voice type You can use the default voice (which is Victoria) on the voice list, or you may want to try another. Most of the voices are less satisfactory, in terms of hearing quality if not fun, than Victoria, but you might want to give Agnes a shout.

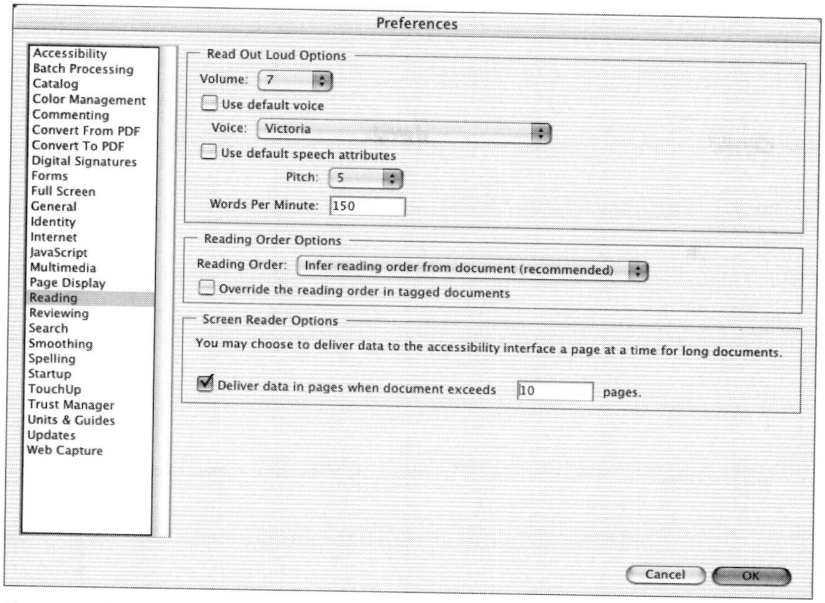

Figure 6.22 Reading Preferences

Speech attributes Here again you can use the default speed and pitch values. However, I do recommend that for most uses you slow the voice speed down to its minimum value, which is 150. This is typically a bit easier, and less tiring to listen to, than high voice speeds, particularly if your sound output quality is poor.

Reading Order Options You will typically want to leave this setting on the default value, Infer Reading Order From Document. If you are unhappy with the reading order in the document, I recommend changing the reading order in the document rather than trying to sort it out here, which is rarely successful. (☞ the section on reflowing PDF contents in "Reflowing (Changing the Order of) PDF Contents" in Chapter 12, "Editing PDF Documents," for information on how to change the reading order.)

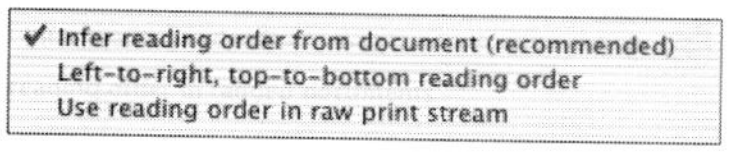

Screen Reader Options This setting affects how the PDF is delivered to the screen reading device. The default is to have this activated with a default value of 10 pages. Leave this setting as is unless your screen reader device's instructions make a different recommendation.

As you become familiar with all of Acrobat's use and navigation tools, you will adopt your own set of tools and techniques, which may include a mix of manual, keyboard shortcut, and automated functions, that work best for you and your capabilities.

PDF Document Management

7

Because PDF documents are page- rather than document-based, you can easily manipulate pages in any wide variety of ways. PDF documents and their pages can be manipulated, compared, optimized, and numbered, and they can have headers and even watermarks added to them. You can work in layers in Acrobat and search their contents to your heart's delight. Heck, Acrobat even has tools to make IT managers smile. It's the page-based nature of PDF documents that makes much of this manipulation and management possible. Let's see how to do all this cool stuff.

Chapter Contents

Manipulating PDF Document Pages

You can manipulate pages in any number of ways in Acrobat. You can add, subtract, crop, rotate, replace, extract, and change the order of pages. Documents can be compared, optimized, and numbered, and can have headers and even watermarks added to them. You can work in layers in Acrobat and search the contents. Acrobat even has tools to interest IT managers. The page-based nature (which we discussed earlier) of PDF documents is what makes much of this manipulation and management possible.

Note: Any pages can be added, deleted, extracted, or replaced easily in a PDF document, without any fear of any other pages in the PDF being affected, due to the page-based nature of PDF. I often use Acrobat and PDF to combine PDF document pages from otherwise unrelated and incompatible documents into one document. For instance, I often want to combine text and graphic page layouts for QuarkXPress, with charts and spreadsheets from Excel, charts from Illustrator, and even presentation materials form PowerPoint. I use watched folders (☞ Chapter 4, "Creating the PDF You Want") in Distiller to create PDFs of all the documents and then use Acrobat to combine and manipulate the final document.

Moving Pages in and out of Your PDF

Manipulating PDF documents in Acrobat is accomplished through page control menus. To access the page controls for adding, deleting, extracting, and replacing pages, do *one* of the following (Figure 7.1):

- Select Document > Pages and, from the submenu, choose the desired command (Insert, Extract, Replace, or Delete).
- Click the Options menu in the Pages tab and choose a command (Insert Pages, Extract Pages, Replace Pages, or Delete Pages).
- Use the keyboard shortcuts for Insert (Shift+⌘+I/Shift+Ctrl+I) or Delete (Shift+⌘+D/Shift+Ctrl+D).

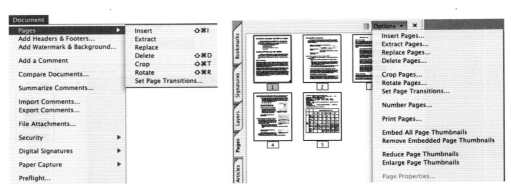

Figure 7.1 Access to page controls

Page Numbering

One issue that can lead to confusion when you start combining PDF documents is page numbering. If the documents you are adding together already have their own page numbering system, you can end up with a confusing mishmash of page numbers. Although it is possible to change the page number of PDF pages (more on that a bit later in this chapter), it is much easier to work out the page numbering system in the original document prior to making PDFs.

If I am using an Acrobat and PDF document as a vehicle to combine document pages from several different sources (as I often do when I make manuals), I create alphanumeric sections such as A-1 through A-25, B-1 through B-34, etc. I assign a different alpha section to each document source. This way if I choose to add or delete pages from any specific section, I do not create a renumbering nightmare for the combined final PDF document.

Depending upon where you are and what you are doing, you can use either of these menus or the shortcuts.

Inserting Pages

To insert pages, follow these steps—and be mindful of the suggestion in the sidebar on page numbering:

1. Open the PDF document that you would like to serve as the base document to which you would like to add pages.

2. Choose Insert Pages using one of the methods offered above. A window will appear (Figure 7.2) asking you to locate and select a PDF document for addition.

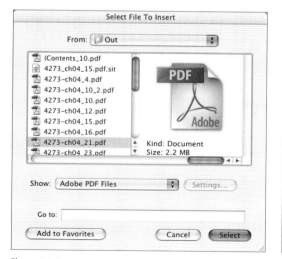
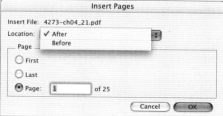

Figure 7.2 Inserting pages into a PDF

3. Select the PDF file you would like to add to the base document and click OK. An Insert Pages window will appear.

4. Determine where you would like your PDF document to be added—After or Before the First or Last page or a specific page number—and indicate this using the Location menu and the Page buttons.

5. Click the OK button and the new document will be added to the base document. The new page count will be updated at the bottom of the Document pane.

Deleting Pages

Acrobat 6 offers two methods of deleting pages. You can designate numerically a range of pages to be deleted or you can delete a selected set of pages.

If you have a simple page-deletion task of one or more consecutive pages, then follow these steps to delete a numeric range of pages:

1. Open the PDF document from which you would like to delete pages.

2. Save your document prior to making any deletions, so you can return to the last undeleted state if you want to.

3. Select Delete Pages using one of the methods offered above. A Delete Pages window will appear (Figure 7.3).

Figure 7.3 Deleting a page range

4. Click the From button.

5. Designate the range of pages (here, pages 3 to 5) you would like deleted.

6. Click the OK button to delete the pages.

If you have a more complicated task of deleting nonconsecutive pages or several sets of PDF document pages, then follow these steps for deleting selected pages:

1. Open the PDF document from which you would like to delete pages.

2. Save your document prior to making any deletions, so you can return to the last undeleted state if you want to.

3. Activate the Navigation pane (Figure 7.4) by clicking the Pages tab (A).

4. Expand the Pages tab until you can see all the pages you would like to delete, by dragging the divider (B).

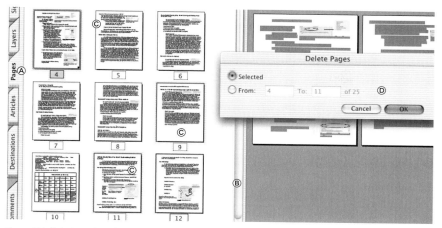

Figure 7.4 Deleting selected pages

5. From the Pages tab, select the pages you would like to delete. Use Shift+click for consecutive page selections, and Shift+⌘+click/Shift+Ctrl+click for nonconsecutive pages. I have selected pages 4, 9, and 11 here (C).

6. Choose Delete Pages using one of the methods offered above; I prefer for speed reasons to use the keyboard shortcut Shift+⌘+D/Shift+Ctrl+D. The Delete Pages window will appear (D).

7. The Selected button should be preselected, and a range of pages from which the deleted pages will be taken should be indicated in the From and To fields even though this section is inactive. Click OK.

Extracting Pages

Acrobat allows you to *extract*, as well as delete, pages to create separate documents. This is particularly useful when you want to use a single PDF page by itself (or range of pages), such as when you want to use a price sheet or order form out of a document.

1. Open the PDF document from which you would like to extract pages.

2. Use the Pages tab (as we did in the preceding section) to select the range of pages you would like to extract.

Note: You can select only continuous pages for extraction.

3. Select Extract Pages using one of the methods offered above. A window will appear asking you to designate those PDF document pages you would like to extract as a separate document (Figure 7.5).

Figure 7.5 Extracting a page range

4. Select the range of pages you would like to extract (4 to 7 here).

5. Decide whether you also want these pages to be deleted from the original document after extraction; check Delete Page After Extraction if you do.

6. Click OK. A new PDF document will be created.

7. Save this extracted document with a new name.

Replacing Pages

Acrobat allows you to replace single or multiple pages in a PDF document. This is useful when you want to swap out pages that change periodically, such as price sheets, without having to redo the entire document.

1. Open the PDF document in which you would like to replace pages.

2. Use the Pages tab (as we did in the preceding sections) to select the range of pages you would like to replace. (Figure 7.6 shows a price sheet on page 26 being replaced.)

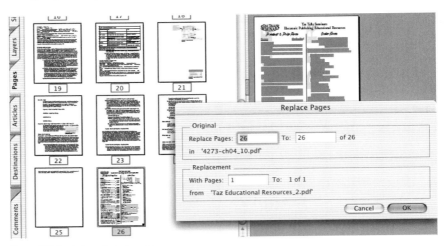

Figure 7.6 Replacing selected pages

PDF Page Sizes and Orientations

Because each page in a PDF document is a completely separate element from all the other pages, you are not limited to a specific size or orientation of your pages. Documents of any size or orientation can be added to documents containing other sizes and orientations of pages. For instance, you can easily add an 11"×17" Landscape PDF page to a PDF document that contains mostly 8.5"×11" Portrait pages. Be careful when you *print* a document with various page sizes and orientations, because the various pages will need to be printed with settings to suit their specific sizes and orientations.

3. Choose Replace Pages using one of the methods offered at the start of the chapter. A Select File With New Pages dialog will appear, asking you to designate the source PDF document containing the pages you would like to put into the original PDF.

Note: The document you choose here will remain unaffected.

4. Select the replacement document and click Select. A Replace Pages window will appear, showing the Original page and the Replacement document page that will be used in the replacement process (Figure 7.6).

5. Check to make sure the Replace Pages window is correct; then click OK.

6. Save your original document with its replaced pages to complete the process.

Cropping and Rotating Pages

The page-based nature of PDF documents once again pays a benefit if you want to crop and rotate pages. Each page in a PDF document can be cropped or rotated on its own. To crop one or more pages, follow these steps:

1. Using the Pages tab, navigate to the page(s) you would like to crop.

2. Using the ⌘/Ctrl and/or Shift keys plus clicking, select discontinuous or continuous pages.

3. Activate the Crop Pages command either by pressing ⌘/Ctrl+Shift+T or by selecting Crop from the Options menu in the Pages tab (Figure 7.7). The Crop Pages window will appear (Figure 7.8).

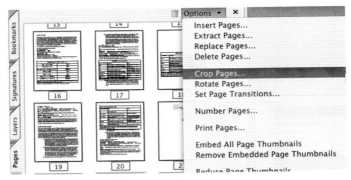

Figure 7.7 Choose the Crop Pages command.

Note: You can also use Document > Pages > Crop, but it is typically slower if you are already in the Pages tab.

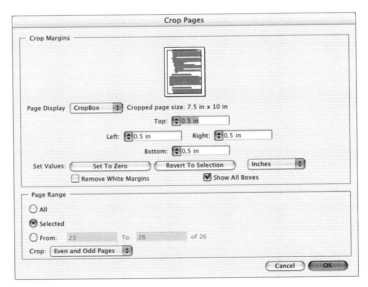

Figure 7.8 Crop Pages dialog

4. Configure the Crop Pages window to suit your needs. The results of your selections will appear in the thumbnail preview at the top of the dialog:

Page Display Select whether you want the Crop, Bleed, Trim, or Art box displayed.

Top, Left, Right, Bottom Indicate the size of the crop that you would like on all four sides. You can have a different crop value on each side.

Remove White Margins If you select this check box, the cropping amount will be decided for you. We will use this feature when we discuss creating presentations in Chapter 8, "Building Presentations and Forms."

Page Range Indicate the page or range of pages to be cropped. If you have preselected pages in the Pages tab, those pages will be already indicated in the From and To fields.

Rotating Pages

To rotate pages, follow these steps:

1. Using the Pages tab, navigate to the page(s) you would like to rotate.

2. Using the ⌘/Ctrl and/or Shift keys plus clicking, select discontinuous or continuous pages.

3. Activate the Rotate command either by pressing ⌘/Ctrl+Shift+R or by selecting Rotate from the Options menu in the Pages tab. The Rotate Pages window will appear (Figure 7.9).

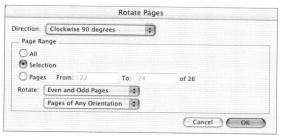

Figure 7.9 Rotating selected pages

4. Configure the Rotate Pages window to suit your needs:

Direction Select the direction of rotation: Counterclockwise 90 Degrees, Clockwise 90 Degrees, or 180 Degrees.

Page Range Identify the pages to be rotated. If you have preselected pages in the Pages tab, those pages will be already indicated in the From and To fields.

Rotate Select Even Pages Only or Odd Pages Only if you want to constrain the action to one type of page. Select a specific orientation if you would like to rotate only Portrait or only Landscape pages.

Changing Page Order

The order of page occurrence in a PDF document can be easily changed. And because of the independent nature of each PDF document page, you can reorder the pages to your heart's content without fear of damaging the PDF document. Here are some tips on how to do this fast:

1. Perform a Save As to create a copy of your document.

2. Click the Pages tab (Figure 7.10) to activate the thumbnail views of the pages.

3. Expand the Navigation pane (A) by dragging the scrollbar divider (B) until you can see all the pages you want to move.

4. Select the page(s) you want to move. (Use Shift+click to select a continuous range of pages and ⌘/Ctrl+click to select discontinuous pages.)

5. Hold down the mouse, click, and drag the selected pages to their new location in the document. Drag the selection(s) between the pages where you want to move them (C). Here, pages 22–24 are being moved to follow page 8.

6. When your reordering is complete, save the document to make the changes permanent.

 Note: If you reorder numbered pages, their page number sequence will be out of order. If you plan to reorder pages in a PDF document, you might want to refrain from assigning the original document page numbers.

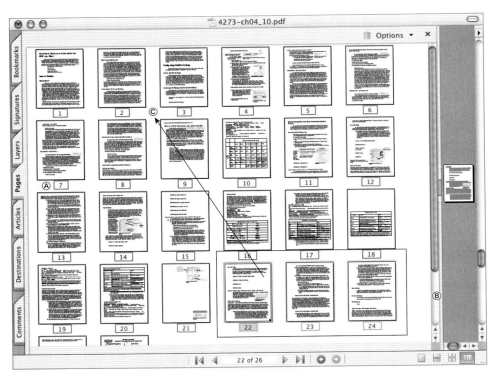

Figure 7.10 Reordering pages

Renumbering Pages

Acrobat allows you to add and/or change the page numbering system that Acrobat uses when it numbers pages. By default Acrobat will automatically number pages sequentially starting with page #1. It is important to distinguish between Acrobat's page numbering system and any original document page numbering that may be used. For instance, if your PDF is a book with front matter that uses a standard lowercase Roman numeral system—i, ii, iii, etc.—then your Acrobat page numbering will not match your original document page numbering.

Acrobat allows you to change the Acrobat page numbering to match the original document numbering system. Here's how:

1. Once again the Pages tab can be a big help here. Using the Navigation pane, navigate to the page(s) you would like to renumber.

2. Shift+click the continuous ranges of pages you would like to renumber—in Figure 7.11, I've selected pages 1–6.

3. Choose Number Pages from the Options menu in the Pages tab. The Page Numbering dialog (Figure 7.12) appears.

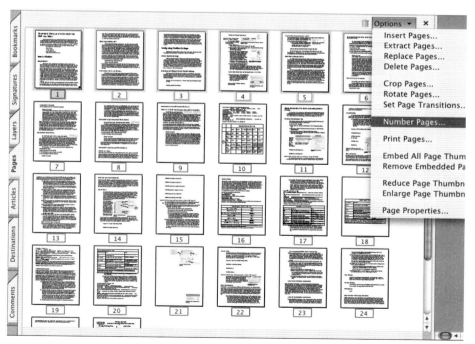

Figure 7.11 Page numbering command and the Pages view

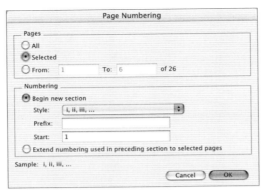

Figure 7.12 Page Numbering window

4. Configure the dialog to suit your needs:

    Pages Select the range of pages you want to renumber. If you have already selected pages in the Pages tab, they will be preselected here and the Selected button will be active.

    Numbering - Style Select the style you would like to use. Here, I have selected lowercase Roman numerals.

    Numbering - Prefix If you want your page numbering to have a prefix such as "A–," enter the prefix here.

    Numbering - Start Enter the first page number for the renumbering here. If you have preselected the page sequence you want renumbered in the Pages tab, the first (current) page number of that sequence will be already entered here.

5. Click OK.

6. Now click the first page of the document in the Pages tab, and check the numbering field in the Status bar. It will now indicate "i (1 of 26)," showing the renumbered page symbol (i) and the absolute page number (1) as well as the total number of pages in the document (26).

See the later section on adding elements to PDF documents to learn how you can *add* page numbers to a PDF document, instead of reordering them.

Comparing PDF Documents

If you work with multiple versions of the same document, one of the handy capabilities of Acrobat is the ability to compare the contents of two PDF documents. I often use this comparison capability when I am working with several versions of a brochure I am making and there has been some time between versions, or several changes have been made and I can't remember exactly what has been changed. Here is how to compare documents:

1. Launch Acrobat.

Note: It is not necessary to have the two comparison files open, but if you do they will appear in drop-down menus in the Compare Documents window for easy selection.

2. Choose Document > Compare Documents. The Compare Documents window appears (Figure 7.13).

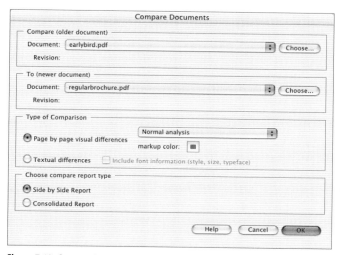

Figure 7.13 Compare Documents dialog

3. Configure this Compare Documents window to suit your needs:

Compare and To Select two PDF versions of the same document for comparison—in this case, two versions of a brochure named earlybird.pdf and regular-brochure.pdf—by clicking the Choose buttons (or by selecting open documents from the drop-down menus).

Type Of Comparison Select whether you want a Page-By-Page Visual Differences analysis (chosen here) or a Textual Differences analysis. If you select Textual Differences, check the box if you want to include any differences in fonts. In some cases you may know that there are style changes between versions, and these may be okay, but you just want to check to make sure the copy is the same, or vice versa.

Note: If I am comparing graphic components between documents, I choose Page-By-Page. If I am primarily looking for text, I select Textural. Sometimes I run both types of analysis if I need to see both graphics and text in detail.

Depth of analysis If you have selected Page By Page… analysis, use the drop-down list at the right to set the depth of the analysis you would like to have done: Detailed, Normal (selected here), or Coarse. Experiment with the depth of analysis to see how much depth is required for your types of documents. I find that the Standard analysis is sufficient for most of my analyses. The Detailed analysis takes considerably longer and sometimes does not yield any more detailed results.

Markup Color Clicking this square opens a dialog to select the color. It is good to choose a bright color that is not prevalent in the documents you are comparing.

Choose Compare Report Type A Consolidated Report presents a marked-up, mouse-activated version of the document indicating areas where text is different. A Side By Side Report (chosen here) creates a new PDF with the two documents presented next to each other in continuous facing mode with the found differences outlined. If you choose the Consolidated Report version, just move your mouse over the markup to view the differences in text.

4. Click OK. Acrobat will analyze the two documents and display the results, as demonstrated in Figure 7.14.

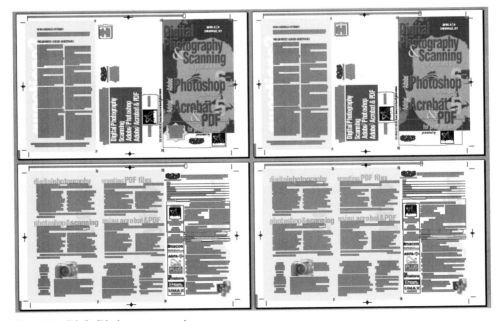

Figure 7.14 Side By Side document comparison

Adding Repeating Page Elements to PDF Documents

Fundamental repeating document page elements such as headers, footers, page numbers, backgrounds, and watermarks can be added to and removed from PDF documents through Acrobat. Because of this capability, in some cases you may want to alter your workflow to handle these page elements in Acrobat rather than your original page layout application.

Adding, Editing, or Removing Headers and Footers

Adding headers and footers is a simple procedure. (Adding dates or/or page numbers is just a variation of adding a header or footer.) Single or multiple items can be added as Headers or Footers as we will see below. To insert or edit these elements, choose Document > Add Headers & Footers and configure the resulting dialog (Figure 7.15).

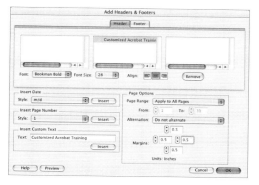

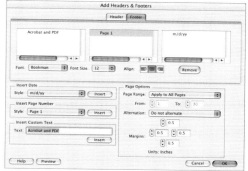

Figure 7.15 The Add Headers & Footers dialog and its preview

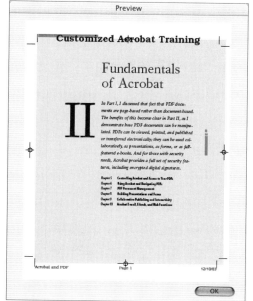

Building Elements in Acrobat Instead of Page Layout

Altering your workflow to control recurring page elements in Acrobat rather than in your page layout application may simplify your original document creation while providing you with some additional document content and versioning flexibility. For instance, you might want to have some of these page elements, such as a watermark, in some versions of a document but not others. Or you may want to wait until after you have edited the order or presence of various document pages in Acrobat prior to adding page numbers. Rather than having to create multiple original versions of documents with your page layout application, you can create one original version there and multiple variations in Acrobat.

To practice using this function, follow these steps. First, we will add text to serve as a header title, but you could insert a date or page number as well:

1. Click the Header tab.

2. Configure the Font, Font Size, and Align choices (immediately under the three scrollable panes). The Align selection you choose will determine which pane will contain the text you type (here, Bookman Bold 28).

3. Under Insert Custom Text, type in the copy you would like to appear in the header (here, Customized Acrobat Training).

4. Click the alignment you would like to see: left, right, or centered (here, centered).

5. Still under Insert Custom Text, click the Insert button. The copy will appear in the Alignment pane you selected in Step 2.

6. Configure the Page Options, including Page Range, Alternation (to direct onto which pages your header will appear), and Margins.

7. It is a good idea to click the Preview button at the bottom left to check to see that your header looks okay.

Next, let's add a footer with a page number, title, and date:

1. Click the Footer tab.

2. To add a page number, click the Insert Page Number Style Menu, and select a Page Number style (here, Page 1).

3. Configure the Font, Font Size, and Align choices for the footer. The Align selection will determine in which pane the text you type will appear (here, Bookman, 12, Centered).

4. Configure the Page Options for the footer, including Page Range, Alternation, and Margins.

5. Now click the Insert Page Number button to place the page number footer text in the middle text field.

6. To add some left-justified footer copy, in the Insert Custom Text field, type the footer copy you want (here, "Acrobat and PDF").

7. Configure this copy as we did above, but this time select a left rather than center justification.

8. Click the Insert Custom Text button to place the "Acrobat and PDF" text in the left window.

9. Last, to add a date to the right side of the footer, from the Insert Date Style menu, select a date style (here, m/dd/yy).

10. Configure this copy as we did above, but this time select a right justification.

11. Click the Insert Date button (Preview) to place the date text in the right window.

12. Finally, click the Preview button to preview both your header and footer inserts, placed on the first designated page of the document.

> **Note:** If you want to change (edit or remove) the header or footer text, it's best to click the text in the Align pane to select it and then click the Remove button (below the panes and to the right of the Align options). Then reenter the correct text and click Insert to insert any new type as we did above.

When you have finished configuring your Add Headers & Footers window, click the OK button and the new header and footer inserts will appear on your PDF document page, as shown in Figure 7.16.

Using Watermarks and Backgrounds in Your PDFs

Just as we added headers and footers in the previous section, you can also add a watermark and background graphics to any PDF document. The procedure for adding backgrounds and watermarks is similar to that in the preceding section. Start by preparing a graphic that you would like to use for your watermark or background, and save it out as a PDF.

Preparing Watermark and Background Graphics

While any PDF can be used as a watermark or background graphic, and this PDF can be scaled in Acrobat to fit the page, I suggest creating the watermark/background graphic at the size and resolution at which you would like to use the graphic. This will guarantee that the graphic will appear as you want it to, especially during high-quality printing. Also, if you intend to rotate your watermark/background graphic in Acrobat, be sure to consider this when you size the graphic. I typically use Photoshop to prepare my watermark/background graphics, and save the image directly out of Photoshop as a PDF.

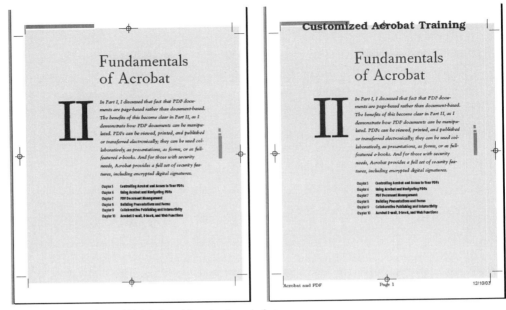

Figure 7.16 (left) Before and (right) after adding a header and a footer

Once you have your graphic ready, choose Document > Add Watermark & Background. Configure the resulting dialog (Figure 7.17) as follows:

Preview Hit the Tab key at any time to view the effects of your selection.

Type Click either the Add A Background or Add A Watermark radio button. The difference is that a background will appear behind the image, but a watermark will appear over the top of any page elements.

Show When check boxes If you want your watermark or background to be visible on screen and/or when the PDF is printed, check one or both of the Show When check boxes.

Source Page Click the Choose button to locate and select the PDF graphic you prepared earlier.

Page Range Select the range of pages on which you would like your graphic to appear.

Position And Appearance Adjust the placement of your graphic vertically (Top, Center, Bottom, or Fit) and horizontally (Left, Center, Right, or Fit). Select Fit if you want Acrobat to scale your image, stretching it to the width or height of the entire page.

Note: Scaling a graphic in Acrobat may lower image quality during printing.

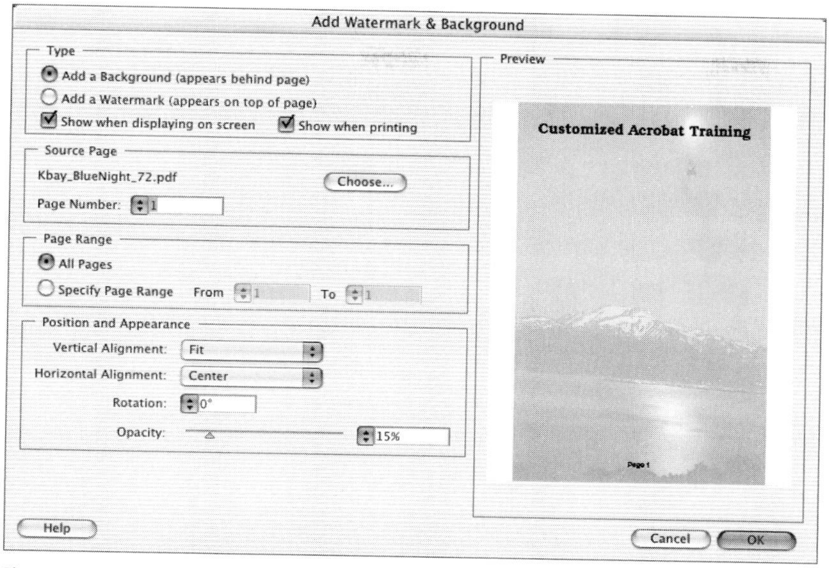

Add Watermark & Background

Type
- ⦿ Add a Background (appears behind page)
- ○ Add a Watermark (appears on top of page)
- ☑ Show when displaying on screen   ☑ Show when printing

Source Page
Kbay_BlueNight_72.pdf   (Choose...)
Page Number: 1

Page Range
- ⦿ All Pages
- ○ Specify Page Range   From 1   To 1

Position and Appearance
Vertical Alignment: Fit
Horizontal Alignment: Center
Rotation: 0°
Opacity: 15%

Preview

Customized Acrobat Training

Page 1

(Help)   (Cancel) (OK)

Figure 7.17 The Add Watermark & Background dialog

Rotation Keep the default 0° if you want the graphic to appear in its original orientation. (Press the Tab key to view the effects of your selection.)

Opacity If you want your image to be visible but still allow text to be clearly seen, I suggest using an opacity in the 5% to 15% range, depending upon the content and brightness of the image. I tend to screen back watermarks a bit more than backgrounds because they are placed on top of page elements. (Press the Tab key to view the effects of your selection.)

When you are finished with all your settings, hit the Tab key one more time to make sure all the settings are applied and view the results in the Preview window. When you are satisfied, click the OK button to view the results in the Document pane.

> **Note:** The results you see on screen probably are not identical to what will print. If you intend to print a background or watermarked PDF, then be sure to run some print tests on the output device prior to your final printing.

Removing or Restoring Watermarks or Backgrounds

Once a background or watermark has been added to a PDF document, it can be easily removed by choosing Edit > Undo Add Background or Undo Add Watermark (or pressing ⌘/Ctrl+Z).

Text on Graphics

If you intend to use a background or watermark image, keep this in mind when you select the font you will be placing on top of your graphics. All too often designers fail to consider this, and the legibility and readability of the copy may suffer.

- Keep text dark and avoid reversed type, unless the background image is very dark.
- Use sans serif type; it is easier to distinguish than serif type on a background.
- Keep your type 12 points or larger.
- Don't track or kern your characters too tightly.

I often see—even in well-known magazines that should know better—small, serif, reversed type placed on top of background images, which pretty much guarantees that your readers will be struggling to read the copy.

Once a background or watermark has been removed from a PDF document, it can be restored by choosing Edit > Redo Add Background or Redo Add Watermark (or pressing ⌘/Ctrl+Shift+Z).

Note: Once a background or watermark has been added to a document that is then saved and closed, the background or watermark cannot be removed with Acrobat. So it is always a good idea to add backgrounds and watermarks to *copies* of your PDFs.

Using Layers in Acrobat

While you cannot create layers using Acrobat, documents created out of applications such as AutoCAD and Visio, which are created in multiple layers, can be saved, viewed, and manipulated as multilayered PDF files. Layers are a handy way to separately display various kinds of data in complex documents, such as different floors in a building blueprint or physical versus cultural information on a map. Layers in PDF documents can be renamed and merged; in addition you can control the properties of layers and adjust how they display through the Default and Initial View settings.

Layers Navigation, Commenting, and Editing

Once you learn how to view and select layers, you can treat the content in those layers pretty much like the elements of any PDF document page. Layers, like any other PDF page elements and locations, can utilize navigation links such as bookmarks and destinations, can receive comments, and can have their text and graphic components searched and edited. All the skills and capabilities, such as the Search function discussed later in this chapter and advanced functions discussed in Chapters 8, 9, and 12, can be applied to layers. ⌒ See these chapters for more details on these topics.

Controlling How Layered PDFs Look

As with any other PDF document, you can control what content will be visible and how it will be displayed when it is opened. Since most of the layered PDFs I see are engineering documents, I typically set my Initial Views a bit differently than I do for my standard facing page documents. Here are some suggestions on how to control a layered document's Initial View:

1. Open the layered PDF.

2. Choose File > Document Properties (⌘/Ctrl+D). The Document Properties window appears.

3. Click the Initial View choice from the list on the left side (or press I). The Initial View controls appear (Figure 7.18).

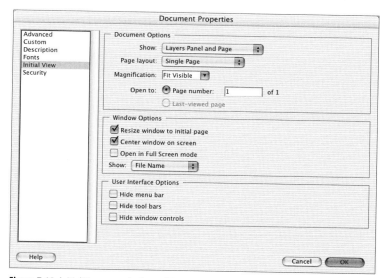

Figure 7.18 Initial View setup for layered PDFs

4. Configure the dialog to control the initial state of this document:

   a. From the Show menu, select Layers Panel And Page. This will not only automatically display the page in the document panel but will preselect the Layers tab so the layers will be automatically visible when the PDF is opened.

   b. From the Page Layout menu, you will typically want to select Single Page rather than one of the Facing Page options.

   c. From the Magnification menu, I usually select Fit Visible to allow the viewers to initially see the entire document and then allow them to choose where to zoom in.

   d. Unless you want a specific page other than page 1 to be the first one viewed, leave Open To set at the default value of 1.

   e. Configure the Window Options to suit. I like to check Resize Window To Initial Page and Center Window On Screen. I check Open In Full Screen Mode only if I intend the PDF to initially open and play as presentation. (☞ Chapter 8 for more information on presentations.)

   f. I prefer to keep all the User Interface Options available, but they can be initially disabled here if you prefer.

5. Click OK. Save the changes to this document, and close the document.

6. Open this newly saved layered PDF, and its initial view should show both the Document pane and the layers in the Layers tab (Figure 7.19).

Note: If you want to see other tab panels, such as the Pages tab, you can drag any additional tabs out so that they become floating panels.

Notice, in Figure 7.19, that there are two kinds of layers:

Individual layers, such as the Grid layer.

Folder layers, such as Serial Number, which contain multiple layers. The contents of multiple layers can be displayed by clicking the triangular tab next to the layer name, which will point that tab down and display the layers contained in the layer folder.

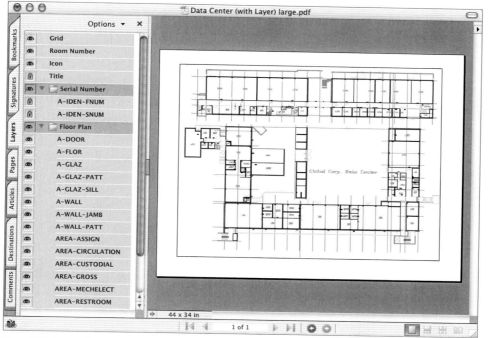

Figure 7.19 Layers tab and Document pane

Controlling the Viewing, Printing, and Exporting of Individual Layers

In addition to controlling how the overall layered PDF looks when it is opened, you can also control the properties of individual layers (or folder layers) on initial viewing and what can be done with those layers after the document is opened. Here's how:

1. Open a layered PDF.

2. Click the Layers tab to make the layers visible.

3. Click one of the layers you would like to control to select that layer. In Figure 7.20, I've selected the layer A-WALL-JAMB.

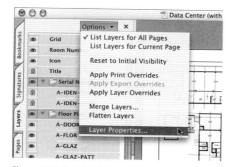

Figure 7.20 Opening the properties for layer A-WALL-JAMB

4. Click the Options menu, or right-click/Ctrl+click the layer, and choose Layer Properties. The Layer Properties window appears (Figure 7.21).

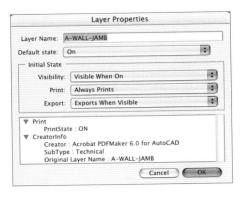

Figure 7.21 The Layer Properties dialog

5. Now each of the Default and Initial properties can be set for this layer:

Default State Turn the Default State for the layer On or Off depending upon whether you want this layer to be on or off when the document is opened.

Initial State - Visibility Select Visible When On if you want the initial state to control the layer's visibility; otherwise, select Never Visible or Always Visible.

Initial State - Print Select Print When On if you want the initial state to control the layer's printability; otherwise select Never Prints or Always Prints.

Initial State - Export Select Exports When On if you want the initial state to control the export of the layer; otherwise select Never Exports or Always Exports or Exports when Visible depending upon how you want the export of the layer to be controlled.

Use various combinations of the Default and Initial State settings to control how a layer will function. For example, if you have a watermark or background layer that you do not want to make visible on screen, but you always want that layer to be exported and to print, then you could set these menus as shown in Figure 7.22.

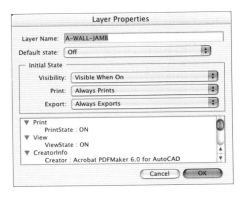

Figure 7.22 Default and Initial State example

Set Your Preferences to Use Layer State Properties

To make sure that any layered PDF you open uses the layer state settings we have just configured, be sure that the Allow Layer State To Be Set By User Information preference is checked in the Startup Preferences in Acrobat: Choose Acrobat > Preferences or File > Preferences (or press ⌘/Ctrl+K) and click Startup.

Viewing Invisible Layer, Print, and Export Content

If you have made some content invisible but still intend to print or export that content, or would even like to just view it, it is nice to be able to temporarily visually check that "invisible" content. You can do this with *overrides*; here's how:

1. Open a layered PDF.

2. Click the Layers tab to make the layers visible.

3. To view the hidden content, click the Layers tab's Options menu (Figure 7.23) and choose Apply Print Overrides, Apply Export Overrides, or Apply Layer Overrides.

The selected invisible content will become visible as long as that menu item is checked.

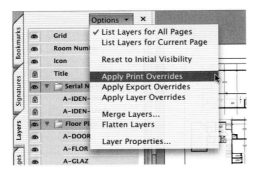

Figure 7.23 Overriding visibility choices

Simplifying Layered PDFs

Once opened in Acrobat, layered PDF documents can be simplified by reducing the number of layers through either merging some layers or flattening all the layers.

Merging Layers

Merging layers is a good way to control the simplification process, by allowing you to merge some layers while leaving others alone. Here's how it works:

1. Open a layered PDF document, make a copy of it, and name the designated new version as merged. I use *name*_m.pdf to indicate a merged PDF file. You will merge layers in the copied document, leaving the original document with all of its original layers.

2. In the copied document, click the Layers tab.

3. Click the Options menu and choose Merge Layers. The three-column Merge Layers dialog appears (Figure 7.24).

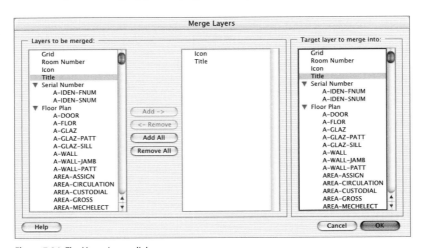

Figure 7.24 The Merge Layers dialog

4. From the left column, select the layers you would like to merge. Shift+click to select a list of continuous layers; ⌘/Ctrl+click noncontinuous layers to select as many layers as you would like to merge together. Here I selected the Icon and Title layers.

5. Click the Add button to add the selected layers to the middle column. If you change your mind and want to remove some layers from the merge list, just select them from the middle column and click the Remove button.

6. From the right column, select the layer into which you would like to merge the layers listed in the middle column.

7. Click the OK button to complete the process. The merged PDF will now have fewer layers.

Flattening Layers

Flattening merges all the layers in a document, leaving you with a simpler and smaller one-layer PDF file. The process is quick and easy, but I recommend that you perform this on a copy of your original layered file, because this process cannot be undone.

1. Open a layered PDF document, make a copy of it, and name the designated new version as flattened. I use *name_*f.pdf to indicate a flattened PDF file. You will flatten all the layers in the copied document, leaving the original document with all of its original layers.

2. In the copied document, click the Layers tab.

3. Click the Options menu and choose Flatten Layers. A message will appear warning you that this process cannot be undone. If you are not working on a copy of the original layered document, click Cancel and go back to Step 1!

Note: The flattening process may take a minute or two if you have many layers to combine, so be patient!

4. Save this newly flattened document.

Playing Search and Find

Acrobat provides some impressive capabilities for searching and replacing elements in PDF documents. Acrobat supports both a simple search function, which is typically used on individual PDF documents, and a more sophisticated function that allows you to search multiple files through the use of a searchable index.

Searching an Individual PDF

To search for something in an individual PDF, follow these steps:

1. Open the PDF you would like to search.

2. To open the Search PDF pane and initiate the search capabilities, do *one* of the following:

    - Click the Search tool in the Tool palette.
    - Choose Edit > Search.
    - Press ⌘/Ctrl+F.

    The Search PDF pane appears, usually to the right of the current Document pane (Figure 7.25).

Figure 7.25 The basic Search PDF pane

3. Configure the Search PDF pane to suit your search criteria:

    a. Enter a word or phrase you would like to search for. Make the word or phrase as specific as possible to narrow the results. Here I have entered the phrase "Distiller Settings."

b. Click the In The Current PDF Document radio button to indicate that you want to search only the open file that is currently active (in the foreground window).

c. Check the Whole Words Only box if you want Acrobat to look for only the complete word or phrase, in this case "Distiller Settings." Otherwise, Acrobat will look for matches for any parts of the words or phrases in addition to the entire word or phrase. In this case, if you do not check Whole Words Only, Acrobat will look for "Distiller," "Settings," "Distill," and "Set," as well as "Distiller Settings."

d. Check the Case-Sensitive box if you want Acrobat to look only for the exact way in which you have typed in the search word or phrase with regard to upper- and lowercase letters.

e. Check the Search In Bookmarks and/or Search In Comments boxes if you want Acrobat to search these as well as the document contents.

4. Click the Search button when you are satisfied with your definition of the search criteria. The search will commence and display the results of the search in a list format, in an updated Search PDF pane (Figure 7.26).

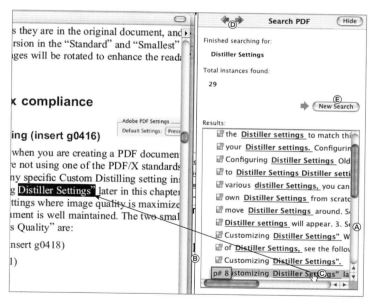

Figure 7.26 The Search PDF pane results

5. You can perform any of the following functions in the Search PDF results pane:

   a. Scroll though the list results, which are displayed as underlined (hyper-linked) words/phrases in their local text context.

   b. Move the cursor over any underlined result, and the page number of its occurrence will display where the cursor is resting.

   c. Click any of the underlined search results to view the actual location of the found results in the Document pane.

   d. Repeat or review previous search panel steps or views by clicking the forward or backward arrows that appear in the Search panels.

   e. Initiate a new search by clicking the New Search button.

Searching Multiple PDFs

You can search multiple PDFs in much the same manner as you searched single PDFs in the previous exercise. The difference is in how you inform Acrobat as to where to look. Here's how to do it:

1. Instead of opening a PDF to search, place all the PDFs you would like to search in a folder; for this example, I use one named PDFs to Search.

2. To open the Search PDF pane and initiate the search capabilities, do *one* of the following:

   • Click the Search tool 🔍 in the Tool palette.

   • Choose Edit > Search.

   • Press ⌘/Ctrl+F.

   The Search PDF pane appears, usually to the right of the current Document pane (Figure 7.27).

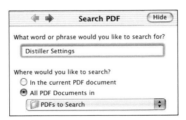

Figure 7.27 Multiple PDF search setup

3. Under Where Would You Like To Search?, click the All PDF Documents In radio button.

4. Locate the folder from Step 1, containing the PDFs you would like to search, using the drop-down menu under the All PDF Documents In button.

5. Configure the rest of the Search PDF pane as we did in the "Searching an Individual PDF" section previously, and then click Search.

The search results will be displayed again in the updated Search PDF pane (Figure 7.28). The difference will be that each document will be listed separately with its own set of results. These results can be selected and displayed just like results in the preceding "Searching an Individual PDF" section. The number of documents searched and total number of search results found are also listed.

> **Note:** The length of the search time will vary depending upon the size and complexity of the document being searched. If you perform many long and/or multiple document searches, which seem to require too much time, you might want to get in the habit of creating searchable indexes prior to initiating your searches. See the next section of this chapter for more information.

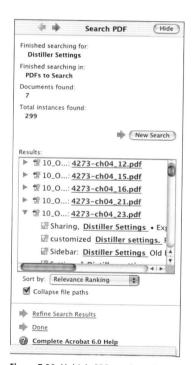

Figure 7.28 Multiple PDF search results

6. You can adjust the ranking of the various result listings by selecting a ranking choice from the Sort By drop-down menu. This is useful due to the fact that multidocument searches often produce a significant number of results.

7. If you prefer to see the file path information rather than the document name information, uncheck the Collapse File Paths check box. By default it is checked *on*, which I usually find to be more useful because the filename is clearly displayed. I will deselect this check box only if I forget where I placed the search folder (which occurs more often than I am willing to admit!).

Performing More Advanced, Refined Searches

If the search results you are getting are not netting the results you want, for instance you may be getting way too many results listed to be practical, you may want to use Acrobat's Advanced Search function. The Advanced Search function will provide you with more search criteria choices to help you focus your search results. Here's how it's done:

Note: For generating indexes and tables of contents, and for creating hyperlinked PDF crosslinks to index and TOC references, I like to use a family of tools called Sonar Bookends from Virginia Systems. Check out the demos of these programs on the companion CD.

Index PDFs Organization and Cross-Platform Naming

Before you begin the process of actually creating any searchable index in Acrobat, you should organize the PDF documents from which you intend to create the index into a folder or a series of nested folders. Each PDF you intend to access as part of the index should be named for cross-platform usage. Cross-platform usage involves naming your documents in a manner that will allow them to be recognized by all operating systems. Current cross-platform naming still follows the old DOS conventions, which include the following:

- Eight characters or less
- Lowercase only
- Only alpha and numeric characters and underscores
- No spaces, dashes, or any punctuation marks other than the (.) dot that precedes the file extension
- A three-character filename extension (.pdf in this case)

Creating a Searchable Index

Although Advanced Searches can be performed on individual or multiple PDF files, as we did with the basic search earlier in this chapter, many Advanced Searches begin with the creation of a searchable index. An index is a list of all the words in a single or multiple document(s) and their relative locations in those documents. Creating a searchable index of the words and/or custom properties in your PDF file(s) provides you with the ability to perform more sophisticated search functions, including Boolean, stemming, and proximity searches, much more quickly and thoroughly than when working with the PDF documents directly. Indexes can also be updated as the documents change.

So first, let's make an index of multiple files. To do this we use the Catalog function in Acrobat's Advanced tool set:

1. Organize, name, and place all the PDFs you would like to index in one folder (mine here is labeled PDFs to Index).

2. Choose Advanced > Catalog. The Catalog dialog appears (Figure 7.29).

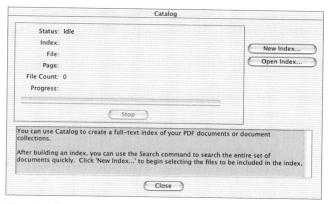

Figure 7.29 The Catalog dialog

3. Click the New Index button. The New Index Definition window appears (see Figure 7.30).

4. Configure this dialog:

    Index Title Name the index. Select a name that encompasses the whole group of files from which you are building the index.

    Index Description Provide any clarifying information about the set of PDF files being indexed.

    Include These Directories Locate and select the files to be indexed by clicking the Add button and navigating to their location—here the PDFs to Index folder created in Step 1.

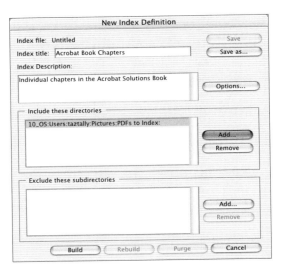

Figure 7.30 The New Index Definition dialog

Exclude These Subdirectories If there are any subfolders that contain any PDFs you do not want to be included in the indexing process, locate and select them here through the use of the Add button.

Options This is an optional button that allows you to refine the indexing process. See the list following Step 7 for tips on refining your index options.

5. Click the Build button  to complete the New Index Definition window.

6. You will be asked to locate where you would like to have the new index file placed. I like to place my index files, at least initially, in the same folder with the PDFs I have indexed, in this case the PDFs to Index folder. Once you select the destination folder, the Catalog window reappears and displays a progress bar as the new index is built (Figure 7.31). An index file will be created with a .pdx extension and a cute little magnifying-glass icon (indicating a searchable index).

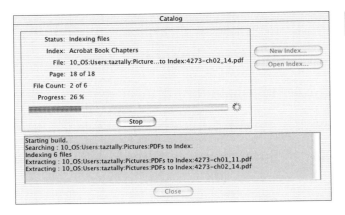

Figure 7.31 (left) The progress is shown while building an index; (right) the icon for a searchable index.

7. Once the index-building process is complete, click the Close button to put the Catalog dialog away.

This .pdx index file is the one we will use to complete our search, but first let's cover the index options that you might want to set prior to clicking the Build button. Click the Options button ⬭ Options... in the New Index Definition dialog (shown back in Figure 7.30) to see the indexing refinement options. The Options window appears (Figure 7.32). Here are some guidelines for refining your index creation through the Index Options:

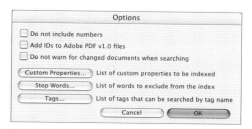

Figure 7.32 The Options dialog

Do Not Include Numbers If you do not want numbers included in your index, check this box.

Add IDs To Adobe PDF V1.0 Files Check this box if the PDFs from which you are creating the index were created prior to version 2.0. These PDFs do not have ID numbers, which are used when long Mac filenames are shortened to comply with the eight-character DOS standard. If you are in doubt about the PDFs' versions, check this option.

Do Not Warn For Changed Documents When Searching Acrobat will automatically warn you during a search if the document has been changed since the last index was made. If for some reason you do not want this warning (you may be aware of this already and you don't want to be nagged by the warning message), then check this on. (The default is off, so that the warning will occur.)

Custom Properties If you have designated any custom document properties (File > Document Properties > Custom), such as the property designated in Figure 7.33, and you would like them to be added to the search index, then click this button; the Custom Properties dialog appears. Type in the searchable custom property you want to add. Designate the Type as either String (shown here), Integer, or Date. Click the Add button and the OK button. This will add the custom property String, Integer, or Date to your index.

Stop Words Click this button if you want to delete certain words from the index. Complete the Stop Words window that appears just as you did for custom properties.

Tags Click this button if you want to add certain document structure tags to the index. Complete the Tags window that appears just as you did for custom properties.

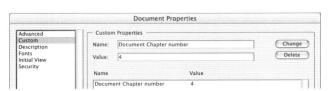

Figure 7.33 If you've defined custom document properties such as the Document Chapter Number shown here, use the Custom Properties dialog to make sure they get indexed.

Searching a Catalog Index

Once you have created a catalog index, as we have just done, you can search this index using the Advanced Search functions. Here is how it works:

1. To open the Search PDF pane and initiate the search capabilities, do *one* of the following:
   - Click the Search tool ![search icon] in the Tool palette.
   - Choose Edit > Search.
   - Press ⌘/Ctrl+F.

   The Search PDF pane appears, usually to the right of the current Document pane.

Document vs. Global Index Settings

In this chapter we have built an index using the Catalog function with designated custom properties using individual PDF documents. So any custom catalog setting we have applied will apply only to this catalog and index. If you would like to make these catalog and index settings global, so that they will apply to all catalogs and indexes, you can set these same settings in the Acrobat Preferences: Acrobat (Mac) or File (Windows) > Preferences > Catalog.

2. At the bottom of the Search pane, click the underlined choice that reads Use Advanced Search Options; Advanced Search options (Figure 7.34) appears in the Search PDF dialog.

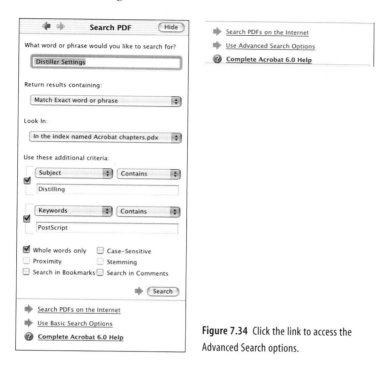

Figure 7.34 Click the link to access the Advanced Search options.

Note: In some cases, such as if you have already initiated a search, this option may read Refine Search Results (compare the bottom of Figure 7.28).

3. The Advanced Search functions can be configured in literally hundreds of ways. And some of the available search options depend upon other search option choices that are made. Here is an overview of the setup categories:

What Word Or Phrase Would You Like To Search For? Type in the word or phrase you would like to search for. You can use the "search for" phrase you placed in the basic Search PDF pane, which will carry over here, or you can type in a new search selection.

Return Results Containing Here you will choose from a list of matching choices, including Boolean searches. Select the match that best suits your search. Your selection here will

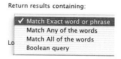

affect some of the available options below. For instance, if you select Match All Of The Words, this will make available the Proximity search criterion.

Look In This menu provides any file selection options, including the ability to select catalog index files. The bottom of this menu provides a Browse option that allows you to search wherever you like. I have selected the Acrobat chapters.pdx index we created earlier.

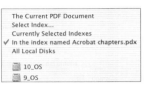

> **Note:** If a catalog index file has already been accessed or used, its name will automatically appear on this list; otherwise you will need to locate that file. You can automatically add an index file to the Search PDF pane and the Look In list by simply double-clicking the index file itself.

Use These Additional Criteria These are two sets of paired drop-down menus that you can use to further define your search. The two left-side menus provide a list of definable search criteria, including metadata such as author, subject, and keywords.

The right-side menus allow you to define whether these search criteria should be inclusive (Contains) or exclusive (Does Not Contain).

You can choose to use one, both, or neither of these additional search criteria by either checking or unchecking their check boxes.

Other search criteria check boxes Check the criteria at the bottom of the pane that will help narrow your search but not exclude items you might want. For instance, if you are not sure that all occurrences of a word or phrase have specific capitalization, you may want to *not* select Case-Sensitive to broaden the search. If you want to search for stems of words, such as "distill" as well as "distiller," you should uncheck Whole Words Only and check Stemming. To find words—such as "distiller settings"—that are close to each other but not necessarily side by side, check Proximity. But remember that Proximity is available for activation only if Match All Of The Words is selected for Return Results Containing.

4. When you are through setting your search criteria, click Search and the results will be reported for you in an updated Search PDF pane similar to the one in Figure 7.28.

> **Note:** The same kinds of searches we have discussed in this chapter can be performed on eBooks and online PDFs. ⌁ Chapter 10, "Acrobat E-mail, eBook, and Web Features," for more information on eBooks and online services.

Distributing Indexes

Creating and distributing indexes is a good way to provide viewers of your PDF documents, particularly multiple PDF documents, rapid access to finding information in your files. It is a good idea to break long documents, such as books, into logical segments, such as chapters, prior to making the index. Then the searches of and access to the found links will proceed much more quickly.

In addition to providing your viewers with the PDF files and the index, it is a good idea to provide them with an Index Readme file that tells them what the index contains, any custom search criteria, any exclusions, and perhaps a bit about how to use the search function in Acrobat to access the index files. Remember, a handy shortcut that is good to include in the Readme file is that double-clicking the index file will automatically add that index file to the Search PDF pane as a selection choice.

Building Presentations and Forms

PDF documents are most commonly used as a medium for transferring a document, such as a page layout or word processing document, into a readily viewable and transferable format. This is usually done without much thought given to how the PDF format can be used to enhance the presentation and/or expand the content and usefulness of the original document. The Acrobat application and PDF document format can be used in almost limitless ways.

Chapter Contents

In this chapter we will explore two common and very useful variations of PDF documents: as presentations and to deliver editable forms documents. Once you see and master the capabilities and tools in this chapter, not only will you know some very useful PDF techniques, but knowing these PDF variations will likely send you off to develop your own special uses for PDFs.

Creating and Using PDF Presentations

The ability to create PDF presentations in Acrobat solves a number of common problems. First, using PDF as a common document format makes it easy to combine information and elements from many different kinds of otherwise incompatible documents and applications. Second, once you have created a PDF presentation, it is typically much smaller than most presentation files, and due to PDF's cross-platform and application-independent nature, PDF presentations are easy to transport across the Internet and/or use on other computers. And to top it off, PDF presentations are easy to create and use!

Creating Presentations from a Single Application or Document

Any PDF file you create can be quickly and easily converted into a slide-show type of PDF presentation complete with transitions. Often you may want to adjust borders and background colors, as well as transitions, all of which are built directly into Acrobat. We will start with the simplest case, a single file source for the presentation, and then discuss multiple-source presentations. Here is how to create a presentation from any PDF file:

1. Open any single-source file from a presentation, page layout, drawing, word processing, or other document. Here I am using an old Adobe Persuasion presentation file, which I would like to keep using, but I am about to run into the end of Persuasion's life span. (Persuasion is no longer made and does not operate in Mac OS X or Windows XP.)

Advantages of PDF Presentations

There are numerous benefits of using PDFs as presentation documents. One is that PDF presentations are often much smaller than the original files. For example, the file size of the original Persuasion document used in this first exercise is 62.6MB, while the file size of the PDF created from this is only 1.9MB, a file size reduction of 97 percent! PDFs are also eminently more transferable from one computer or platform to another. All the recipient needs to have is Adobe/Acrobat Reader. You can even, as I have done in our first exercise in this chapter, convert to PDF to salvage and resecure older presentation files created in now-defunct applications.

2. Print this document as a PostScript file to a watched folder in order to create a PDF document. I typically use a watched folder configured for viewing and low-resolution printing, such as the Standard Distiller setting. This provides me with plenty of on-screen viewing quality and enough resolution and image quality to print decent handouts on a desktop printer, while minimizing the file size of the final PDF document (Figure 8.1). (☞ Chapter 4, "Creating the PDF You Want," for more information on distilling and on watched folders.)

Figure 8.1 Original vs. PDF file size

> **Note:** If the Standard setting does not provide you with enough resolution and/or image quality for the printing you need, you can always modify the resolution and/or compression settings to suit your needs.

3. Open the PDF you created in Step 2. Each page or slide, if you printed the PDF from another presentation file, will have its own page on the new PDF document. These new PDF pages will often need to be tweaked a bit to prepare them for presentation. For instance, as you can see in Figure 8.2, your PDF pages may have borders or other unwanted page elements surrounding them that you would like to remove.

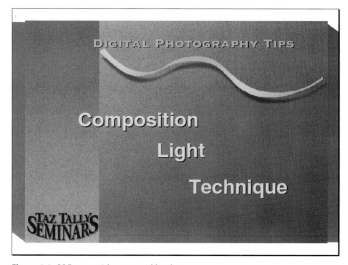

Figure 8.2 PDF page with unwanted border

4. To remove unwanted borders, select the Crop tool 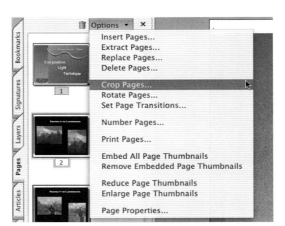 by choosing Crop Pages from either the Document menu or the Pages pane's Options menu (Figure 8.3) or by double-clicking the Crop tool in the Tool palette. Then either double-click the Document pane or click and drag to create an initial crop area. The Crop Pages dialog appears (Figure 8.4). Configure this window as follows:

Preview You can view a thumbnail of the Document pane at the top of the window. Any border alteration will show up there.

Figure 8.3 Pages pane, Options menu, Crop Pages command

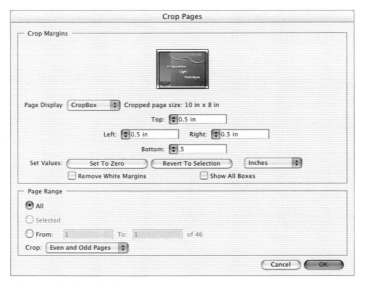

Figure 8.4 Crop Pages dialog

Page Display Set this to show the CropBox. You can view the BleedBox if you want to see what would print on a commercial print device, the TrimBox to view what will be seen after commercial trimming, or the ArtBox to see the entire image without cropping.

Margins Adjust the border values to crop off the areas you want to remove. If you have initialized the crop window by dragging with the Crop tool, the initial crop area created with the Crop tool will appear in the crop value fields. Check the actual Document pane, as well as the Crop Pages window thumbnail, for the placement of the crop lines, because it is likely to be easier to see and show the crop more accurately.

Set Values To start all over or remove the crop entirely, click Set To Zero. If you have tried several crop values and want to return to the last preview of values, click Return To Selection.

Remove White Margins If all you have around your page is a white border, check this box to remove it. Sometimes this works okay, but sometimes it does not.

Show All Boxes Uncheck this option so that only the CropBox will show in the preview window. This will be less confusing and facilitate viewing the crop area.

Page Range Select the pages to which you would like to apply the crop. Here I have selected All and Even And Odd Pages.

When you have finished setting up the Crop Pages window, click the OK button to see the results (Figure 8.5).

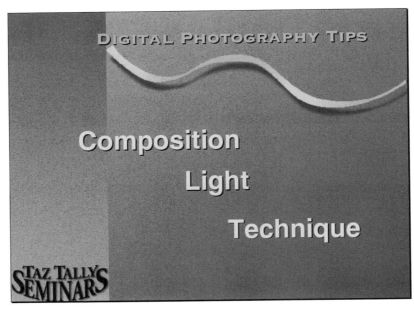

Figure 8.5 Crop results

5. Using the rotation tool (Page pane > Options > Rotate), rotate any necessary pages, such as Landscape-oriented charts, graphs, or images in an otherwise Portrait-oriented document, so that all pages will read right side up.

6. Once you have the PDF document pages oriented and cropped, it is time to configure the presentation characteristics. Open the Acrobat Preferences (choose Acrobat > Preferences on the Mac, File > Preferences in Windows, or press ⌘/Ctrl+K). Select Full Screen from the list of preferences at the left (Figure 8.6). Configure the options to suit your presentation preferences, and click OK when you're satisfied:

Advance Every If you intend to have your presentation run automatically, set the transition time. Make the times longer if you have text for viewers to read. Try 5 seconds for images and 10 seconds for text as starting points.

Loop After Last Page If you want your presentation to start back at the beginning after the last page, check this box.

Escape Key Exits Check this to give the Escape (Esc) key the ability to stop the Presentation mode and return to regular PDF viewing.

 Note: ⌘/Ctrl+L will work to both start and stop your presentation.

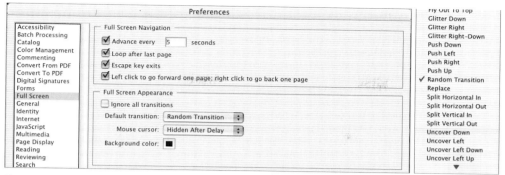

Figure 8.6 Full Screen Preferences, including the list of available Default Transitions

Left Click To Go Forward... If you have a two-button mouse, check this box to allow you to move forward and backward by clicking.

> **Note:** I use the Right and Left arrow keys to move forward and backward manually through a PDF presentation.

Full Screen Appearance Assign your transitions. As you can see, the list is long. I typically use Random Transitions to allow Acrobat to randomly show a transition and to add some variety to my presentations.

Mouse Cursor Tell Acrobat what to do with the visibility of your cursor after the presentation has begun: Always Visible, Always Hidden, or Hidden After Delay. I typically hide the mouse to remove any on-screen distraction and use a laser pointer if I want to call attention to something.

Background Color Click the swatch to set a color. The default is black.

7. Preview your presentation. To start the presentation (in Full Screen mode), simply press ⌘/Ctrl+L or choose Window > Full Screen View. To stop the presentation, press the Escape (Esc) key or press ⌘/Ctrl+L again.

Creating Presentations from Multiple Applications or Documents

One of the great benefits of the world of Acrobat and PDF is that the once-arduous task of combining information or pages from multiple documents created in different applications is now pretty much a snap. This has been a godsend for me, because I often want to take QuarkXPress pages and combine them with information I have organized in PowerPoint presentations, graphs from Illustrator, spreadsheets from Excel, and images from Photoshop. Or I may have pages from two different page layout applications that I would like to include in one document. PDF to the rescue—here's the workflow:

1. Set up watched folders with the proper settings to create the type of PDF pages needed for your final output device (☞ Chapter 4).

2. Open all the applications and documents you would like to use in your combined final PDF.

3. Print all these documents to the watched folder to convert them to properly configured PDF documents. (Be sure to pay attention to page number issues; ☞ Chapter 7, "PDF Document Management.")

Next, you could combine all the PDFs using the "Adding Pages" techniques discussed in Chapter 7. But if you have many PDF documents to combine, consider using the Create PDF From Multiple Files capability. It's a real time-saver, and here's how it works:

4. Do *one* of the following:

   • Open all the PDFs you would like to combine.

   • Place all the PDFs you want to combine into a single folder.

5. Select File > Create PDF > From Multiple Files. The Create PDF From Multiple Documents dialog appears (Figure 8.7; yes, the dialog name is different from the menu command).

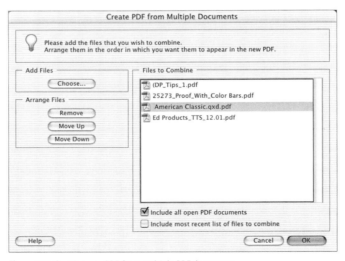

Figure 8.7 Creating one PDF from multiple PDF documents

6. Arrange the list of PDFs to combine, in the desired order:

    a. If you have already opened some or all of the documents you want to include in the combined PDF, check the Include All Open PDF Documents box.

    b. If you want to add other documents to the list of PDFs to combine, click the Choose button to locate and select more PDFs.

    c. Reorder the files in the list using the Move Up and Move Down buttons.

Note: The order in which the documents appear in the Files To Combine list is the order in which they will appear in the final PDF.

7. When you have all the documents you want to combine arranged in the order in which you would like to combine them, click OK to begin the combination process. A progress bar will appear on screen to show you how the combination process is progressing.

When the document combination process is complete, a new PDF with the name Binder1.pdf will be created on screen. Save this PDF. A Save As window will appear asking you to name and save this new file.

Presentation Navigation

Many times PDF presentations are used in multimedia productions for kiosks and/or distributed CD-ROMs. These applications often require the development of on-screen interface buttons for controlling navigation, printing, initiating searches, or launching other files or applications. The use of forms buttons duplicated across multiple pages meets these needs. (See the sections on creating interactive forms later in this chapter.)

Converting PowerPoint Files to PDFs with Animations

As we discussed in Chapter 4, you can easily convert any Microsoft Office document—including Word, Excel, Outlook, and PowerPoint document files—to PDFs with the use of the one-button, built-in PDFMaker. You can even preserve the transitions you create in your PowerPoint presentations so that they appear in Acrobat—but this is best accomplished through the Print dialog box rather than the one-button PDF method. Here's how:

1. Open a complete PowerPoint presentation.

2. Choose File > Print to activate the Print dialog box. Choose Microsoft PowerPoint from the drop-down list of option categories (Figure 8.8).

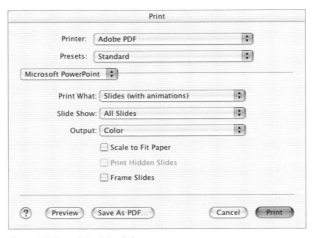

Figure 8.8 PowerPoint Print dialog

Note: Your Print window may appear somewhat different than this one, depending upon your operating system, printer driver, and application version, but all the essential elements will still be there, even if they are organized somewhat differently.

3. Configure this window as follows:

   a. Select Adobe PDF as your Printer driver.

   b. From the Print What drop-down, choose Slides (With Animations).

   c. Choose the slides you want to print (All Slides selected here).

Note: If you want to print handouts, notes, or your outline in PDF format, the Print What drop-down is also where you would choose to do that.

4. Before clicking the Print button, you may want to check your PDF Distiller settings. Working in the same Print dialog, choose PDF Options from the dropdown list of options categories (Figure 8.9), and then from the Presets menu select the Distiller setting you would like to be used during the PDF creation process. (See Chapter 4 for more information on Distiller settings.)

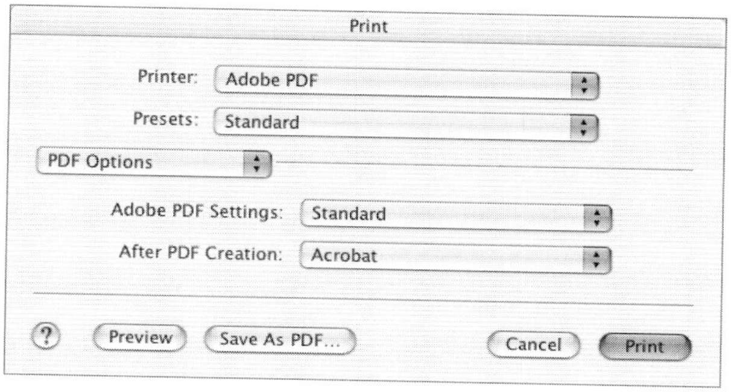

Figure 8.9 PDF Print Options

5. Click the Print button to initiate the final process of printing to PDF. You will be asked to select a location where your PDF file will be created.

6. Open your newly created PDF in Acrobat. You will notice that each transition—in this case, both lines of text and slides—has become a separate PDF document page (Figure 8.10). See the following sections on editing your PDF presentations for tips on how to order pages and control transitions between them.

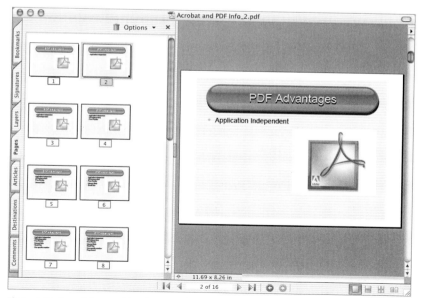

Figure 8.10 PowerPoint transitions in PDF

Editing Slide Order in PDF Presentations

Adding, deleting, or changing the order of your presentation pages is a snap:

1. Open the PDF presentation document in Acrobat.

 Note: Prior to editing any presentation, I think it's a good idea to make a backup copy and work on that...just in case!

2. Click the Pages tab to view the pages in the Navigation pane.

3. Drag the divider between the Pages tab and the Document pane to enlarge the Pages tab until you can see all of the PDF pages you want to edit.

4. Edit the slides as follows:

    a. Click any page that you want to remove from the document; then either click the trashcan or hit the Delete key.

    b. To change the order in which your PDF pages will appear in a presentation, simply drag the page(s) you want to move beside the page in front of which you would like to move them.

 Note: The standard Shift+click (for sequential page selection) and ⌘/Ctrl+Shift+click (for nonsequential selection) works just fine here.

5. When you have finished editing your presentation, save your changes. I usually save my edited presentations with sequential numbers, such as Presentation_1, Presentation_2, etc., so that I can easily pick out my most recent version without having to look at creation dates.

Setting Page Transitions

Once you have completed the creation and editing of your presentation contents, you can control the transitions that will occur between the pages when the presentation is played back in Full Screen mode. Earlier in this chapter we discussed controlling transitions for the entire presentation through the Full Screen Preferences (Acrobat/File > Preferences > Full Screen > Transitions). But if you don't want all the transitions to be the same throughout your presentation, and you would like to have a bit more control than just selecting Random, here's how it's done:

1. Open your PDF presentation document.

2. Click the Pages tab and enlarge it so that you can see all of the presentation pages.

3. Select the pages for which you would like to set transitions (1–3 are selected in Figure 8.11).

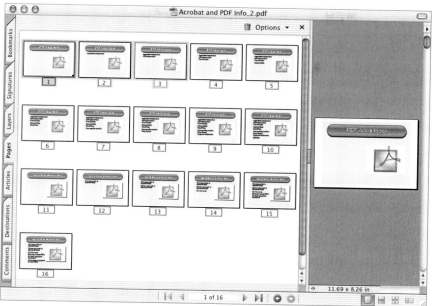

Figure 8.11 Pages 1–3 selected in the Navigation pane

4. Choose Document > Pages > Set Page Transitions or choose the same command from the Pages tab's Options menu; the Set Transitions dialog appears (Figure 8.12).

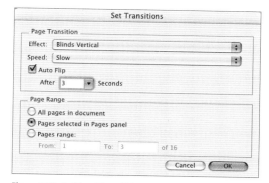

Figure 8.12 Set Transitions dialog

5. Start at the *bottom* of this dialog box: Define the pages to which you will apply a certain transition. If you have already selected a page or pages in the Pages tab, those will automatically be selected, and the Pages Selected In Pages Panel button will be activated.

 Note: If you would like to choose pages from Pages Range fields in this window, you can, but I usually find that making page selections in the Pages tab is easier and much more convenient.

6. Set up the transition for the Page Range you've defined:
   a. Select a transition type from the Effect menu (Blinds Vertical is selected here).
   b. Choose a Speed at which you would like that transition to occur.
   c. Check the Auto Flip check box if you want the pages in this selection to automatically transition from one to the other. Then select the time delay between the transitions.
7. When you have completed defining this set of transitions, click OK.
8. Repeat Steps 3–7 for as many sets of PDF pages as you would like.
9. When you are through assigning transitions, save your document with the new transitions.
10. Test your new presentation and enjoy your transitions by using ⌘/Ctrl+L or Window > Full Screen View.

Controlling Presentations When You Send Them Out

Often after you have created your PDF presentation, you may well move it to another computer by sending it across the Internet or possibly copy it to a laptop to take to a conference. Here is how you can make sure that your presentation will always open up and behave like a presentation when you send it or take it somewhere else.

1. Choose File > Document Properties (or press ⌘/Ctrl+D). The Document Properties dialog appears.
2. Select Initial View from the list of Document Properties on the left side of the window (Figure 8.13).
3. Configure the window as follows:
   Open In Full Screen Mode Select this check box (in the middle of the dialog, under Window Options); it is the most important setting to make sure that your PDF will open and display in Presentation mode. In fact, if you just click this button, your presentation display should be okay. However, I go ahead and configure the remainder of the window as follows, just in case the Full Screen mode doesn't work.

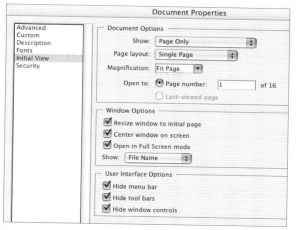

Figure 8.13 The Initial View properties

Other Window Options Select both Resize Window To Initial Page and Center Window On Screen.

Document Options Select Show: Page Only; Page Layout: Single Page; and Magnification: Fit Page. If you want the presentation to start on something other than the first page, set that page number here. However, typically if I am sending out a presentation, I remove any pages that I do not want displayed.

User Interface Options Check all of these boxes to disable these elements, because they are not important in Full Screen Presentation mode.

> **Note:** By default, the User Interface Options don't show when the Full Screen mode is properly activated. However, I disable them anyway just to make sure.

4. Set the Security Options: If you want to control who has access to your presentation and/or you want to make sure that your PDF can only be viewed and not altered in any way and/or no content can be printed or extracted from it, set the Security Options (Document > Security > Restrict Opening and Editing…) on your file prior to distributing it. (See Chapter 5, "Controlling Acrobat and Access to Your PDFs," for complete details on how to control the security of your PDFs.)

5. Save the changes you have made and close the file.

6. Open the file to make sure that it launches in Full Screen Presentation mode.

Acrobat Preferences vs. PDF Document Properties

Acrobat Preferences control the way in which a particular copy of Acrobat behaves. PDF Document Properties affect specific PDF files. PDF Document Priorities take precedence over—that is they overrule (at least initially)—any Acrobat Preferences that may be set. For instance, if your Full Screen mode presentation PDF is opened with a copy of Acrobat whose preferences are set to Continuous Facing Pages, your document property will take precedence, forcing your presentation to open, as you want it to, in Full Screen mode. And if you have set the PDF security so that the properties on your PDF cannot be altered, it will always start in Full Screen mode.

Creating and Using PDF Forms

One of the many great features of Acrobat and PDF is that they can be used to create, fill in, and distribute forms. This solves that common problem that is created when a form is generated in a custom forms program or extension that most people do not have, requiring that they print the form in order to fill it out and then send it by mail or fax. The PDF capabilities of Acrobat and PDF allow you to create the final form in Acrobat and then edit and distribute that form electronically, keeping the entire process digital. And of course, using Acrobat's Security features allow you to control access and use of your PDF form. The following sections tell you how forms work.

Creating Form Templates

You will typically design the template or background for a PDF form in a document creation application such as InDesign or Word. This form layout will then be made interactive in Acrobat using the Forms tool.

1. Design and lay out the form you would like to create, preferably in a page layout application. The one I will use here is an order form I laid out in QuarkXPress. When designing a form template/background, build one that will display well on a screen at 600×800, and leave enough room to add form fields in Acrobat.

2. Convert this form to a PDF document. To minimize errors and speed up the PDF creation process, I prefer printing my page layout documents to a watched folder controlled by a Distiller setting that will be appropriate for the form's use. (☞ Chapter 4 for information on creating watched folders and selecting Distiller settings.)

   After you have a PDF form template, you will basically have a series of two-step processes: define a form element; then configure that element. The following sections describe the typical steps and provide a few form element examples.

PDF Version for Forms

Although you can save a PDF form in the most recent format—Acrobat 6 (PDF 1.5)—I recommend that you select an earlier version of Acrobat (PDF 1.3 or 1.4) so that a wider audience will be able to open, view, and fill in your PDF-based form. Many people don't have the most recent version of Acrobat or Reader, so assume that many of your readers will be a bit behind the times. Of course, if you must use Acrobat 6 (PDF 1.5) due to the level of security you need, by all means save it in the latest format.

Creating Fields in Forms: Text Fields

To create a form in Acrobat, we will first open a form template (this is typically created in another page layout application), to which we will then add form fields. During their creation, we will control the characteristics of these form fields so that they will behave as we want them to. Acrobat allows us to create a variety of form fields; here we will start by creating and formatting text fields:

1. In Acrobat, open the PDF form template you created in the previous section. I'm using one of my Calibration Kit order forms, and you can open this very file from the companion CD-ROM to follow along (it's FormTemplate.pdf in the Chapter 8 folder). I'll show you how to build the fields on the Order Information panel at the bottom of the form (Figure 8.14).

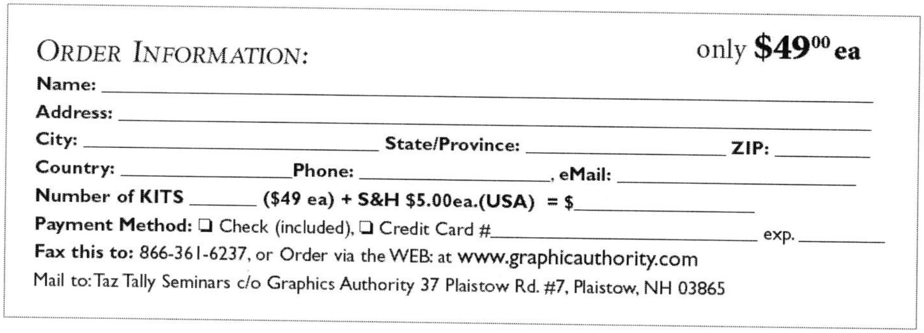
ORDER INFORMATION: only $49^{00} ea
Name: ______
Address: ______
City: ______ State/Province: ______ ZIP: ______
Country: ______ Phone: ______, eMail: ______
Number of KITS ______ ($49 ea) + S&H $5.00ea.(USA) = $______
Payment Method: ❑ Check (included), ❑ Credit Card #______ exp. ______
Fax this to: 866-361-6237, or Order via the WEB: at www.graphicauthority.com
Mail to: Taz Tally Seminars c/o Graphics Authority 37 Plaistow Rd. #7, Plaistow, NH 03865

Figure 8.14 A PDF form template

2. Click the down-arrow to the right of the Button tool (Figure 8.15) and choose Show Forms Toolbar; the Forms tools will appear in their own floating tool palette. This toolbar can be left floating or dragged up to become a stationary part of the main toolbar.

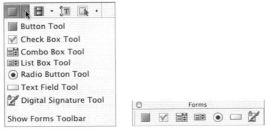

Figure 8.15 Open the Forms tools and let them remain a floating toolbar.

This Forms toolbar contains the various Forms tools used to create the forms elements—such text fields, check boxes, radio buttons, and signature fields—that are used to create your form. The tools you use and how you configure them will vary with the types and contents of the forms you want to create.

3. Let's start with creating a text field. Click the Text Field tool ⬚.

4. Double-click the location where you would like to place the form field to create a default-sized field, or click and drag your cursor across the portion of the form template where you would like to create an interactive text field, in this case the Name line. Be sure to draw the text field long enough and tall enough to accommodate the length and size of text you will want to use in this field. When in doubt, err on the side of making the field bigger. A red rectangle will appear around the text field area, and the Text Field Properties dialog will appear (Figure 8.16). This is where you configure the characteristics of the form field you have just drawn.

Distiller Settings and Graphics Formats for Forms

If you have used pixel-based images in your forms and intend to use your forms in an electronic fashion only, then a low-resolution, moderate image quality Distiller setting such as Standard will be fine. If you intend to print these forms commercially as well as use them electronically, you may want to consider making two versions of the forms, a smaller, lower-resolution/image quality version for electronic distribution and one with higher resolution/image quality for commercial printing. But here is a graphics tip: If you use a vector (EPS) format for your graphics, such as logos that appear on your forms, they tend to be significantly smaller than pixel-based graphics such as TIFFs, and unlike the pixel-based images, vectors are not affected by the distilling process. Vector graphics will both look good on screen and print well on high-resolution printing devices. So if the only graphics you use in your forms are vector-based, you can use the same PDF form for both screen viewing and editing, as well as high-resolution printing. But whichever graphic route you take, be sure that the font files are included/embedded in your PDF so that the typesetting integrity of your form will be maintained.

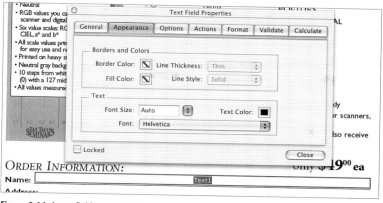

Figure 8.16 A text field area and its Appearance Properties

Note: You can fine-tune the position and dimensions of the form field by dragging the interior of the field to move the field or dragging one of the field edge control points to change the dimensions of the field.

5. Click the Appearance tab, which controls the look of the field area and, in this case, the text within the field:

   a. Decide whether you want to have a Border Color and/or Fill Color (background) for your field. Click an outlined color swatch to assign a color.

   b. If you assign a border color, select a Line Thickness and Line Style.

   c. Assign a Font, Font Size, and Text Color for the text in the field.

6. Click the General tab (Figure 8.17), which controls field characteristics and behavior. These properties are usually the same for any type of form field:

Name Type in the name of the field.

Tooltip Enter text if you want to provide mouse-activated instructions for the form user.

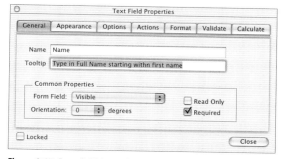

Figure 8.17 Form field General Properties

Font Selection

Most PDF forms will be viewed on screen at some point, so it is a good idea to select fonts that will be easy to read on screen. Typically, sans serif fonts that have prominent horizontal and vertical swashes, such as Helvetica and Arial, are good choices. Also try to keep the point size at 10 points and above, so that they will be easier to read by viewers of all ages.

Form Field Select visibility and printability characteristics from this menu: Visible, Hidden, Visible But Doesn't Print, or Hidden But Printable.

Orientation If you want the field to be placed at an angle, set that angle here.

Read Only If you want the field to be read-only, such as a text string, check this box.

Required If this is a required form field, check this box.

Locked If you want to prevent any further editing of these properties, check here.

Note: Text fields can contain input fields like this one, but they can also contain strings of text that are intended to be read but not modified, such as instructions. You may want a text string to be visible but not necessarily print.

7. Click the Options tab (Figure 8.18), which controls field features and limits. These properties differ according to the type of form field being configured:

Alignment Set the alignment of text within the field to either Left, Center, or Right.

Default Value If you want to enter default text for the field, do so here.

Multi-Line Check this option if you want to allow multiple lines (not appropriate for a Name field).

Scroll Long Text If you will have or allow a scrolling list, check this box. If you check this, the Field Is Used For File Selection option becomes available.

Allow Rich Text Formatting To allow form users to apply formatting to their text entries, such as bold and underlining, check this option.

Limit Of _ Characters If you want to place a maximum on the number of characters you will allow—for instance, this might be dictated by the field space limit in a database that will receive this form's data—enter that number here. I have placed a limit of 30 characters here.

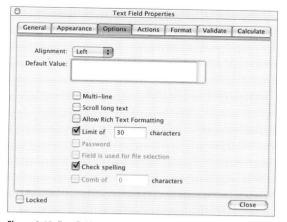

Figure 8.18 Text field Options Properties

Password Check this box if you want to restrict access to this form field to those who have password authorization to use this form.

Field Is Used For File Selection This option works with the Scroll Long Text control above, and it would be selected if this text field would be used to select from a list of filenames.

Check Spelling Check this option if you want Acrobat to spell-check text entries. (This is not appropriate for a Name entry.)

Comb of _ Characters Select this box to evenly distribute characters across the text field, and enter the number of characters that will be allowed. This is useful for single-character text fields.

8. Click the Close button to complete the formatting of the input text form field. Your newly created text form field will appear as you have formatted it with the name you have given it. The text field will still be selected.

ORDER INFORMATION: only **$49⁰⁰ ea**
Name: [Name   ]

9. Click the Hand tool or press H. Your newly created text form field will be deselected and will appear without a name or resizing handles.

ORDER INFORMATION: only **$49⁰⁰ ea**
Name: [   ]

Selecting Form Fields

Once you have deselected your form field, it is not available for editing. To prepare an already created form field for editing, do *one* of the following:

- Select the Object tool and double-click the form field you would like to edit.
- Select the Forms tool that matches the form field you would like to edit (for example, the Text Field tool for a text field), and click the field you would like to edit.

The Field Properties window, described in the preceding section, will appear again for you to reconfigure.

In Figure 8.19, I've selected six form fields: Name, Address, City, Zip, Phone, and eMail.

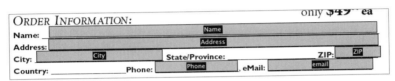

Figure 8.19 Six separately named text fields

Duplicating Form Fields

Once they are created, form fields can be duplicated once or multiple times. This can save an enormous amount of time if you are creating multiple variations of the same type of field. This situation is common, for instance, when creating form fields for contact information such as name, address, postal code, etc.

With either the Object tool or appropriate Forms tool (in this case, the Text Field tool), select the form field. Then do *one* of the following to duplicate this field:

- To make one copy, you can simply copy and paste the selected form field(s).
- To make one copy in a particular location, Option/Alt+drag the selected form field(s) to where you would like the copy to be placed. (This is my favorite way to make one copy.)
- To make single or multiple copies, Ctrl/right-click the selected form field(s) and choose either Duplicate or Create Multiple Copies. A Create Multiple Copies Of Fields dialog appears (Figure 8.20). You can control the number, size, and placement of the duplicate fields and even preview them with this dialog.

Note: You can select single or multiple fields for duplication using any of these methods.

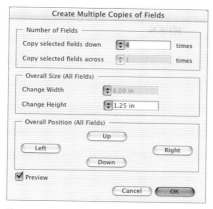

Figure 8.20 Creating multiple copies of one or more fields

If you use the Create Multiple Copies option, configure the window to create as many copies of the original field as you will need. In Figure 8.20, I'm making four additional copies of each of the selected fields.

Creating Choice Lists in Forms: Combo Box and List Box Fields

In addition to creating input text fields, Acrobat offers you the ability to create preset lists of choices. These are good to provide for those form entries that require very specific text or formatting for which there could be many variations. A list of state name abbreviations is just such a list, because each state has its own two-character abbreviation, they should always be uppercase, and some of them are easily confused. (Is the state abbreviation for Alaska AK or AL—and what is Arkansas?) We typically use a combo box to create and implement such a structured list. Let's add this to the order form we have been creating:

1. Select the Combo Box Forms tool ▦.

2. Drag the Combo Box tool over the form area designated for a choice-list form, such as State/Province. The Combo Box Properties dialog appears, opened to the General tab (this was shown back in Figure 8.17).

Auto-Forms Filling of Duplicate Named Fields

Acrobat supports an auto-forms filling capability; this uses the names of the form fields to identify which fields should respond to auto-filling. Identically named form fields, such as all those named (Name), will have the same input as the first Name text field in which text is entered.

3. Type in the field's name and Tooltip (such as "Select your state from this list") and set its Common Properties; then click the Appearance tab and configure it as we did earlier in the "Creating Fields in Forms: Text Fields" section.

4. Click the Options tab (Figure 8.21). This is where you create your list of choices. Here's how:

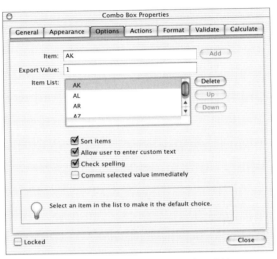

Figure 8.21 Options properties for a combo box form field

Item Type in a list entry. Here, I'm adding a two-character state symbol, AK, to the combo box.

Export Value If you want to Acrobat to export this choice as something other than the text shown (here, AK) when the form data is exported—perhaps the full name of a state, or even a number if you assign each list item a numeric value in your database (as I have done here assigning a numerical export value of 1 to AK)—then enter that value in this field. I have matched the two here.

Add button and Item List Once you have set the Item text and the Export Value, click Add, and the item is added to the Item List. Select one of the values in the Item List—typically the first one in an alphabetical list—to be the default value.

Sort Items Check this box if you want Acrobat to sort your list.

Allow User To Enter Custom Text If you want to provide users with the ability to enter custom values (not appropriate for a list of states or provinces), check this box.

Check Spelling Activate this option if users will add any custom text, other than names.

Commit Selected Value Immediately Check this option if you want the combo box value saved as soon as the value is entered. If left unchecked (the default state), the value will not be saved until another field is selected or the Tab key is hit.

5. Click the Close button to apply your combo box list. The combo box field will be added to the form, with the default list value (AK here) appearing in the form. You will also see a down-arrow indicating the presence of a manual selection list (Figure 8.22).

Note: When making a state list, be sure to list all 50 states and the District of Columbia. Plus you might want to include entries for Canadian provinces. And if you provide alternative export values, be sure that each list value is assigned a proper export value.

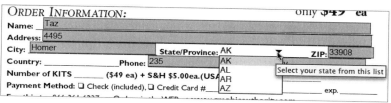

Figure 8.22 Combo box complete with state list and Tooltip

6. To try out your field, switch to the Hand tool or type H. Click the Combo Box menu to activate the state choice list.

The Country field area in this order form is another good candidate for the use of a combo box with a list of specifically named countries. Let's duplicate this State field to create a Country field:

1. Option/Alt+drag the State combo box to another area to create a duplicate field.

2. Double-click the copied combo box field, click the General tab, and change the Name and Tooltip as shown in Figure 8.23.

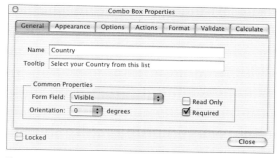

Figure 8.23 Country combo box, General tab

3. Click the Options tab and edit it as follows (Figure 8.24):

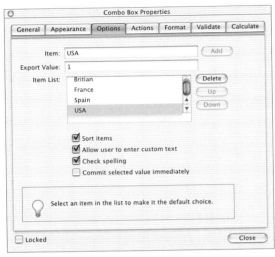

Figure 8.24 Country combo box, Options tab

a. Select and delete the state list entries.

b. Create a list of countries, as we did the list of states in the preceding combo box exercise. Here, I have assigned numbers as export values for each country.

c. Be sure the Sort Items box is checked.

d. Click the country name (here USA) that you would like to make the default field value choice.

e. Check the Allow User To Enter Custom Text option.

 Note: Unlike the state names list, there are likely to be countries that may not be on the list, or may change their names over time, so allowing custom values is appropriate here.

4. Click the Close button to compete the Combo Box Properties windows.

5. Select the Hand tool and click the Country field to view your new list.

The List Box Tool

The List Box tool works in much the same manner as the Combo Box tool, but instead of providing a menu, it places the entire list on screen and provides for multiple selections. Neither of these features are appropriate for a state or country list, but they might be appropriate for a more limited list of related items such as products and accessories.

```
AK
Al
AR
AZ
```

Adding Special Field Types

Acrobat provides some built-in special formatting options for common formats, including general number formats, special number formats (such as phone, zip code, social security, and currency numbers), percentage value displays, date formats, and time displays. Acrobat also supports the creation of custom values for JavaScript.

> **Note:** Which special formatting values are available will depend upon the field character values entered in the Options window.

Creating Phone Number Fields

Since phone numbers are written so many different ways, it would be nice to have a common way for phone numbers to appear. Here is how we do this:

1. Using the Text Field tool , drag across the Phone area on the form. The Text Field Properties window will appear for you to reconfigure.
2. Click the General tab and configure it as follows:
   a. Enter **Phone** in the Name field.
   b. Enter **Type in your phone number** in the Tooltip field.
3. Click the Format tab (Figure 8.25).
4. Select Special from the Select Format Category drop-down menu.

> **Note:** Select Format Category includes predefined format categories, such as Number, Percentage, Date, Time, and Custom, each of which has a list of optional choices.

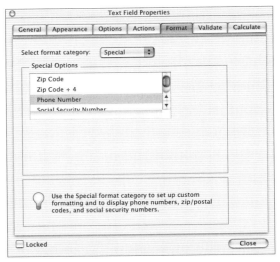

Figure 8.25 Phone field, Format tab

5. Click the Phone Number choice from the Special Options list.

6. Click the Close button to complete the Phone field properties.

7. To try out your field, switch to the Hand tool or type H. Click the Phone field and type in 10 digits without punctuation. Press the Enter key to apply the phone number, and note that Acrobat automatically formats the phone number with parentheses, spaces, and dashes.

Creating Lists of Numbers

A common item on many forms is a list of numbers. This is useful not only for numeric items, such as product codes, but also for quantity fields. Here is how we would add a list of numbers to this order form:

1. Create a combo box form field (as we have done previously in this chapter).

2. Click the General tab and enter the following:

Name field   **Number of Kits**

Tooltip field   **Select a number or type in a value**

3. Click the Options tab and configure it as follows (Figure 8.26):

   a. Add Item numbers and Export Values (here, they are identical for numbers 1–10), just as we did in creating the State and Country combo boxes earlier.

   b. Uncheck Sort Items so that the number 10 does not appear second on the list.

c. Check the Allow User To Enter Custom Text box in case someone wants to order more than 10 kits!

d. Uncheck the Check Spelling option.

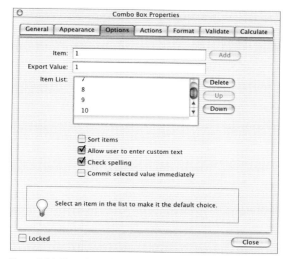

Figure 8.26 Numeric combo box field, Options tab

4. Click the Format tab (Figure 8.27), and choose Number from the Select Format Category drop-down list. The following options appear:

a. Select the number of decimal places you want (0 here).

b. Choose your Separator Style.

c. If you accept negative numbers (certainly not allowed for an order quantity!), you can format the Negative Number Style.

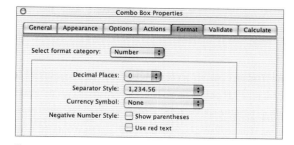

Figure 8.27 Numeric combo box field, Format tab

5. Click the Close button to complete the setup of the Combo Box properties.

6. To try your new field, switch to the Hand tool or type H. Click the Number of KITS field to see the list of numbers 1 through 10.

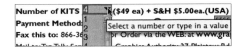

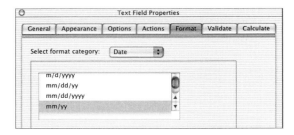

Note: Since we have allowed the input of custom values in the Options tab, users can either select a number from this list or type in their own (numeric) value.

Creating Date Fields

At the bottom of my order form, I've created a simple text field for the credit card number and another text field with a date format for the expiration date. You can set up this type of field by creating a text field, opening its Properties dialog's Format tab, and choosing Date from the Select Format Category drop-down list. Then pick a date format from the scrolling list.

Adding Hidden Values for Calculations

Many order forms contain some standard or set values that need to be used in calculations. In this form we have a kit price ($49) and a shipping and handling charge ($5 each), which are standard values that do not change. In this section, we will add them to the form as hidden values that we can then use for calculating the total price in the next step. Here's how we do it:

1. Select the List Box tool ⊟⬆.

Note: We use the List Box tool here rather than the Combo Box tool because no menu is required, we have only one value to add, and it will be hidden anyway. The List Box tool is preferable to a hidden text field here because it will not be automatically added to a tab sequence (as a text field would).

2. Drag the List Box tool over some relevant copy; in my order form, I've positioned this field over the area containing the "($49 ea) + S&H $5.00 ea" copy. Exact placement is not critical because these will be hidden values.

3. Click the General tab and format as follows (Figure 8.28):

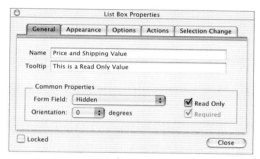

Figure 8.28 Hidden cost field, General tab

a. Type **Price and Shipping Value** in the Name field.
b. Type **This is a Read Only Value** in the Tooltip field.
c. Select Hidden from the Form Field menu.
d. Check the Read Only option.

Note: Hidden and Read Only will hide this field value from users and prevent them from altering the value.

4. Click the Options tab (Figure 8.29) and enter the number **54** (the sum of $49 + $5) in the Item and Export Value fields, and then click Add. No other formatting is necessary.

5. Click the Close button to complete the List Box Properties window.

6. Switch to the Hand tool 🖐 or type H; the field will be hidden from view. To view the field and gain access to it, click the Item tool ⬆, which makes all hidden fields visible.

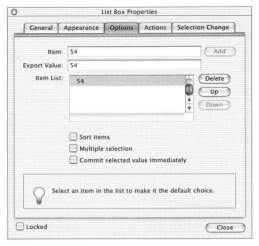

Figure 8.29 Hidden cost field, Options tab

Creating Calculation Fields

Acrobat allows you to create fields that will contain values calculated from other fields. In this case, we are interested in the calculation of the number of kits ordered times the price per kit plus shipping and handling (which is in the hidden field created in the preceding section). Here is an example of how you might go about creating a calculation field:

This will be another text form field:

1. Create a text form field next to the $.

2. Click the General tab and format as follows:

   a. Type **Total Cost** in the Name field.

   b. Type **Your total cost will appear here** in the Tooltip field.

   c. Be sure the Form Field value is set to Visible.

   d. Check the Read Only and Required check boxes.

3. Click the Format tab and set it up as follows (Figure 8.30).

   a. Choose Number from the Select Format Category list.

   b. Choose the number of Decimal Places you want displayed.

   c. Choose your style of punctuation from the Separator Style list.

   d. Choose a Currency Symbol.

4. Click the Calculate tab (Figure 8.31).

5. Click the Value Is The radio button, and choose Product from the drop-down menu of math functions.

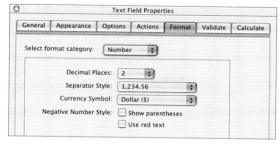

Figure 8.30 Calculation field, Format tab

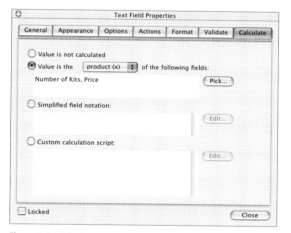

Figure 8.31 Calculation field, Calculate tab

6. Click the Pick button. The Field Selection window appears (Figure 8.32). Select the field values you would like to have multiplied (in this case, the Number Of Kits field and the Price And Shipping Value field). Then click OK to close the Field Selection window.

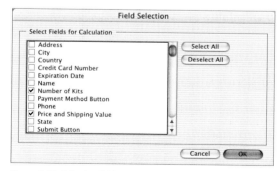

Figure 8.32 Selecting fields to use in the calculation

Complex and Custom Calculations

As you can see in the Calculate tab of the Text Field Properties dialog, Acrobat supports the creation of simple math calculations such as addition, subtraction, multiplication, and division of field values. Applying more complex or customized calculations generally requires the creation and use of JavaScript. The Simplified Field Notation and Custom Calculation Script buttons available in the Calculate tab can be used instead of the simple arithmetic functions we have used here. To learn more about creating and using JavaScript in Acrobat, refer to the following website:

        http://partners.adobe.com/asn/acrobat/index.jsp

One word of caution and encouragement for simplicity: Remember that not all applications—and Adobe Reader is one of them—can handle JavaScript. The simpler your forms are, the more readily they can be used. Whenever possible, I attempt to design my forms so that I can use Acrobat's simple built-in arithmetic functions.

7. Click the Close button to finish the setup of the Calculation Text Field Properties.

8. To test your new calculation field, select a value of 4 from the Number Of Kits field. Acrobat should calculate 4 × $54 = $216.00.

Number of KITS 4 ▼ ($49 ea) + S&H $5.00ea.(USA) = $ $216.00

Now any time that a user enters or changes the value in the Number Of KITS field, the Total Cost will be recalculated.

Adding Radio Buttons and Check Boxes

There are often circumstances where all that is needed is to choose between a few limited numbers of items, such as the payment method on our order form. This can be nicely handled with one of the Forms Button tools. In this case we will use the Radio Button tool because it provides us with the ability to create exclusionary buttons, so only one option can be selected at a time.

Note: The Check Box tool ☑ works in the same way as the Radio Button tool, but it should be used when you want to create nonexclusive lists where more than one item can be selected.

Here's how to create a set of radio buttons:

1. Click the Radio Button ⦿ tool.

2. Zoom into the Payment area of the order form, to improve the accuracy of your placement of the button.

3. Drag the tool across the top of the square check box labeled "Check (included)". The Radio Button Properties dialog appears.

4. Click and set up the General tab as follows:

   a. Type in a name of the button (I used **Payment Method Button**).

   b. Enter a Tooltip if you wish (such as **Click one of these buttons**).

   c. Select Visible in the Form Field.

   d. Uncheck Read Only. It is important to turn off this option, because this will make the buttons interactive.

   e. Click the Required box.

5. Configure the Appearance tab as we have done in the previous exercises.

6. Click the Options tab and configure it as follows (Figure 8.33):

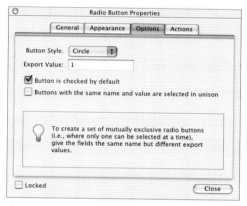

Figure 8.33 Radio Button Properties, Options tab

   a. Choose a Button Style: Check, Circle, Cross, Diamond, Square, or Star.

   b. Enter an Export Value (**1** here), which you designate to represent the choice of a check when this form data is exported.

   c. Check the Button Is Checked By Default option if you want this button to be the default choice.

   d. Uncheck Buttons With The Same Name And Values Are Selected In Unison, because there will be no buttons with the same name and values.

7. Click Close.

8. Now duplicate this button by Option/Alt+dragging the button you just made over the top of the Credit Card # area on the form. This action will duplicate the original button with all of its properties.

9. Double-click the new button to reopen the Radio Button Properties window, and click the Options tab.

10. Place a value of **2** in the Export Value field (Figure 8.34). This is the only change we will make to this button's properties (☞ the sidebar on "Mutually Exclusive Buttons").

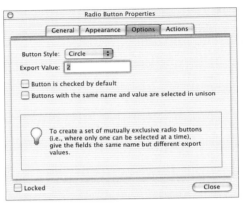

Figure 8.34 The Options tab for the second radio button

11. Click the Close button to complete the creation and configuration of the two radio buttons.

12. To test your set of radio buttons, click the Hand tool ✋ or type H. Click first on one button and then the other. You will notice that you can select only one button at a time.

You can, of course, create more radio buttons in one set than the pair we've built here. And you can have multiple sets of radio buttons, and multiple sets of mutually exclusive radio buttons (by using different sets of Export values).

Mutually Exclusive Buttons

By assigning the same name to both buttons (by copying the first button and its properties) and changing only the Export Value between the two buttons, you make them mutually exclusive, so that only one of them can be selected at a time.

Adding a Submit Button

After you have finished constructing your form, you have a variety of options on deciding how a user can handle that form; the form can be printed, or it can be sent electronically. Built in to Acrobat is the ability to submit that form in a variety of ways.
Here's how to add a "submit" capability to a PDF form:

1. Select the Button tool ▊ and drag it across a clear area near the bottom of the
   form. The Button Properties window appears.

2. Click the General tab and configure it as follows (Figure 8.35):

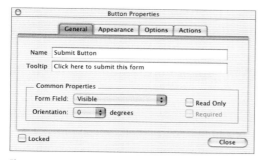

Figure 8.35 Button Properties, General tab

   a. Type **Submit Button** in the Name field.

   b. Type **Click here to submit this form** in the Tooltip field.

   c. From the Form Field drop-down, choose Visible.

   d. Be sure the Read Only box is *unchecked*.

3. Click the Appearance tab and configure it with these guidelines (Figure 8.36):

   a. Select bright and contrasting colors for the Fill and Border Colors.

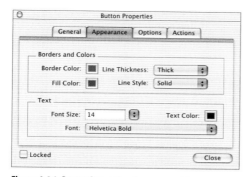

Figure 8.36 Button Properties, Appearance tab

b. Add a thick, solid border if you think this will attract attention to your submit button.

c. Select a larger Font Size than is common in your other form fields.

d. Choose a bold san serif font for your typeface.

 Note: Always make the Submit button large, brightly colored, and easy to find.

4. Click the Options tab, and configure it like this (Figure 8.37):

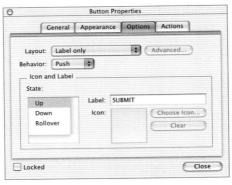

Figure 8.37 Button Properties, Options tab

a. Select the type of Layout you would like the button to have: whether it should a text label, icon, or both, and how they should be arranged. If you opt for one of the Icon choices here, you can select a graphic by clicking the Choose Icon button (which is grayed out here).

b. Select a button Behavior: None, Push, Outline, or Invert. This will define what will happen when a mouse is clicked on the button. Here we have defined Push.

c. Select the Up State option. (Not all behaviors offer options. State options define what will display in the button area when a specific state is active. The states available will depend upon which Behavior has been selected in the previous steps. Here Up, Down, and Rollover are available.)

d. Type in an identifying text label, **SUBMIT**. This will determine that when the button is not just sitting there unmolested; it will have a label of SUBMIT.

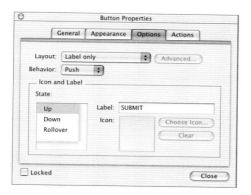

e. Next, select the Rollover State option and type in a label of **Click Here**. This will cause the Submit button to show the instruction "Click Here" when a mouse is moved/rolled over the button (not clicked on, just rolled over the button).

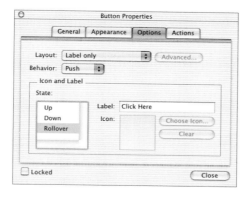

f. Next select the Down State option and type in a label of
Release. This will cause the Submit button to show the
instruction "Release" when a mouse is clicked on the button.

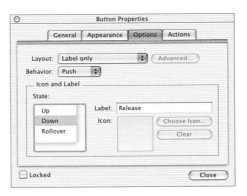

5. Click the Actions tab to prepare what will happen when the Submit button is
clicked (Figure 8.38). Set up this window like this:

a. Click the Select Trigger drop-down menu and select one of the trigger mech-
anisms (Mouse Down here).

b. Click the Select Action drop-down menu and choose Submit A Form from
the list of actions that can be initiated by the trigger.

Once you've chosen a trigger and an action, click the Add button to add this
action to the Actions list. The Submit Forms Selections dialog appears.

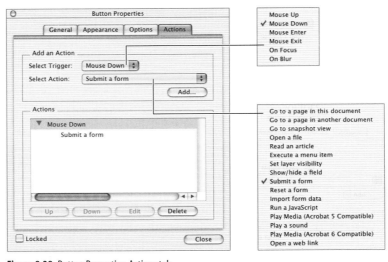

Figure 8.38 Button Properties, Actions tab

6. Set the Submit Form Selections dialog (Figure 8.39) to deliver your form's data in a manner and to a destination of your choosing. Here are some guidelines:

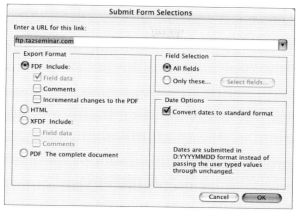

Figure 8.39 Submit Forms Selections dialog

a. Type in the address (Web, FTP, e-mail intranet server) where you want this data to be submitted.

b. FDF (Forms Data Format) here will include Field Data only, since this is a form and we don't have any comments anyway.

Note: See the collaborative publishing section of Chapter 9, "Collaborative Publishing and Interactivity," for more information on distributing Comments data.

c. If you want to export the form's data in HTML, XFDF format, or as a complete PDF, click the appropriate button.

d. Under Field Selection, check All Fields or choose to export only certain specified fields.

e. Under Date Options, check Convert Dates To Standard Format so that any date data will be submitted in a consistent format.

HTML and XFDF Data

If you export your forms data in HTML or XFDF data, you must be sure that the receiving website or other server contains a CGI application that can accept and route the data properly. To dig deeper into the use of HTML and XFDF data, refer to the "FDF Toolkit Overview" on the Adobe website.

7. Click the OK button to complete the Submit Form Selections window. The Submit A Form action will be added to the Actions list in the Actions tab window.

8. Click the Close button at the bottom of the Actions tab to complete the creation, formatting, and editing of the Submit button.

9. View your finished form (Figure 8.40)!

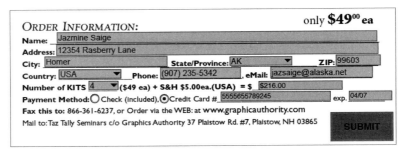

Figure 8.40 The completed order form

Note: My finished PDF order form is also on the companion CD-ROM: CompletedForm.pdf in the Chapter 8 folder.

To edit or remove an action you have already created, simply reopen the Submit button Properties Actions tab, click the action in the Action list, and then click the Edit or Delete button.

Checking and Editing Form Field Sequence

When creating form fields, it is best to create them in the order in which they will be used, because Acrobat will automatically link the form fields in that sequence. This linked sequence of form fields will allow users to tab through the field boxes in a logical order. However, if you need to change the field order linking, here's how you do it:

First, test the form field sequence as follows:

1. Click the Hand tool or type H.

2. Click the first form field, Name. A cursor will appear in the Name field.

3. Press the Tab key to move through the fields, place some sample data to test the form fields, and view the field sequence. *Record* the order in which the fields are selected.

Let's say the tab sequence for the order form winds up as follows: Name, Address, State/Province, Zip, City. This sequence is out of order; the City field should precede the State/Province field (compare this order with Figure 8.40). Here's how to change the tab order of a field:

1. Activate the Tags tab: View > Navigation Tabs > Tags.

Note: If no tags are present in your PDF form document, you can add tags by choosing Advanced > Accessibility > Add Tags To Document.

2. Click the down-arrow to expand the Tags display, which will show you the structure and order of all the contents in the document. Click more arrows until you can see the City and State form fields (Figure 8.41).

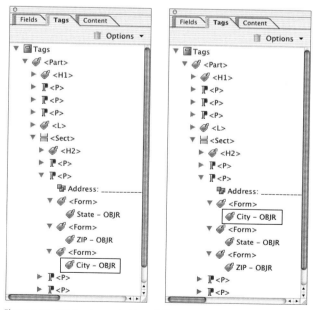

Figure 8.41 Initial and corrected form field sequence

Setting Forms Security

The final step in creating a PDF forms document is to set the document security so that users can view and fill in the form but not edit it. ↪ Chapter 5, "Controlling Acrobat and Access to Your PDFs," for information on setting document security.

3. Drag the City tag until it appears between the Address and State/Province tags.

4. Navigate through the form fields again to check that the fields are now in the proper order.

Filling Out PDF Forms

Acrobat provides for both mouse and keyboard navigation of forms. Text fields, if they are properly constructed, should allow users to move logically and progressively throughout text and text fields simply by pressing the Tab key. Also be aware of and look for mouse-activated menus and actions as well as signature locations.

Automatically Filling in Form Fields

Acrobat provides the ability, through its Application Preferences, to allow you to automatically fill in repetitive form data, saving you time, typing, and spelling mistakes. Once this feature is activated, when you begin to fill in identical data, such as your name or address, in a form field, Acrobat will offer up the data for you. Here's how to activate the auto-forms:

1. Choose File > Preferences or Acrobat > Preferences. The Preferences window will appear.

2. Select the Forms category from the list on the left side of the window (Figure 8.42).

3. Among the options in this dialog, choose either Basic or Advanced from the Auto-Complete drop-down list to activate this function. You can edit Auto-Complete entries.

Note: Advanced Auto-Complete offers more options and will flow text in automatically without selection if it "thinks" it has a really good match.

4. Click OK, and Acrobat's Auto-Complete feature will be active.

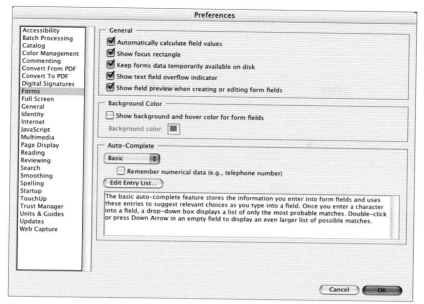

Figure 8.42 Forms Preferences settings

Spell-Checking Forms

Checking the spelling on a form is a simple procedure. Do this:

1. Choose Edit > Check Spelling > In Comments And Form Fields (or press F7). The Check Spelling window appears (Figure 8.43).

2. Click the Start button. Acrobat will find suspect words, list them in the top window, and list suggested corrections in the bottom window.

3. Apply any changes with the buttons at the right.

4. Click the Done button when you are through.

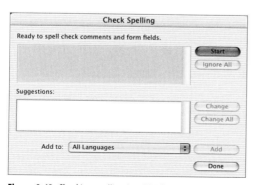

Figure 8.43 Checking spelling in a PDF form

As you have seen, the features for creating and using forms in Acrobat are powerful and, once you get the hang of them, easy to use. Remember that a good form starts with a good form *design*. When you create your initial background page layout document, leave yourself plenty of room to create your form fields in Acrobat. And when ever possible, keep your forms simple, so that the largest number of users can view and fill in your forms.

Collaborative Publishing and Interactivity

9

In addition to allowing you to repackage and redistribute text pages in a flexible format, Acrobat provides a wide variety of interactive features, including collaborative publishing tools and multimedia capabilities.

Chapter Contents

Guiding your viewers with bookmarks

Collaborating with comments

Adding multicolumn and multidocument navigation

Adding sounds and movies to your PDFs

Guiding Your Viewers with Bookmarks

PDF documents can serve as a very flexible work-in-progress document format. With Acrobat's collaborative publishing tools you can lead your collaborators though a document, make comments and suggestions, share comments, track document versions, and even use digital signatures to track and protect your work's progress.

Note: You need Acrobat, not just Adobe Reader, in order to use the collaborative publishing features described here. ☞ Chapter 5, "Controlling Acrobat and Access to Your PDFs," for details on digital signatures; ☞ Chapter 10, "Acrobat E-mail, eBook, and Web Features," for information on web and e-mail collaboration.

If you would like to direct your PDF viewer to various parts of your document and focus on specific sections, then Bookmarks is the tool to use. Here's how it works:

1. Open the PDF document you would like to bookmark. I'll use a first draft of a chapter of this book as a sample file; I've included it on the companion CD (in the Chapter 9 folder) as Chapter8Sample.pdf in case you'd like to follow along with the illustrations here.

Note: The CD also includes a "final" version of that file, named Chapter8SampleCommented.pdf, full of comments and media.

2. Click the Bookmarks tab. A bookmarks panel will appear to the left of the current (first) page.

3. Navigate to the page *and* the zoom/magnification level you would like to capture as a bookmark. In Figure 9.1, I have zoomed into the lower-right margin of page 3.

Note: For speed reasons, I like to use keyboard shortcuts to navigate to the pages and zoom levels I prefer. ☞ Chapter 6, "Using Acrobat and Navigating PDFs," for some tips on how to zip around PDF documents quickly.

4. Create a bookmark of this view by doing *one* of the following:
   - Click the Create New Bookmark icon.
   - Select New Bookmark from the Options menu.
   - Press ⌘/Ctrl+B.

   A new bookmark symbol will appear in the Bookmarks tab, labeled Untitled.

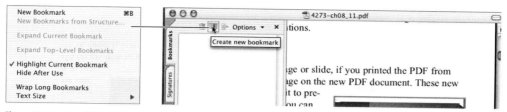

Figure 9.1 Bookmarking tools

5. Label your newly created bookmark in a logical fashion. I used the caption of the obvious illustration visible here to name this bookmark (Figure 8.2 PDF Page With Unwanted Border).

> **Note:** If you select some text in the bookmark area *before* making the bookmark, this copy will be used to label the bookmark.

6. If, like mine, the bookmark name is too long to appear in a single line and you would like to see the entire name, then right-click/Control+click the bookmark and select Wrap Long Bookmarks from the context menu, as shown in Figure 9.2. This will wrap the bookmark names so they fit within the Bookmarks tab. (You can also use this context menu to rename, delete, and set the properties of your bookmarks.)

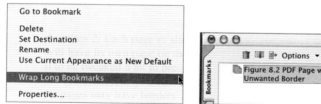

Figure 9.2 (left) The Bookmarks context menu; (right) a wrapped bookmark name

Now you can navigate to other views (pages and magnifications) and create bookmarks wherever you want to direct a viewer's attention.

Bookmarks Views

Acrobat's bookmarks will record not only the page and the specific location on the page but also the zoom or magnification level of the view you choose to bookmark. So select exactly the view you will want your viewers to see prior to making a bookmark.

Reordering and Nesting Bookmarks

Bookmarks can be ordered in any way you like, and they can be grouped together in a nested fashion to show relationships between them. For instance, if you have two bookmarks on separate pages but they relate to each other topically, you can nest one bookmark under the other one. Or, as we will do here, you may have two bookmarks that occur on the same page that you would like to nest to show their spatial relationship in the document.

To move a bookmark, click its *name* and drag it to a new position in the list of bookmarks. A small (red) tick mark appears to indicate the destination bookmark—the bookmark that the one you're moving will follow when you release the mouse. Release the mouse button, and the bookmark you dragged will move to its new location, as shown in Figure 9.3.

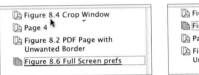

Figure 9.3 Moving the Figure 8.6 bookmark directly under the Figure 8.4 bookmark

 Note: The actual bookmarked view itself does not change; only the entry in the bookmarks list changes.

To nest a bookmark to show a relationship, follow these steps:

1. Click the bookmark *icon* (rather than the name). You can highlight multiple bookmarks to move together by Shift+clicking each icon. In this case I will select the icons for the bookmarks named Figure 8.8 and Figure 8.9 and move them under the Page 8 bookmark in the hierarchy.

2. Drag the two bookmarks' *icons* under the *icon* of the bookmark under which you would like them to nest. A small, one-sided red arrow appears to indicate where the nesting will occur (Figure 9.4).

3. Release the mouse button, and the selected bookmarks will be nested under the destination bookmark.

Figure 9.4 Nesting a bookmark

Collapse or display the contents of nested bookmarks by clicking the gray triangular tab to the left of the parent bookmark (here, Page 8).

Creating Bookmarks Automatically from PDF Structure

There are methods for automatically creating bookmarks from the content in a document. Two of the most common and useful methods involve using the document structure of a PDF file and using the contents of a web page.

To create a set of bookmarks from a PDF file's structure:

1. Choose Advanced > Accessibility > Add Tags To Document. This will locate all the structures in your document, including style sheets.

2. From the Options menu in the Bookmarks tab, select New Bookmarks From Structure. A Structure Elements window appears (Figure 9.5).

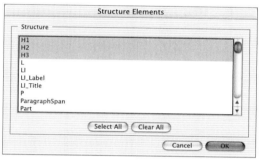

Figure 9.5 Selected style sheets to use as bookmarks

Style Sheets Again!

Way back in Chapter 2, "Document Construction and Preflighting," I discussed the speed, consistency, and editing benefits of using style sheets when creating original page layout documents. I also stated back then that there would be additional benefits to be gained from initially constructing your documents using style sheets once you converted your page layout document into PDFs. Well, here's a benefit: If you have used style sheets to create your original documents, you can use these style sheets to automatically create bookmarks, which in turn can be used as a hyperlinked interactive table of contents, as I have done here.

To take ease of navigation to the next level, the third-party program Sonar Bookends Activate (from Virginia Systems) creates hyperlinks in Acrobat PDF files for an index, table of contents, URLs, e-mails, figure and table references, and page references. I've included a trial version of this software on the companion CD.

3. Select the document elements you would like to use as bookmarks. Style sheets are commonly used elements for creating bookmarks. In Figure 9.5, the three main heading style sheets are selected to use as bookmark elements: H1, H2, and H3.

4. Click OK when you have completed selecting your bookmark elements.

5. View the bookmarks created from the selected document structure elements. Initially, the bookmarks created from this command are all nested bookmarks under an Untitled main parent bookmark, as shown in Figure 9.6. These bookmarks can be renamed, moved, and nested.

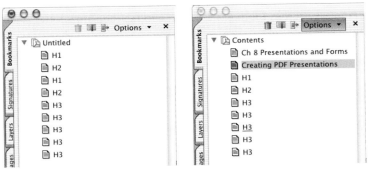

Figure 9.6 Bookmarks made from document structure default to a list under Untitled, but I'm renaming these so they serve as a table of contents.

Creating Bookmarks Automatically from Web Pages

Web pages can very easily be made into PDF documents; Chapter 10 describes this process in detail. But you should also know that all the pages of a website can be bookmarked on-the-fly. To convert web pages into bookmarked PDFs, get online and follow these steps:

1. Get online; then in Acrobat, choose File > Create PDF > From Web Page.

2. Configure the Create PDF From Web Page dialog as described in Chapter 10, but before you click OK, click the Settings button. The Web Capture Settings dialog appears.

3. Select the following check boxes in the PDF Settings section:

    Create Bookmarks This will create a bookmark for each page you convert.

    Create PDF Tags This will tag the PDF pages as they are being created, allowing you to make additional bookmarks from the tagged constructed elements, as we did in the previous section using style sheets.

4.   Click OK in the Web Capture Settings window, and then click Create in the Create PDF From Web Page window. Your selected website pages will be converted into a multipage PDF document, with each page having its own bookmark.

Collaborating with Comments

In addition to leading viewers around a PDF document with bookmarks, you can comment on various aspects of a PDF document and use those comments to navigate through a PDF. Acrobat provides two levels of Review and Commenting tools—basic and advanced. Here is a guide on how to use them:

There are four basic Commenting tools: the Note, Text Edits, Stamp, and Highlighting tools. To activate these tools if they're not already visible, click the Review & Comment icon in the main tool palette, and choose the Commenting Toolbar option (Figure 9.7).

Figure 9.7 Open the Commenting toolbar.

You can drag this toolbar out of the main tool palette to float on its own, as shown. Also, the Text Edits, Stamp, and Highlighting tools have multiple variations and can be further detached to their own even smaller toolbars.

> **Note:** When you are through commenting on a document, be sure to save all of your comments, additions, and changes. In fact, it's a good idea to do a save periodically as you progress through your document.

Highlighting Text to Suggest Edits

If you want to bring attention to some text and even suggest an edit to it, the Highlighting tools are your best bet: Highlighter, Underline Text, and Cross-Out Text. These are the simplest of the Commenting tools. Here's how they work:

You can access them from the basic Comments tool palette or activate the floating Highlighting toolbar by selecting Show Highlighting Toolbar.

To mark text, just select a tool and drag across the text you would like to highlight, underline, or strike through.

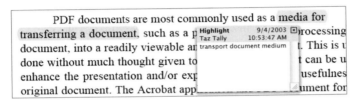

If you would like to add a comment to go along with that highlighted text, you do not have to reselect the text. You could add a note next to the text, as described in the following section, but the easiest method is to select the Hand tool (press H) and double-click the highlighted text. A Highlight note field will appear in which you can enter your comment.

PDF documents are most commonly used as a media for transferring a document, such as a p | Highlight   9/4/2003 ⊠ |rocessing document, into a readily viewable ar | Taz Tally   10:53:47 AM | done without much thought given to | transport document medium | t. This is u done without much thought given to   t can be u enhance the presentation and/or exp   usefulnes original document. The Acrobat app   ument for

When you are through making your comment, click the X in the upper-right corner to close the field; you or your readers can reopen your note by double-clicking the highlighted text again.

Adding "Sticky" Notes

The Note tool is probably the most used commenting tool. It works like a digital sticky note:

1. Click the Note Tool icon   Note Tool .

2. Click and drag your cursor over the area where you would like the comment to be placed. A Note field appears on screen.

3. Type in the comment text.

4. When you are through making your comment, click the X in the upper-right corner of the note to close the note, or press the Esc key to deselect the note but

leave it open. Once it is closed, a small sticky-note icon will be placed on the page at the point from which you initially dragged out the note.

> CHAPTER 8 PRESENTATIONS AND FORMS

5. To edit your comment, double-click the collapsed sticky-note icon to open it.

Suggesting Text Deletions and Insertions

The Text Edits tool allows you to make a variety of text-editing comments, including deletions and changes, while keeping the original text there for everyone to see.

1. Click the Select Text tool [IT] Select Text (press V) or the Text Edits tool [T_A] Text Edits (press E).

2. Select the text you would like to edit by dragging over it, or insert your cursor in the text.

3. Click the down-arrow next to the Text Edits tool icon, and choose an option (Figure 9.8).

For example, if you select some text and choose the Cross Out Text For Deletion option, the text will appear with a red line through the middle.

To insert text instead of deleting or editing it, you don't need to select any text first. Just place the cursor where you would like to make a note about a text edit, and then choose the relevant command. For example, if you use the Insert Text At Cursor menu choice, an Insert Text window field will prompt you for the new text. Type it in, and then click the X in the upper-right corner to close the window. The Text Insertion icon will remain visible (Figure 9.9).

Figure 9.8 Select the text or place your cursor in the text, and then choose a Text Edits option.

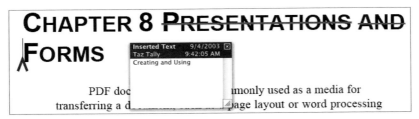

Figure 9.9 I've marked two words for deletion and added a note about some new text.

Adding a Text Comment Box

Sometimes you may want just a simple box of text comment that does not collapse but remains visible all the time. This is when you will want to use the Text Box tool.

To use this tool, first select Tools > Advanced Commenting > Show Advanced Commenting Toolbar. This will add the Advanced Commenting tool set to the main tool palette, allowing you to select tools there without having to return to this menu. Then, if you choose, you can float the Advanced Commenting toolbar by dragging it out of the main tool palette.

Select the Text Box tool ![Text Box icon] and drag the cursor across the area where you would like the text box to be located. Type in your comment, and press the Enter key when you have finished. The text box will automatically shrink to fit the size of the copy.

This box will remain visible at all times, unlike the other text commenting tools such as the Note and Text Edit tools, which have disappearing text field windows.

Adding Graphic Comments with the Stamp Tool

You can also add graphic comments, either from a built-in set of graphics or from a graphic you make. Use the Stamp tool to add a comment with a built-in graphic:

1. Click the down-arrow next to the Stamp tool, and use the menu and category submenus to choose a stamp, as shown in Figure 9.10.

2. With the stamp icon ![stamp icon] that appears as your cursor, click where you would like to place the stamp on the PDF document page. The stamp will appear where you place it.

Two of the Stamp tool categories have special features:

Dynamic (time/date) stamps These preset graphic stamps include your name and the time and date of your stamping action (they're called Dynamic stamps to indicate their time-sensitive nature). The five Dynamic stamps read Approved, Confidential, Received, Reviewed, and Revised.

REVIEWED
By Taz Tally at 12:23 pm, 9/4/03

Sign Here stamps These stamps make it easy to "sign" a document graphically in some standard formats; they read Rejected, Accepted, Initial Here, Sign Here, and Witness. When you stamp with one of these tools, you can initial or sign the document by double-clicking the stamped comment with the Hand tool (keyboard shortcut H), as shown in Figure 9.11.

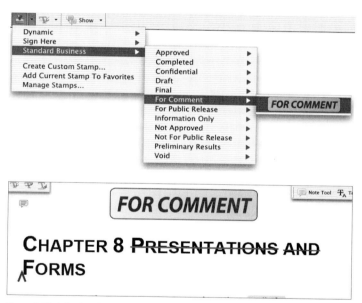

Figure 9.10 Left, choosing a graphic stamp from the Stamp Tool menu; right, the stamped page

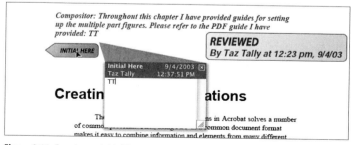

Figure 9.11 Opening an Initial Here comment on a page

Creating and Using Custom Graphic Stamps

You can easily create and use your own graphic stamps, and here's how:

1. Prepare a graphic that you would like to use as a PDF stamp, and save it as a one-page PDF file.

 Note: It is a good idea to create your custom stamps at close to the size you will be using them, to reduce the size of the stamp file.

2. From the Stamp Tool menu, choose Create Custom Stamp.
3. Click the Select button. In the Select dialog, browse to the PDF file you would like to use as your custom stamp; then click OK to return to the Create Stamp dialog.
4. Choose or create a Category for your new graphic stamp to appear under in menus. (In Figure 9.12, I've created a category called Taz Business.)

Figure 9.12 Identifying and selecting a custom graphic stamp

 Note: If you intend to use many custom graphic stamps, it is a good idea to organize your custom stamps into logical categories (such as Logos, Faces, Hand Signals, etc.) to make finding and using your stamps faster and easier.

5. Name your custom stamp.
6. Click OK. This will add your new custom stamp (and a new custom stamp category if you created one) to the Stamp Tool menu, as shown in Figure 9.13.

Use your new stamp just like the built-in ones, as described in the preceding section. From the Stamp Tool menu 🦫, choose the category and then the stamp name. When your cursor changes to the stamp icon, click where you want to place the stamp graphic on the PDF document page.

Figure 9.13 The custom stamp added to the tool menu

Adding Lines and Arrows to Your Comments

In some cases, it is helpful to be able to point at or link various comments and document elements. For instance, you may want to add arrows to link a comment text box with a specific location in a PDF document. To add arrow comments to a PDF, follow these steps:

1. From the Advanced Commenting toolbar, choose the Arrow tool or Line tool.

Note: You can float the Drawing tools in their own toolbar by choosing Show Drawing Tools from the Drawing Tools menu.

2. Click and drag arrows or lines *from* the object to which you would like to point *to* the comment text box.

3. Select the Hand tool ✋ or press H, and click the arrow or line. A Line comment field will appear, allowing you add a text comment to your arrow.

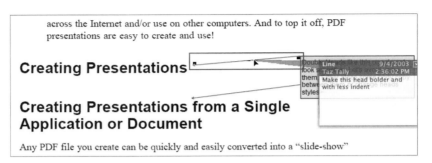

4. Type in your comment, and hit the Enter key to complete the line/arrow commenting process.

Adding Shapes to Your Comments

In some cases you may want to make a comment about a general area of a document, such as suggesting the addition of a graphic in a general area rather than a specific location. Acrobat offers a variety of tools to allow you to do this, including several shape tools and a Pencil tool (both in the Advanced Commenting tool set). Here we will use the Cloud tool (new in Acrobat 6) to demonstrate their use. To designate an area follow this process:

1. Select the Cloud tool ☁ from the Drawing tools.

2. Using a series of clicks and drags, draw around the area you would like to include.

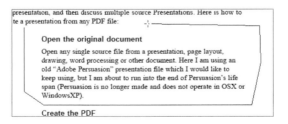

3. Double-click when you get to the end of the area selection to complete the selection. A cloud shape will appear around the selected area.

4. Select the Hand tool  or press H, and click any part of the edge of the shape. A Polygon comment field will appear, allowing you add a text comment to your shape.

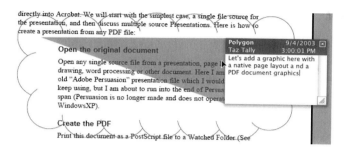

> **Note:** The Polygon tools and Pencil tool work in much the same fashion as the Cloud tool. The Pencil tool even allows you to erase sections you don't want. Use the area-selection tool that best suits your needs.

Adding Sound Comments

Sound based comments can also be added to a PDF. The Sound Comment tool allows you to either record your own message on-the-fly or attach a sound file. Select this tool and click the spot where you would like to place the comment icon; the Record Sound dialog appears.

> **Note:** To use a previously recorded sound file, click Choose to locate the file. Unlike the Add Media button (covered later in this chapter), a sound file added to a PDF with the Sound Comment tool cannot be compressed. If you try to add the FireIceSong.aif file provided on the CD with the Sound Comment tool, you will get the error message: "Only uncompressed WAVs or AIFFs are importable."

To record your voice or other sound on-the-fly, click Record. When you are through recording, click Stop. You can click the Play button to play back your recording.

Once you have finished recording, click OK to complete the creation of the sound comment. A small speaker icon will be added to the PDF document page at the point where you initially clicked with the Sound Comment tool. Once created, a sound comment will be added to the Comments tab just like any other comment but with a small speaker icon.

This sound can then be played back by double-clicking its icon on the PDF document page with the Hand tool.

Moving, Deleting, Resizing, or Editing Comments

To select a comment for either moving or deleting, simply click *once* on the comment symbol with the Item tool (press R). This will select the comment and, if appropriate to the comment, open a note window. Then do one of the following:

- To move the comment, click and drag it.
- To delete the comment, simply hit the Delete key.
- To resize a stamp comment, click and drag the control points along the edges of the graphic.

- To edit the text of the comment, click in the note window.

Hand Tool vs. Item Tool

If you select a comment, such as a graphic comment with a text field, and the text field is visible but not editable, you probably have the Item tool rather than the Text tool selected. If you want to edit the copy in a comment text field, make sure you have the Hand tool selected. Remember that you can switch back and forth between the Hand tool and the Item tool by typing **H** and **R**.

Setting Commenting Preferences

Once you have worked with the Commenting tools for a while, you will get a feel for how they work and how you would like them to behave. Then you might want to set your Commenting tool Preferences and Properties to fine-tune them to work the way you want them to. (Some of these Preference settings won't make any sense until you have used the Commenting tools a bit, which is why I'm bringing them up at the end of the Commenting section rather than the beginning.)

When you set the Commenting Preferences, you are making adjustments that affect all comments. To use the global Commenting Preferences, choose File/Acrobat > Preferences, and select Commenting from the list on the left side of the window (Figure 9.14). There are quite a few Preferences, many of which are self evident, but I will review a few key ones here:

Font Set a font size that is appropriate for your audience. If you know that there are folks over the age of 16 who will be looking at these comments on screen, don't select Small.

Pop-up Opacity Set a value that suits you, but anything below 50 percent is typically hard to read.

Automatically Open Pop-ups On Mouse Rollover Turn this option on if you want to see text comments pop up as you move your mouse around. This can be a benefit if you are doing a quick overview, but it can also drive you crazy if you are in the process of adding rather than reviewing comments. So it is one that I turn on and off to suit my current work mode.

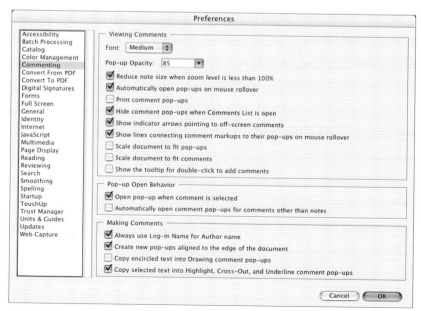

Figure 9.14 The Commenting Preferences

Popup Open Behavior check boxes As with the preceding "Automatically open..." option, I often like to have these turned on when I am reviewing and turned off when I am creating comments.

Copy Selected Text Into Highlight, Cross-Out, And Underline Comment Pop-ups I like to turn this one on, so that any text that I select with a Highlighting tool will automatically be included in the text edit field if I choose to use one. This saves me typing time, and I can quickly delete any copy I don't want.

Setting Comment Tool Properties

In addition to setting overall or global Commenting Preferences, you can adjust each tool separately and even each comment separately.

To access the properties of a specific tool, do *one* of the following:

- Choose Advanced Commenting > Properties Bar.
- Right-click/Control+click the tool in the toolbar and choose Properties Bar.
- Press ⌘/Ctrl+E.

The tool's Properties bar appears on screen. This bar is context-sensitive: Its contents change depending upon which tool is selected. The name of the tool is listed at the top of the Properties bar. Select the property you would like to adjust and click that portion of the Properties toolbar.

Setting Properties for Individual Comments

To access the properties of an individual comment, right-click/Control+click the comment and choose Properties from the context menu (Figure 9.15). A Properties dialog will appear, allowing you to set up that specific comment to suit your needs.

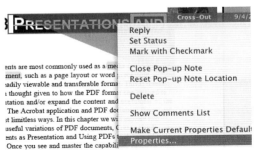
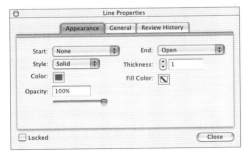

Figure 9.15 Accessing the properties for a Commenting tool

Here again the properties you see will depend upon the type of comment you have selected. A Line Properties dialog has many more settings than a Cross-Out Properties dialog, for example.

> **Note:** I use these individual comment properties quite frequently when I am working with lines and polygons to control colors, line weights, and transparency.

Viewing and Navigating Comments

Once you have created comments you can use them in a wide variety of ways. Comments can be viewed, organized, summarized, and shared.

Comments can, of course, be viewed by simply looking for them as you navigate through the document panel, but you might find using the Comments tab handy and faster. Here's how:

1. Open the PDF document that contains comments you would like to view. I'm using the Chapter 8 document (Chapter8SampleCommented.pdf) to which we added comments in the earlier sections of this chapter.

2. Click the Comments tab, located to the left of the Document pane. A pane will appear below the Document pane listing the pages that contain comments.

3. If you remain in this view, you can drag the bar between the panes to resize the Comments and Document panes.

4. I usually find this default arrangement, with the document on top and comments on the bottom, to be a bit awkward, so I like to separate the two. To do so, drag the Comments tab until it separates from the Document pane, as in Figure 9.16. Here are some ways to navigate the Comments tab:

- To view the comments on a particular page, click the + sign located to the left of the page number (here, the Page 1 comments are expanded and the Page 2 comments are collapsed). A list of the comments on that page will appear, and the + sign becomes a – sign.

Figure 9.16 Floating the Comments pane

- To activate a comment, click its text in the Comments tab. Both the comment in the Comments tab and the comment in the Document pane will be located and highlighted. In the figure, the For Comment stamp at the top of the page is activated.

- To view the details of a comment, click the + sign to the left of the comment.

- To move from one comment to the next in order, press the Up and Down arrow keys on your keyboard.

Comments as Bookmarks

Comments serve not only as tools for commenting but as simple bookmarks as well. Whenever you click a comment in the Comments tab, Acrobat will automatically take you to the page where that comment exists and will display and select that comment in the Document pane.

Comments, however, do not provide the zoom-view capabilities that the regular bookmarks do. But bookmarks and comments can be used in concert to draw attention to an item of interest. If you think that a zoom view is important, feel free to create and place a zoomed-in bookmark in addition to your comment in the Document pane. In this way a reader could navigate to the zoomed in view using the Bookmarks tab, and then read the comment from there.

Managing Comments

As you review comments made by someone else, you may want to sort or filter the comments, track the status of those you have viewed, mark up a comment, make your own remarks to a specific comment, or summarize all the comments.

Sorting comments The default sorting mechanism is by page. To sort the comments in a document by another order, click the Sort icon in the comments panel and choose another sort mechanism. When several people are working on a document, I often like to sort by Author so that I can easily review all of the comments by a particular person together.

Filtering comments With collaborative projects with multiple authors and reviewers, the sheer volume of the comments can get a bit overwhelming and tedious to slog through. Filtering allows you to limit the display of the comments you see on screen at any one time. Click the Filter icon and select your preferred filtering mechanism(s) (many of the filtering selections offer subsets of choices). I often like to sort by Reviewer so that I can see just one set of comments at a time.

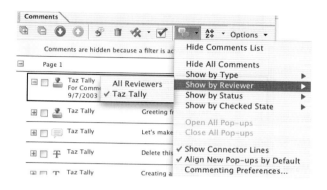

Note: Acrobat tracks the date and time when many of the following comment events occur.

Marking comments as reviewed Particularly when you have many comments from multiple authors, and you know it will require more than one session to review them all, it's handy to be able to place a simple check mark on the comments you have seen. Select the comment to be checked, then click the check box icon in the Comments pane toolbar or check the box next to the comment itself.

Setting the status of comments Keeping track of how a comment has been received and treated is much easier in Acrobat 6. Simply click the status icon and choose a status, which will be noted under that comment in the list.

Note: Once you begin assigning status to comments, you can also sort and filter by status.

Remarking on others' comments In addition to managing your own comments (covered in detail earlier in this chapter), you can make return remarks on someone else's comments. Simply select the comment from the list, click the remark icon 📝, and then type your remark in the field that appears under the comment. The remark will appear next to the name of the author making the remark. Here I have remarked on my own comment and decided to agree with myself!

Spell-checking comments Prior to sharing or exporting comments, you may want to spell-check them. To do this, choose Edit > Check Spelling > In Comments And Form Fields. The Check Spelling window will appear; click the Start button.

Sharing Comments

Comments can not only be created and manipulated in various ways, as we have seen in the preceding sections, but they can be shared as well. The four most common methods of sharing comments are as follows:

- Share the entire commented PDF document
- Summarize comments and send those around
- Import and export comments
- E-mail and web collaboration

You can simply send around the entire commented PDF document as an e-mail attachment or place it on a web page or FTP site for others to download. Although this is perhaps the easiest way to share comments, it is not always the best way. Complete PDF documents are typically much larger than either the comment summaries or exported comment data—plus the whole document will not have the benefit of the organization or brevity provided by the summary.

Note: As I've said elsewhere in the book, PDF documents are by their very nature Internet-safe—that is, made to be sent around the Internet. However, sometimes even PDF files get corrupted in transit. If this happens, consider compressing them in ZIP or SIT archives (and ensure that your recipients have the "unzip" or "unstuff" application that will open your archives).

Summarizing Comments

It is often handy to be able to create a summary of all of the comments in a document for a simplified review, form printing, or sharing comments with someone else. A summary will nearly always be smaller than the entire PDF document but contain all the comment data and information.

To build a summary, click the Options menu in the Comments tab and choose Summarize Comments. A Summarize Options dialog appears (Figure 9.17).

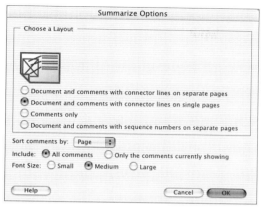

Summarize Options

Choose a Layout

- ○ Document and comments with connector lines on separate pages
- ● Document and comments with connector lines on single pages
- ○ Comments only
- ○ Document and comments with sequence numbers on separate pages

Sort comments by: [Page ▼]

Include: ● All comments   ○ Only the comments currently showing

Font Size: ○ Small   ● Medium   ○ Large

[Help]   [Cancel]   [OK]

Figure 9.17 Options for a comment summary

Choose A Layout Select what you would like included in your comment summary. Acrobat 6 allows you to create a text summary of just the comments, or you can include a view of the PDF document pages as well as the comments. If you choose to include a view of the document pages, you can also include lines linking the comment text to the comment locations in the document pages. You can separate your comment summary and document view on different pages or keep them on the same page.

Sort Comments By Select how you would like to have comments sorted in your summary: by Author, Date, Page, or Type.

Include Select which comments you would like to have included in the summary.

Font Size Select the size of the font you would like to be used in the text summary.

Click OK to initiate the creation of the comment summary. A new PDF document containing your comment summary will be created. Figure 9.18 shows an example summary configured with the text summary and the linked document view on the same page.

Single-Page vs. Separate-Page Summaries

If you intend to print your summary and want to include the document page, I suggest that you consider creating "single pages" summaries so that the comments and document view will print together. If, on the other hand, you intend to review these summaries on screen, then I suggest that the "separate pages" will serve you better, because Acrobat will display the related document view and text summaries on facing pages. The text will be larger in the separate pages and therefore much easier to read on screen, and the separate pages will always be tighter in the document.

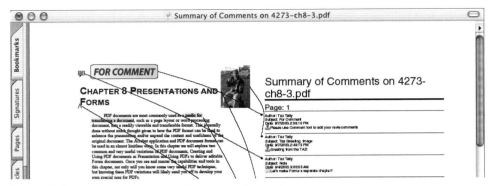

Figure 9.18 A comment summary, set up to show connector lines on single pages

Exporting Comment Data

The "lightest"(smallest file-size) way to share comment data is by exporting your PDF document comments to someone else who will then import them into their copy of the PDF document. Exported comment data uses a very small file that can be quickly and easily shared with another person. Here is how it works:

1. Initially send a copy of the PDF document to be reviewed to all those who will be participating in the collaboration.

2. From the list of comments in the comments panel, select the comments you would like to share.

3. At the top of the comments panel, select Options > Export Select Comments. An Export Comments dialog appears (it looks much like a standard Save dialog).

4. Browse to where you want to save your exported comments, and click Save. Your comments will be exported as an .fdf file, which is the forms data format in which any forms or comment data are exported from Acrobat.

4273-ch8-3.fdf

5. Send this .fdf file to the other folks in your group whom you want to see this comment data, and tell them to follow the instructions under "Importing Comment Data" (next).

Importing Comment Data

Once comment data has been exported from a PDF document (see the preceding section), that data can easily be added into a PDF document for review and manipulation.

1. Open your copy of the collaborative PDF document.

2. At the top of the comments panel, select Options > Import Comments. An Import Comments dialog appears.

3. Browse to the exported .fdf file that was sent to you.

4. Click Open; the comments from the .fdf file will be added to your copy of the PDF.

You will now be able to view and manipulate the comments just as you would any other PDF comments.

Adding Multicolumn and Multidocument Navigation

In addition to using bookmarks and comments to navigate through a PDF document, Acrobat has another level of sophistication that allows you or your document viewer to navigate interactively through a multicolumn PDF or several PDFs. Tools such as articles, links, and destinations allow you to lead a viewer through a very specific course of linked information, which may or may not be sequential in the document and may not even be limited to one document. You can easily lead a viewer through multiple columns of text and to jump page locations for copy that continues on another page. Or, you can skip around a PDF document or documents to show a viewer a series of related topic elements that have no relationship to the original document organization.

Using Multicolumn Navigation Links—Articles

When you want to lead a viewer through multiple columns and/or jump pages in the same document, you can use the Article tool to define a series of sequential locations and views, known as an article. To create an article, follow these steps:

1. Open a multicolumn multipage document. For this section, I'm using an old copy of *Design Tools Monthly*, which is a four-column multipage document. You can follow along by opening DTM06_03.pdf from the Chapter 9 folder of the companion CD. We will link the "News & Rumors" columns across two columns and two pages.

> **Note:** The CD also includes a "final" version of that file, named DTM06_03Commented.pdf, so you can examine the resulting articles.

2. Click the Article tool in the Advanced Editing toolbar. Your cursor will become a small cross hair [⇩], which you will click and drag to define sections of your article.

> **Note:** If the Advanced Editing toolbar is not visible, select Tools > Advanced Editing > Show Advanced Editing Toolbar.

3. Create the article with these steps:

   a. Click and drag over the first part of the "News & Rumors" section titled "Photoshop 8 Won't Run on Mac OS 9." A rectangle labeled "1-1" (indicating the first part of the first article) will appear when you release the mouse. There will be a small + sign in the lower right-hand corner, indicating that this article can be continued.

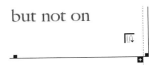

   b. Click and drag over the "QuarkXPress 6" section to create the second portion of the article, which will be labeled "1-2" (indicating the second part of the first article).

   c. Click and drag over the "Spam" section to create the third portion of the article, which will be labeled "1-3."

   d. Navigate to page 2 (the jump-page finish to the "News & Rumors" section) to create the jump-page portion of the article.

   e. Click and drag over the extension of the "Spam" section to create the fourth portion of the article, which will be labeled "1-4."

   f. Click and drag over the "X-Ray" section to create the fifth and final portion of the article, which will be labeled "1-5."

4. Hit the Enter key to complete the article. An Article Properties window will appear, with Title, Author, Subject, and Keyword fields.

5. Fill in the properties and click OK. Your PDF article is now ready for use.

Note: Any words you place in the Keywords field can be used for searching the PDF file as well as for the creation of an article index. (↩ Chapter 7, "PDF Document Management," for more information on searches and indexes.)

Reading PDF Articles

To see whether a document has any articles, click the Articles tab. The articles panel will appear, showing a list of available articles (Figure 9.19).

- To begin reading an article, simply double-click the article's icon ⬚ in the Articles tab. The document panel will immediately jump to an enlarged view of the beginning of the article.

- To read the next section of an article, move your mouse over the lower end of the article. The cursor will change to a small hand with a down-arrow 👆. Click the mouse button, and the next block of the article will appear.

- To move backward in the article sequence, hold down the Shift key (the cursor becomes a small hand with an up-arrow 👆) and click. The previous article block will appear.

- To skip all the way to the beginning of the article, hold down the Alt/Option key (the cursor becomes a small hand with an arrow pointing upward at a bar 👆) and click. You will be taken to the initial view of the article.

- To view the article rectangles and labels, select the Article tool .

Figure 9.19 (left) The Articles tab; (right) the initial article view, after clicking the article in the tab

Deleting Articles or Article Boxes

An article can be deleted in several ways, but perhaps the easiest method is as follows:

1. Select the Article tool .

2. Click one of the article boxes (if you want to delete just one of the boxes, click that box).

> **Note:** If you delete one article box in the sequence, the article will automatically reflow and renumber the remaining boxes.

3. Click the Delete key on your keyboard. A Delete dialog appears.

4. Click the appropriate button, depending whether you want to delete just the box or the entire article.

Resizing and Reflowing Articles

You can change the size, shape, and order of the boxes in articles. For all of these actions, first select the Article tool :

- To change the size or shape of an article box, click the box, and then drag one of the control handles found around the edge of the article box to resize the box.

- To create a new box to extend an article in another location, click the small + sign at the bottom-right corner, and then click in a new area and drag out the new box.
- To combine two articles, click the small + sign at the bottom-right corner of a box, and then click the box of an already created article into which you would like the article to flow.

 Note: If you add or combine article boxes, the boxes in the resultant article will automatically reflow and renumber.

Adding Links to Other Locations or Actions

Another way to navigate through and between PDF documents and other locations such as web pages is via links. There are two related ways to create links between locations (either within a document or between documents):

- The first and simplest way is to simply create links with the Link tool. This solution works fine when you are creating links between pages in a document.
- The second method, which also uses the Link tool, is to use destinations. You can think of destinations as secure links between documents. Links with destinations remain secure even if the linked document is changed substantially through the addition or subtraction of pages, while simple links between pages may be lost. In addition to being more secure, destination links can be tracked and managed.

Creating Simple Links from PDF Document Pages

One common use is to create a link to another resource, such as another PDF document, from a specific location on a PDF page:

1. Open a PDF from which you would like to create a link.
2. Navigate to the page and location where you would like to place the link.

 Note: You will typically find it a bit easier if you zoom in a bit on the location where you would like to create a link.

3. Select the Link tool .
4. Click and drag the Link tool across the area where you would like to place the link.

Note: Make the link area large enough so that it will be easy to locate if you make the link invisible.

5. The Create Link dialog appears (Figure 9.20). Click the radio button for the type of link you would like to create, setting any additional options that become active (such as a page number and zoom characteristic to control the view of an Open A Page In This Document link or the URL of an Open A Web Page link). You usually shouldn't choose Custom Link; I'll explain why not in just a moment.

Figure 9.20 Creating a link

Note: If you create a web link, the parent PDF should always have access to the Internet. Also, a fast connection is preferable so that the response to clicking the link is rapid.

6. If you chose Open A File, skip to Step 7. For other choices, click OK.

7. To establish a link to another document, click the Browse button and navigate to the target document to which you would like to link. (I'll be linking to a PDF map of Hawaii, which is included in the Chapter 9 folder on the CD as Hawaii.pdf.) Click the Select button to create the link to that file. The Specify Open Preference window appears (Figure 9.21).

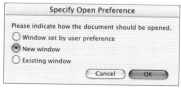

Figure 9.21 Specifying the preference for opening a link

8. Set your preference for how you would like this linked document to open when the link action is activated, and click OK. The Link Properties dialog will appear (Figure 9.22).

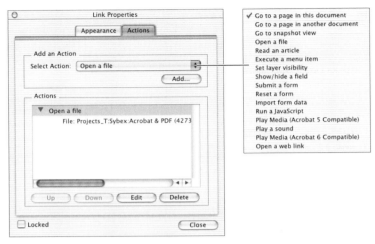

Figure 9.22 Setting a link's action

9. Click the Actions tab, and examine the Select Action drop-down menu to make sure that Open A File is selected.

Note: If you click the Select Action menu, you will see the wide variety of action choices available. This is the menu that will appear if you select Custom Link in the Create Link dialog back in Step 5. So, you can access this list of action choices without having to select Custom Link, and you can change the nature of the link at this point without having to return to the start of this process.

10. Click the Appearance tab (Figure 9.23), and configure the options there for the look and style of your link. For Link Type, choose whether you want the link to be visible or invisible; I often make my links invisible for presentations. For Line Style, I like to use bright colors if I want to draw attention to the location of this link.

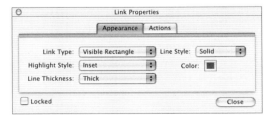

Figure 9.23 Setting a link's appearance

11. Click the Close button to complete the link-creation process.

Your new link will be visible (if you made it so) at the location where you created it.

To try out your new link, click the Hand tool or press H. Move your cursor over the link location. The cursor will turn into a pointing finger, indicating that an active link is under the cursor. Click the link. The action should be executed, and the linked file (in this case, the map of Hawaii) should appear on screen in its own document window.

> **Note:** You can edit a link at any time by selecting the Link tool and double-clicking the link location.

Creating Linked Destinations between Documents

Destinations are stable links between documents that can be managed. Creating a destination is similar to creating a link, but the first few steps are bit different. In fact, you start by opening the target document to which you would like to link rather than the source document. Here is how to create a stable linked destination.

The first part of creating a destination link is to establish a target file that Acrobat can recognize:

1. Open a target document to which you would like to create a stable linked destination (here I will open the Hawaii map as the target document).

2. Click the Destinations tab to activate it, and drag it out to form its own window if you prefer.

> **Note:** Like all the other tabs, the Destinations tab can be dragged out of its document to form its own window (generally my preference).

3. From the Destinations tab's Options menu, select Scan Document.

> **Note:** Whenever you create a new destination, you must scan the document first, even if you know there are currently no destinations assigned to it. Remember that Acrobat tracks and cares for all of its destinations, and this is the way you update Acrobat as to what is currently linked to what.

4. Either click the new destination icon or select Options > New Destination.

5. A new destination will appear in the Destinations list. Type a name for this destination (here, Hawaii Map) and press the Enter or Return key.

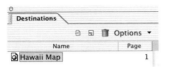

You have now tagged the Hawaii map so that Acrobat can recognize it as a destination location.

The second part of creating a destination link is to work through the source document from which the link will be established to the target file designated in the previous process. From here, the procedure is very similar to creating a simple link, with a few variations specific to recognizing a destination link:

1. Open a PDF from which you would like to create a destination link.

2. Navigate to the page and location where you would like to place the link.

3. Select the Link tool.

4. Click and drag the tool across the area where you would like to place the link. The Create Link window appears.

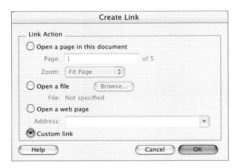

5. Click the Custom Link radio button and click OK. The Link Properties dialog opens.

6. In the Actions tab, from the Select Action drop-down list, choose an action, and then click Add. For this example, let's use Go To A Page In Another Document.

Note: Here we are going to another document; if you were creating a link in the same document, you would select Go To A Page In This Document.

7. In the next dialog, configure the options, which are specific to the action type you chose. The options for the Go To A Page In Another Document dialog (shown in Figure 9.24) are described in the following steps.

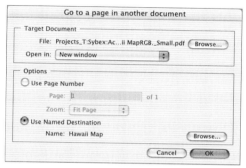

Figure 9.24 Choosing a page in another document to link to

8. Click the Browse button at the top and locate the target document (here Hawaii Map). Click OK to return to the action's dialog.

9. Select your Open In preference.

10. Click the Use Named Destination radio button. (You could specify a page number at this point instead of a named destination.)

11. Click the Browse button at the bottom, and select the destination of your choice. Click OK to return to the action's dialog.

Note: Step 11 specifies a specific named destination within the target file. A target file may have more than one destination, if they have been previously created.

12. Click OK in the action dialog (here the Go To A Page In Another Document window). The Link Properties dialog reappears, with the destination page action included in the Actions list (as shown back in Figure 9.22).

13. Click the Close button to complete the process.

Once established, destination links can be used just like any other link to activate linked resources. Destination links can also be sorted by name or by page using the destination panel's Options menu.

Adding Sounds and Movies to Your PDFs

In addition to text and graphics, PDF documents support the addition of other media as well, including sound and movies. If you have been through the previous exercises of adding links to your PDFs, you already have acquired the skills to add sound and movies.

You can add either sound or movies to your PDF document. They are added and configured pretty much the same way, and I'll work with a sound file to show you how it's done.

 Note: I've included a sound file (FireIceSong.aif) and a movie file (Intro 1 Avoiding The Blues 2.mov) on the companion CD for you to experiment with.

Adding Media Buttons

Adding sound is just like creating a link but with the Sound tool. Here's how:

1. Select the Sound tool 🔊 from the Advanced Editing toolbar.

2. Click and drag across the area where you would like to have the button for activating the sound file.

3. In the Add Sound dialog (Figure 9.25), click the first Choose button to locate the sound file you would like to link to your PDF.

4. Configure the rest of the Add Sound dialog as follows:

    Select New Content's Compatibility Select whether you want your sound files to be compatible with Acrobat 6 only or compatible with Acrobat 5 and earlier versions.

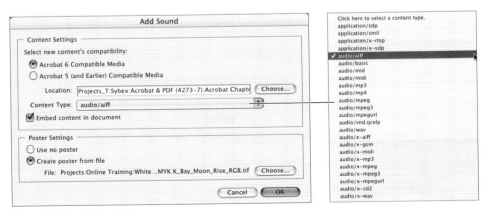

Figure 9.25 The Add Sound dialog

Content Type Open this menu to see the wide range of sound file types supported by Acrobat.

Embed Content In Document Check this box if you would like to have the sound file embedded in the PDF document.

Poster Settings If you would like to have a poster graphic to represent the sound file, you can activate it here; you must select a file to provide that graphic by clicking the Choose button in this area.

5. When you have completed the Add Sound dialog, click OK.

The sound button, with the poster graphic you chose (if you did), will appear on the PDF document at the size and location where you performed your initial click and drag with the Sound tool.

To play the sound, simply click the Hand tool or press H, move the tool over the sound button, and click.

Configuring Media Buttons

After you have created the initial button, you can further configure your media. To do so, select the Item tool (press R) and double-click the media button. The Multimedia Properties dialog (Figure 9.26) will appear.

- On the Settings tab, you can edit the Annotation Title or provide an Alternate Text title, open the List Renditions For Event drop-down menu to edit the action that will activate the sound, and select and add renditions of sounds that you can use.

To Embed or Not to Embed

Embedding your linked sound and movie files is a good idea if your PDF file is not locationally static—that is, staying in one place. If the PDF will be moved around or copied and moved, the links will likely be broken and therefore not work. But be aware that embedding media, and particularly movie files, will dramatically increase the size of your PDF document. Media files are often many times larger than the PDF file itself. It is certainly a good idea to compress and sample your sound and movie files as much as quality degradation will allow, in order to reduce the size of the linked media files.

- On the Appearance tab, you can configure the look of the button.
- On the Actions tab, you can choose a trigger that will start the sound playing and choose the action/sound that is played by the trigger. You can also highlight actions in the Actions list to reorder or delete them.

With the tools and skills you have learned in this chapter, you will now be able to create a whiz-bang interactive multimedia PDF document that will surely impress! In the next chapter, we will cover Acrobat's online capabilities.

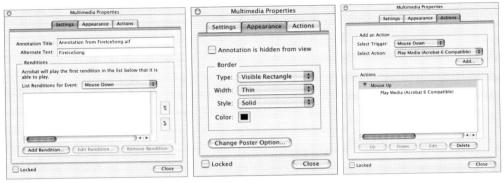

Figure 9.26 Settings for a sound or movie

Acrobat E-mail, eBook, and Web Features

10

In addition to working with standard PDF files on individual computers, Acrobat offers some very useful e-mail, web, and eBook capabilities. PDF documents can be created and immediately sent across the Web and can even be created over the Web. Collaborative publishing can occur in real or delayed time, across intranets and the Internet; standard PDFs can be reformatted into eBook documents and used on a variety of devices.

Chapter Contents
E-mailing PDF documents
Collaborating via E-mail
Web-oriented PDF capabilities
Using eBooks

We are really just starting to think about and use documents in a variety of non-traditional ways, making it easier and more flexible for us to work and communicate. And the flexible cross-platform and page-based nature of Acrobat technology and PDF documents makes them excellent vehicles for exploring and expanding ways in which we can use documents.

E-mailing PDF Documents

PDF documents are designed to be sent over the Internet. PDFs are what we call "Internet-safe"—that is, they are designed to be sent across the Internet without being all bundled up. There are several ways to accomplish this.

Most Microsoft applications (at least the more recent versions) support the one-step creating and sending of a PDF file as an e-mail attachment. See the section "Creating One-Button PDFs with PDFMaker" in Chapter 4, "Creating the PDF You Want," for easy instructions.

You can, of course, just attach a PDF file to any e-mail message as an attachment, from within your e-mail application. Creating a standard e-mail attachment allows you to wrap your PDF in a protective archive if needed (☞ the sidebar on corrupted PDFs).

However, if you are already working in Acrobat and would like to e-mail the current PDF file, you can simply use Acrobat's built-in e-mail capability:

1. Complete and save any additions and/or changes you may have made to your Acrobat document.

Corrupted PDFs

Although PDF files are by their very nature Internet-safe, sometimes even PDF documents can be damaged or corrupted when they are sent across the Internet. This most commonly occurs when they pass through some abusive corporate heavy-duty security firewalls. If this happens, prior to attaching the PDF you can encase or archive your PDF in a protective sheath using one of the common lossless compression/protection applications such as WinZip (more common on Windows) or StuffIt (more common on Mac). This lossless compression will not harm your PDF file. If you zip your PDF, it will take on a new extension, .zip, while stuffed archives will become .sit files. Be sure the person who is receiving your file has the unzip and/or unstuff applications (and versions) needed to open the compressed archive.

2. In Acrobat, either choose File > Email or click the Email button from the Tool palette. This will automatically launch your default e-mail application, open up a new e-mail document, and attach your PDF file to the e-mail.

3. Address the e-mail, type in a message, and send it.

The name of the PDF document is automatically inserted as the subject of the e-mail, further streamlining the process, but you can change that if you like.

Collaborating via E-mail

In Chapter 9, "Collaborative Publishing and Interactivity," you learned how to use the collaborative publishing tools, such as commenting, that PDF has to offer. As we discussed, you can send Acrobat comments either as part of an entire PDF document or as much smaller .fdf files. These collaborations can also occur directly via e-mail.

Note: Using Acrobat's collaboration tools requires either the Standard or Professional version of Acrobat.

Sending Comments for Review

Once you have added comments to a PDF, you can initiate an e-mail-based review session by using Acrobat's built-in e-mail-savvy review tools. Here's how:

1. Open and add your comments to a PDF document. You can follow along here with the PDF document we used in the preceding chapter, Chapter8Commented.pdf. (Look for it in the Chapter 9 folder of the companion CD.)

MAPI-Savvy E-mail Applications

Acrobat's e-mail capabilities work only with e-mail applications that are compatible with MAPI (Messaging Application Program Interface). Not all e-mail applications are MAPI-savvy; many versions of AOL are not. Many more recent e-mail applications, such as Microsoft's Entourage and Apple's .Mac, are MAPI-savvy. If you want to use these auto-e-mail features in Acrobat but your default e-mail application is not compatible with MAPI, then you will need to assign a different default e-mail application. In Mac OS X, you can do this through the Internet section of the System Preferences; in Windows use the Internet Options in the Windows Control Panel.

2. Choose the Send By Email For Review command (either from the File menu or from the Review & Comment button on the toolbar).

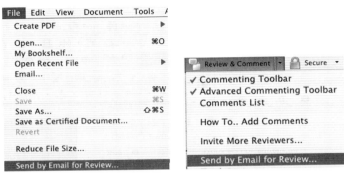

Your default e-mail application will be launched (☞ the sidebar on MAPI-savvy e-mail applications). Your collaboration-oriented e-mail will be preconfigured for you in several ways (Figure 10.1).

- The Subject line contains a reference to both the PDF file and the fact that it is being sent for commenting. In this case, the Subject line reads, "Please Review the Attached Document: 4273-ch8-3.pdf."

- A special .fdf file containing both the comments to be sent and the commented PDF file is created and automatically attached to the e-mail. (☞ Chapter 9 for more information on Acrobat's data format (.fdf) files.)

- The message portion of the e-mail contains basic instructions on how the receiver/reviewer of the PDF should proceed.

3. Add whatever you want to the message field, and click the Send Now button.

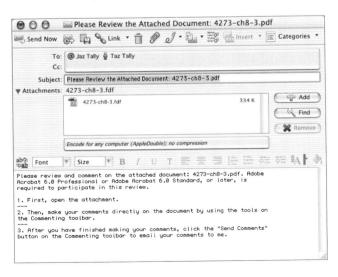

Figure 10.1 A preconfigured review e-mail

Including Other Reviewers

After you have sent a PDF out for review to one person, it is easy to send it out to others. Do this:

1. From the Review & Comment button on the toolbar, choose Invite More Reviewers. Again, your MAPI-savvy e-mail application will launch a preconfigured e-mail with your attached PDF.

2. Add as many e-mail addresses as you like to the To field.

3. Add whatever additional message you want to the message field, and click the Send Now button.

Note: In all cases, it is a good idea to leave the instructions provided by Acrobat in your e-mail.

Receiving Comments for Review and More Comments

You can receive as well as send PDFs for review. The key is to keep your MAPI-savvy e-mail application involved. Here's how it's done:

Note: You can easily identify a "PDF for review" e-mail, because it will have a subject and instructions similar to those seen in Figure 10.1.

1. When you receive a PDF file for review, *open the PDF from within the e-mail application* by double-clicking the PDF attachment. This establishes the link between Acrobat, your PDF, and your e-mail application. The PDF for review will open in Acrobat.

2. Acrobat will ask you if you want to load the included comments; say Yes!

3. Add your own comments. (☞ Chapter 9 for instructions on using the Comment tools.)

4. Choose File > Send Comments To Review Initiator.

Your default e-mail application will be launched (☞ the sidebar on MAPI-savvy e-mail applications). Your collaboration-oriented e-mail will be preconfigured for you in several ways (as shown back in Figure 10.1).

This built-in e-mail review process dramatically simplifies the file sending and receiving process, and it greatly reduces the likelihood that wrong version of PDFs is sent or received. You can go back and forth as many times as you like with as many reviewers as you like using this e-mail review procedure. If you go back and forth a few times with several reviewers, as you might imagine, the commenting process could become a bit confusing and complicated. This is why Acrobat has a built-in comment-tracking tool.

Keeping Track of Comments

Once a collaborative document has been commented on and the comments have been shared and marked up, remarked on, and otherwise managed, it can get a little confusing as to who said what to whom and when, so Acrobat has a tracking feature that allows anyone who has access to a commented PDF to see an organized summary of what has been said by whom and when.

To keep track of the review process, open the PDF document whose history you would like to track, click the Options button at the top of the Comments panel, and choose Open Review Tracker. The Review Tracker panel will become active (Figure 10.2).

You can now display and manage your comments as follows:

1. Click the Show menu to control which reviews you would like to have visible: All, Active, Completed, Sent, or Received.

2. All the visible reviews will appear in the Showing area in the upper panel. Select the review you would like to manage.

3. Information about the selected review is displayed in the lower panel. Use the Open or Remove button at the top to open or delete selected reviews.

4. Continue the review process with the Manage menu, where you can send out for more reviews by selecting Invite More Reviewers or Go Back Online.

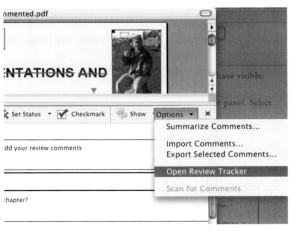

Figure 10.2 Opening the Review Tracker panel

Converting Web Pages into PDF Documents

In addition to working in Acrobat on your own workstation, you can take advantage of PDF-oriented services available over the Web. You can create PDF documents from web pages, search them, and even preflight them.

> **Note:** You need Acrobat, not just Adobe Reader, to participate in most web-oriented services.

It's easy to convert websites and pages into PDF documents. When you do so, all internal and external links can be maintained, and the PDF format is easy to manage and navigate. You can convert internal links into bookmarks, which makes navigating some web pages faster, easier, and more intuitive as PDF documents than they are as a website. The conversion into PDF also makes the printing of the web pages a more dependable and predictable event since the web pages are divided into standard page sizes.

Here's how it's done. Connect your computer to the Internet and launch Acrobat. Then do *one* of the following:

- Choose File > Create PDF > From Web Page.
- Click the Create PDF From Web Page button in the toolbar.

The Create PDF From Web Page window appears (Figure 10.3).

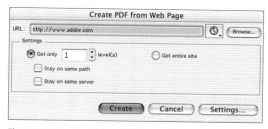

Figure 10.3 Create PDF From Web Page dialog

Configure this window as follows:

URL Type in the address of the website you would like to convert into a PDF document, *or* click the Browse button to find the site you want.

Get Only _ Levels Designate the number of layers you would like to capture. For big sites, 1–3 levels is a safe initial bet. Add more on other tries.

Get Entire Site Be careful of this one. I rarely check this option unless I am very familiar with the site. Some websites have many levels and may take hours to download, especially if you do not have a broadband connection.

Stay On Same Path and Stay On Same Server On big sites—and particularly if I am looking to capture only a specific portion of a site, such as product sales information for printers but not copiers—I often check both of these options. Checking Stay On Same Server will limit the download of pages to the same domain name. Checking Stay On Same Path will further restrict the download to pages that occur on the same address path, such as the path leading to printer sales (http://ABC/products/printers/sales.html) but not the path to copier sales (http://ABC/products/copier/sales.html). Large websites often contain so many internal and external hyperlinks that if you do not restrict the download parameters, you may end up trying to download most of the Internet, which would be pretty slow at dial-up speeds.

Click the Create button to begin the download and conversion process. If it is a large site, be prepared for an extended download.

Fine-Tuning Settings for Web-to-PDF Conversion

The first time you capture a website, you will likely just use the default settings. But you may want to fine-tune the results you get, and here's how you do it:

1. Click the Settings button in the Create PDF From Web Page dialog (shown back in Figure 10.3). The Web Capture Settings window will appear (Figure 10.4).

2. Click the General tab. Here are some tips on setting up this portion of the dialog:

   Create Bookmarks Check this option to automatically create linked bookmarks to each web page that is converted into a PDF document page. This creates a very handy way to navigate a website.

   Place Headers & Footers On New Pages Check this option to place a header with the Web Page title name and a footer with the URL name, page number, and date and time of download.

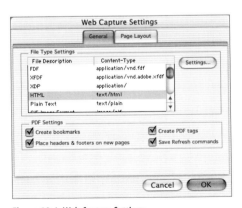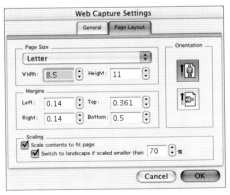

Figure 10.4 Web Capture Settings

Create PDF Tags Check this option to tag all the page elements (paragraphs style sheets, graphics, etc.) for later use. (☞ Chapter 9 for information on how PDF tags can be used to restructure a PDF file.)

Save Refresh Commands If you intend to use and reuse the external hyperlinks preserved from the web page to the PDF, check this box. This will require you to create a list of HTML links, which can then be updated later.

3. Click the Page Layout tab, where you can set the dimensions, margins, and orientation of your PDF document's pages.

Note: The page orientation will *not* automatically change if you swap width and height measurements.

Scaling If the web pages are of different sizes and orientations, you may want to have Acrobat scale the contents to fit your page size and/or have Acrobat flip the orientations if the scaling would exceed a certain value (the default is 70%).

4. Click the General tab again and, under File Type Settings, click HTML or Text.

5. Click the Settings button in the upper-right corner of the General tab (alternatively you can just double-click the HTML or Text setting). This will activate a Conversion Settings window for the appropriate file type (Figure 10.5).

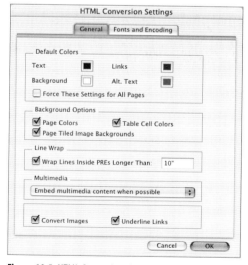

Figure 10.5 HTML Conversions Settings, General options

Web and PDF Pages

You can designate any page size, orientation, and margins for your PDF document pages. The web pages' content will be automatically formatted to fit into the space you create. Often there will not be a one-to-one match between the numbers of web pages and PDF pages, because larger web pages will be converted into multiple PDF document pages. Remember that web pages of varying size and orientation (some Landscape and some Portrait) are not a problem for a PDF document, which can accommodate both in the same document.

6. Select the General tab, and set it up as you wish. For HTML, the options are as follows:

Default Colors Choose your preferred colors (by clicking the color swatches associated with each) for Text, Alt. Text, Links, and Background. If you want your color selections to apply to *all* the specified page elements throughout the web page, then check the Force These Settings For All Pages box. Otherwise, the colors you specify in the swatches will be applied only to page elements to which no colors have been previously applied. I typically want to see and use the supplied colors in a website, so I usually leave this box unchecked.

Background Options Web pages often have background colors or graphic elements, some of which may be tiled. Include these elements by checking these boxes, or exclude them by not checking them.

Line Wrap Some web pages have really long lines of text. If the one you are converting has long lines of copy, you will want to set a limit (the default is 10″) here.

Multimedia You will want to decide how to handle any multimedia links:

- Choose Disable Multimedia Capture if you intend to primarily print or just use the text content.

- Choose Embed Multimedia Content When Possible if you want to use the multimedia content offline.

- Choose Reference Multimedia Content By URL if you want to use it but the PDF will have access to the content online.

Convert Images and Underline Links If you want to include the website images in the converted PDF and underline any active URLs, check the appropriate boxes.

 Note: Embedding the multimedia content can significantly increase download and conversion times as well as the size of the final PDF document. You will need to decide how important those links are to your use of the converted website.

Background Elements

Backgrounds and background colors often enhance the look and feel of a web page when viewed on screen. Retaining these elements can significantly increase download and conversion-to-PDF times if they are included (and particularly if you do not have a broadband connection). If you intend to print your resulting PDF document pages, it may be to your benefit to exclude (uncheck) these background elements, because they can muddy the look of a printed piece.

Note: Including graphics files will increase download time and PDF size but usually not as much as embedding multimedia content.

7. Click the Fonts And Encoding tab (Figure 10.6). Here are some guidelines for configuring this window:

    Input Encoding Select the language set of fonts you want to use.

    Language Specific Font Settings You can adjust the font characters that will be used to apply text in your converted PDF document by clicking the Change button and setting your choices for Body Text, Headings, and Pre-formatted text.

    Font Size You can assign a base or minimal font size here. I adjust this if the website has really small type on it. (This will alter the look and line breaks of the web pages, but it may be an okay price to pay for better readability.)

    Font Embedding If you want your PDF version of the converted website to look as much like the original as possible, check this box.

Fonts and Websites

Most websites are constructed with commonly used fonts, such as Arial, Helvetica, Times, and Times New Roman on sites using European languages. This is done to promote easy and consistent viewing of web pages on many different computers. Display text created with special fonts is often converted into and displayed as graphics to prevent any mismanagement, such as font substitution, when the websites are viewed. Sometimes you may encounter a website with different fonts or variable font use (usually the sign of a technically challenged website designer). These are the times when you might want to either embed the font files or simply create some consistency on your own by designating your own font choices in the Select Fonts window (File > Create PDF From Web Page > Settings > General Tab > Plain Text (File Type Settings list) > Settings > Fonts And Encoding).

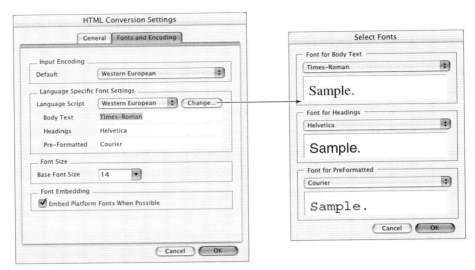

Figure 10.6 HTML Conversion Settings, Font And Encoding options

Controlling Captured Web Elements

Some web conversion controls are located in the Acrobat Preferences settings. These affect how web links in PDFs are opened and viewed and how Acrobat should handle secured web pages and stored graphics. Open the Acrobat Web Capture settings: Acrobat/File > Preferences > Web Capture (Figure 10.7). The following are descriptions of these preferences:

Verify Stored Images If you are interested in having your captured PDF file updated with respect to its graphics content, and you are regularly connected to the Web, then you can specify how often Acrobat will check for updated graphics content here.

Open Web Links You can designate whether web links in your PDF documents will open in Acrobat or in a web browser (if the browser is PDF capable). If you just want to quickly view the pages, the browser is okay. But if you want to have access to Acrobat's substantial navigation, management, and adjustment tools, select In Acrobat.

Show Bookmarks Panel… I suggest checking this option because it will automatically present the panel with all the bookmarked web pages. Many people do not think to look at the Bookmarks panel, and checking this will encourage them to use this very helpful navigation feature.

Conversion Options Some web pages are secure, that is, not downloadable. The Skip Downloading Secured Pages setting controls when Acrobat will skip these pages and move on to capturing and converting pages to which it has access.

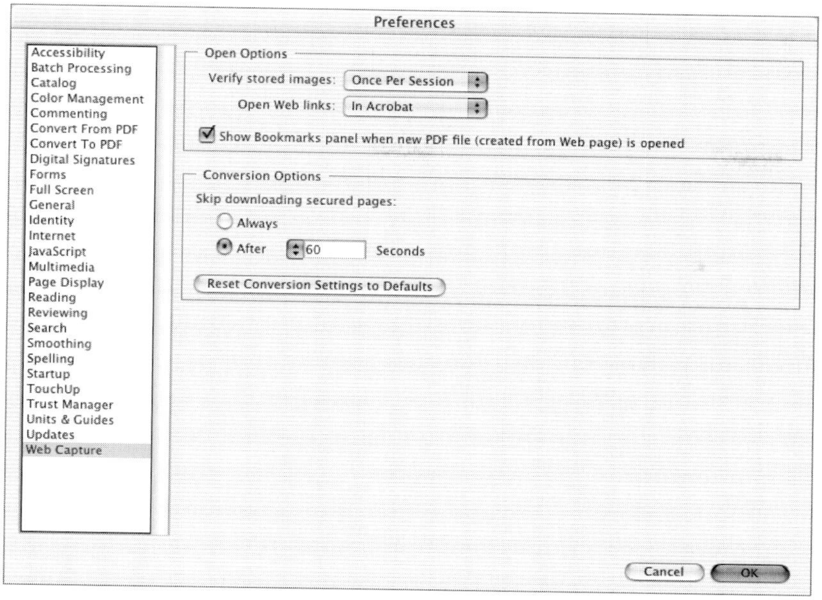

Figure 10.7 Acrobat Web Capture Preferences

Searching PDFs over the Internet

We discussed performing simple searches and creating and searching multiple PDF indexes in Chapter 7, "PDF Document Management." Searches for, and through, PDFs can also occur over the Internet. Here's how:

1. Choose Edit > Search or simply click the Search tool Search .

2. The Search PDF panel will appear Search PDFs on the Internet (usually to the right of the Document panel). Click the Search PDFs On The Internet link located at the bottom of the Search panel. A second Search PDF panel will appear (Figure 10.8; look for the Powered By Google logo).

3. Type in the word or phase for which you would like to search.

4. Click the Search The Internet button Search the Internet .

When you use the Search PDFs On The Internet capabilities, remember that you are searching PDFs located all over the Internet. There are millions of them out there, so it's a good idea to use qualifiers to narrow your search. For instance if you are looking for information on Corvettes in the Omaha area, instead of just looking for "Corvettes," you might search for certain years and locations such as "Chevrolet, Corvette, 1963, Omaha." By specifying "Chevrolet" Corvette, you will eliminate any references to Corvette boats, which are used by the Australian Navy.

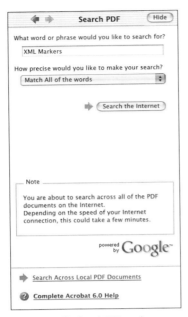

Figure 10.8 The Search PDF panel

The good news is that the Internet Search function used by Acrobat uses Google, which as of this writing is by far the best, meaning it delivers the most useful results of any search engine I have seen.

Using eBooks

eBooks, or electronic books, are documents that are intended to be viewed and used primarily on screen, rather than printed. Unlike web pages, which are typically static in their dimensions and formatting, eBooks can be formatted in a variety of ways and be viewed in a variety of formats depending upon the eBook reader being used.

Adobe Acrobat and Adobe Reader can serve as eBook readers. They can also be used to manage eBooks through reflowing contents, adding comments, and sharing eBooks. One of the first steps to use these functions is to establish an eBook account with Adobe, because this will activate Acrobat's eBook capabilities. Once you have activated your Adobe eBook account (which is free), you will be able to purchase and borrow eBooks, which you can open, read, and manage through Acrobat.

Although the world of eBook publishing is still small compared with that of analog/paper book publishing, as our display system gains in quality and flexibility, eBooks will become increasingly popular and, in some cases, preferable to paper published books.

Activating Acrobat's eBook Capability

Here's how to establish an eBook account, activate Acrobat's eBook feature, and download and open your first eBook:

1. Click the eBook tool and choose Get eBooks Online.

> **Note:** If you do not see the eBook icon in the taskbar, you can activate it by selecting View > Task Buttons > eBook.

> **Note:** If there are any "uncertified" plug-ins installed in Acrobat 6 when launching the eBook Online function, a dialog box appears stating that the function will not work until uncertified plug-ins are disabled (these plug-ins appear under a separate Plug-ins menu item). The dialog box also gives the user the option of restarting Acrobat 6 with all uncertified plug-ins disabled. Be careful because those disabled plug-ins might be important to you.

2. Your default browser will launch. If you have not activated the eBook capabilities, a page will appear suggesting that you establish an eBook account. Agree to do this.

3. You'll be taken to the Adobe website, where you create an Adobe customer ID number and password (or enter these if you already have them).

> **Note:** Record your Adobe ID and password, because you will find them useful in many circumstances when using the Adobe website.

4. Once you have entered or created your Adobe ID and password, an Activation Profile page will appear (Figure 10.9), asking you for your name and e-mail address. Enter this information and then click the Create Profile button.

5. A new page will appear (Figure 10.10) asking you to activate Adobe Reader or Acrobat on this computer or Adobe Reader on a Palm device. Here click the Activate button for Acrobat.

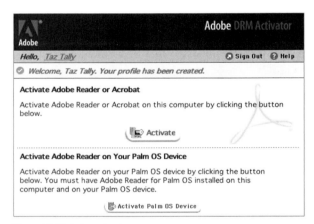

Figure 10.9 The eBook Activation Profile page

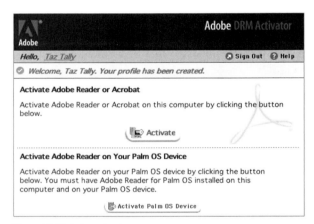

Figure 10.10 Activate Acrobat

6. A Hello page will appear, indicating that the activation process has started (Figure 10.11). During activation, a document activation data file will be downloaded; be patient while this process proceeds.

7. When the download is completed, a pop-up window will appear informing you, "Your Adobe software has been activated." Click the OK button.

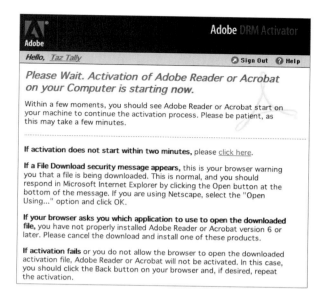

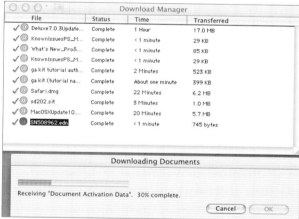

Figure 10.11 Activating Acrobat involves downloading a data file.

8. The next page will inform you that your computer has been activated, *and* it will provide you with the ability to download a migration utility. If you have been using eBooks with a previous version of Acrobat, you must "migrate" them for use with Acrobat 6. This is an easy option to miss (Figure 10.12), so be sure to download this utility (select the Mac and/or Windows version depending upon your needs).

9. A good place to start learning about and exploring eBooks is the Adobe eBook Mall, also known as Adobe Digital Media Store. Click the link that will take you there.

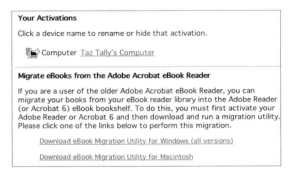

Your Activations

Click a device name to rename or hide that activation.

Computer Taz Tally's Computer

Migrate eBooks from the Adobe Acrobat eBook Reader

If you are a user of the older Adobe Acrobat eBook Reader, you can migrate your books from your eBook reader library into the Adobe Reader (or Acrobat 6) eBook bookshelf. To do this, you must first activate your Adobe Reader or Acrobat 6 and then download and run a migration utility. Please click one of the links below to perform this migration.

Download eBook Migration Utility for Windows (all versions)

Download eBook Migration Utility for Macintosh

Figure 10.12 If you have eBooks from an earlier version of Acrobat, migrate them.

10. The Adobe Digital Media Store page will appear (Figure 10.13). All sorts of information and links to other sites are here. A good place to start might be to download your first eBook from the Adobe eBook site (shown at the lower left on this page), which always has a couple of free eBooks that you can download to get you started.

11. Download your first eBook and view it in Acrobat.

Figure 10.13 The Adobe Digital Media Store

Note: The eBook Central and Digital Media Store websites may appear different than seen here, since these sites have been frequently altered and updated.

Note: To test-drive the My Bookshelf feature, you might want to download free eBooks available online, including many classics, from Aesop's Fables to Ulysses. One site that features over 50 free classics is accessible through the homepage PlanetPDF (www.planetpdf.com/). These eBooks are provided in tagged versions to enable expanded accessibility on handhelds and to use screen-reading software (see Appendix A, "Resources and Shortcuts," on the CD for other Acrobat and PDF resource sites).

Purchasing eBooks

After you've gone through the activation process, clicking the eBook tool in Acrobat and choosing the Get eBooks Online command will take you directly to the Adobe Digital Media Store, which is a good place to see whether the title you want is available as an eBook title and to start looking for eBooks to purchase.

However, eBooks can be purchased online at a variety of sites. Nearly all of the major, and many of the minor, booksellers offer online eBook sales.

Note: Links to all the major sellers of eBooks are on Adobe's site, and you can perform searches for eBook titles there.

PDFs vs. eBook Documents

You will see that eBooks look and feel much like PDF documents. You can view and navigate an eBook using the same tools, techniques, tabs, panels, and windows that you use with a standard PDF document. If you open an eBook in Acrobat, rather than Adobe Reader, you can add, copy, and paste text items (sometimes with time and frequency restrictions) and add comments to them as well. However, you will not have all the editing capabilities that you have with a standard PDF document. (☞ Chapter 9 for a complete overview of using commenting tools.)

Lending eBooks

eBooks can be lent and borrowed just like books from a traditional library. Borrowed eBooks have set borrowing time periods as with books from any other library. The nifty thing about borrowed eBooks is that they will expire automatically after a certain time period, so that they do not have to be returned. Here's how to learn about lending and borrowing eBooks:

Access an online library that provides (lends) eBooks. If this is your first experience with lent/borrowed eBooks, start with the Adobe site by choosing Advanced > eBook Web Services > Adobe eBooks Central (Figure 10.14). Click the Lend From A Library link `· Lend from a library` to learn about setting up a lending library.

Note: You can access the Adobe eBook website directly at http://www.adobe.com/epaper/ebooks/library.html.

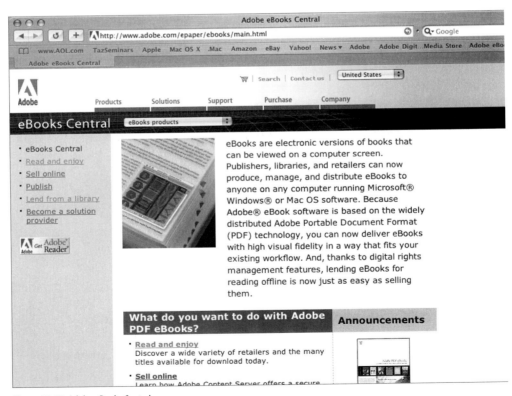

Figure 10.14 Adobe eBooks Central

Keeping Track of Your Borrowed eBooks

You can organize and keep track of your borrowed eBooks by using your eBook Bookshelf. Click the eBook tool and select My Bookshelf; the My Bookshelf window will appear (Figure 10.15). Thumbnails of the covers of any eBooks that you have borrowed or purchased will appear in this My Bookshelf window. Borrowed eBooks will have a small clock icon in the upper-right corner of the thumbnail; click the clock icon to see the document's expiration date.

Figure 10.15 eBooks in the My Bookshelf dialog show an icon to indicate a time limit.

Organizing and Sharing Your eBooks

The My Bookshelf window in Acrobat also provides a full range of eBook management features. Here are some of the key eBook management tools available to you (Figure 10.16):

Adding eBooks to your Bookshelf When you add purchased or borrowed eBooks through Acrobat, they are placed in a default directory, which allows them to be automatically visible and available through the My Bookshelf window.

- You can add eBooks stored in other locations on your system or network by clicking the Add File button at the top left and then navigating to the files.

- You can go directly online from My Bookshelf to access more eBooks by clicking the eBooks Online button.

View as thumbnails   View as list

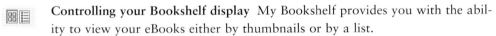

Figure 10.16 Your Acrobat Bookshelf contains all the controls for using and managing eBook files.

Getting information about an eBook Select an eBook by clicking its thumbnail. Look in the information window in the lower-left corner to see information about the eBook, including its title, author, and number of pages.

Controlling your Bookshelf display My Bookshelf provides you with the ability to view your eBooks either by thumbnails or by a list.

Reading your eBooks You can open an eBook for reading by selecting the eBook and clicking the Read button at the top of the My Bookshelf window or simply by double-clicking the eBook thumbnail.

Sharing your eBooks To send a selected eBook to someone else, click the Email button at the top-right, which will launch your default e-mail application and attach the eBook. Be aware, however, that not all eBooks are sharable. If an eBook is not intended to be shared, a message will appear informing you of this.

 Note: If an eBook is not sharable, you can always forward the web address from which you borrowed or purchased it instead.

Copying an eBook Select the thumbnail of an eBook, and then click the Save A Copy button at the top right. Locate the folder where you would like to save a copy of your eBook.

Categorizing your eBooks You can organize your eBooks into categories using the drop-down menus at the bottom right. In My Bookshelf, you can assign your eBook one or two categories. Here I have assigned *The Raven* the categories of Mystery & Thrillers and Literature & Fiction. You can create your own categories by choosing Edit Categories from the All drop-down list at the top of the dialog, where you can also view your eBooks by category.

Backing up your eBooks To make a backup copy of *all* of your eBooks, simply click the Backup button at the bottom right and locate the folder where you would like those backups placed.

Reading eBooks Out Loud

Like any other PDF document, an eBook accessed through Acrobat can take advantage of Acrobat's Read Out Loud capabilities. To activate Acrobat's Read Out Loud capabilities, just open the eBook in Acrobat and choose View > Read Out Loud > Read This Page Only or Read To End Of Document.

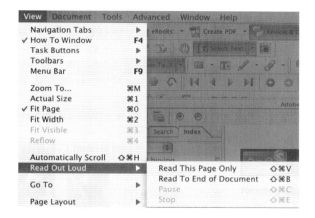

See the last section in Chapter 6, "Using Acrobat and Navigating PDFs," for more details on reading out loud.

Improving the Readability of eBooks

Acrobat provides, through its Preferences, a set of display tools to help you improve the way text and images appear on your screen. To do so, open the eBook in Acrobat and choose Acrobat/File > Preferences > Smoothing. ↩ Chapter 5, "Controlling Acrobat and Access to Your PDFs," for more information on setting up this window.

Reflowing eBooks

Sometimes when a PDF document makes the transition from a standard PDF document to an eBook, its content doesn't flow properly from page to page on your screen, or document or page elements may appear out of order. You can adjust this if the original

PDF is properly tagged. This tagging must have been performed when the original PDF was created and prior to it being made into an eBook.

To reflow an eBook, simply choose View > Reflow. If the content order needs to be changed, you will need to edit the tagged order of page/document elements in the PDF document. ✍ Chapter 12, "Editing PDFs," for instructions on how to accomplish this.

Selling Your Own eBooks

To learn more about eBooks and keep up-to-date on the latest eBook technology trends and offerings from Adobe, including getting information on how you can sell your own eBooks, you might want to bookmark the Adobe eBook Central website. To access this site initially, choose Advanced > eBook Web Services > Adobe eBook Central. Click the Publish link • Publish to learn about selling your own eBooks.

Advanced Acrobat

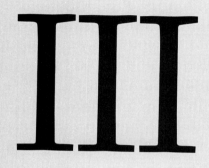

Acrobat 6 offers a wide variety of evaluations, adjustments, and manipulations that can be performed on PDF documents. PDFs can be preflighted to determine their suitability for various uses. Both the structure and content of a PDF can be edited. These capabilities are expanded by specialized and useful third-party applications and plug-ins. And once you learn all you need to know about creating, manipulating, evaluating, and editing PDF documents, you'll want to learn how to streamline those tasks through automation.

Preflighting PDFs

As you have seen throughout this book, PDF documents can be created and modified for a wide variety of uses. This inherent flexibility and specificity can result in a PDF being used for purposes other than the one for which it was originally intended. Preflighting allows you to check how well suited a PDF is for a particular use and in some cases correct some document problems without direct editing.

11

Checking the Accessibility of Your PDFs

Acrobat 6 offers two tools for checking how accessible your PDF documents are for use by visually impaired users and for eBook use. These accessibility-checking tools can check document structure as well as document content. You can perform either a Quick Check or a Full Check.

Quick Accessibility Check and Adjustments

Acrobat 6 allows you to run a Quick Check on the accessibility of your PDF. This check will look for document structure or the presence of tags. If tags are present, then your document will get a clean bill of health for basic accessibility.

Open the PDF document you would like to check for accessibility, and choose Advanced > Accessibility > Quick Check. Acrobat will tell you whether your document is tagged (Figure 11.1).

Figure 11.1 If your document already contains structure tags, you'll see the message on the left; if it doesn't, the one on the right will appear.

If your document does not contain structure tags, which are used by eBook readers to organize and deliver PDF contents, you have these choices:

- You can add tags to your document so that its current structure can be automatically read, by selecting Advanced > Accessibility > Add Tags To Document.

- You can, as the second Quick Check window above suggests, specify a reading order in the Reading Preferences: Acrobat/File > Preferences > Reading.

- Or, you can do both. Try using the automatic ordering with the Add Tags To Document command, and if that does not provide you with the order you want, you can then go to plan B and override the automatic tagged order using the Reading Preferences.

If these options don't provide you with the reading order you want, you will have to manually edit the tag order. ↝ Chapter 12, "Editing PDFs," for more information on editing tag order (that is, "reflowing" your PDF).

Note: It is a good idea to always create tagged PDFs so that anyone who views your PDF will at least have the automatic tagged reader to use in case they want to view your PDF in an eBook reader or other device.

Enhanced Accessibility Check

In addition to a simple document structure check provided by the Quick Check tool, Acrobat 6 provides a more thorough accessibility check. To run this check, open the PDF document you would like to check for accessibility and choose Advanced > Accessibility > Full Check. The Accessibility Full Check dialog appears (Figure 11.2).

Configure this window as follows:

Create Accessibility Report Browse to the location on your hard drive where you would like to have the accessibility option report placed.

Include Repair Hints In Accessibility Report Have the report include suggestions if you would like some tips on improving the accessibility.

Create Comments In Document In addition to a separate accessibility report, you can have Acrobat add comments to the document. (This is very handy!)

Page Range Select the PDF document pages you would like to test for accessibility.

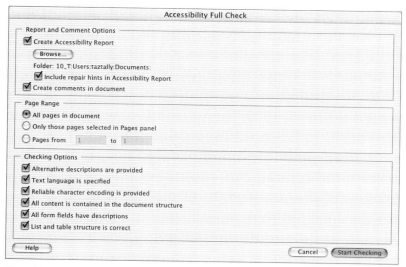

Figure 11.2 Accessibility Full Check options

Note: A Full Check of a long document may take some time. If there are any pages that will not be included in the final PDF, you may want to exclude them from the Full Check process.

Checking Options Select the options for which you would like the Full Check process to examine and report. Unless you are very familiar with the accessibility items and know that you would like to exclude one or more, I suggest that you check all of these boxes.

When you're all set, click the Start Checking button to initiate the Full Check process. An HTML report will be generated (a sample named AmericanClassic.html is included in the Chapter 11 folder on the CD), containing the same included information and placed in the location you chose. You will also see a report on screen listing any accessibility problems found (Figure 11.3).

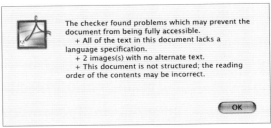

American Classic.html

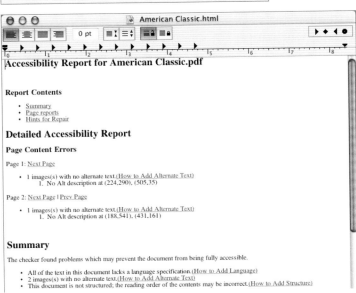

Figure 11.3 Results of an accessibility Full Check

If you selected the Create Comments In Document check box, you can activate the Comments panel to view the location and description of all the accessibility report items (Figure 11.4).

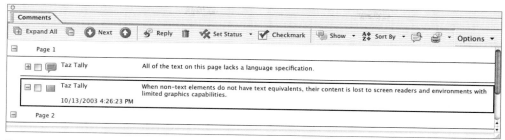

Figure 11.4 You can ask Acrobat to insert comments about the file's accessibility.

Note: The comments will show suggestions—in addition to reporting problems—if you have activated the Include Repair Hints In Accessibility Report option.

If the only thing that is necessary is for structure to be added to this document, then adding tags, as demonstrated earlier in this chapter, will fit the bill. Other corrections such as adding alternative text will require more extensive editing. 𝒢 the sections in Chapter 12 on the reflowing (changing reading order) of PDF contents and on adding alternative text to enhance accessibility.

Preflighting PDFs

Acrobat provides a sophisticated preflighting tool that allows you to check the content and structure of your PDF documents in a very detailed manner. This preflighting tool is most commonly used for checking PDF document contents for commercial printing, and there are separate preflight profiles and controls for PDF/X output. The tool can also be used to test the suitability of a PDF for other uses, through the use of custom preflighting profiles.

Note: The preflighting functions in Acrobat 6 are available only in Acrobat Professional.

Running Preflight on PDFs

Run through the following steps to preflight a PDF:

1. Open the PDF you would like to preflight (here we will use a document called AmericanClassic.pdf, which is provided in the Chapter 11 folder on the companion CD).

2. Choose Document > Preflight. The Preflight: Profiles window appears (Figure 11.5), which contains a list of preconfigured profiles that can be used to check for a wide range of document characteristics. As mentioned above, these profiles have been designed with commercial printing in mind.

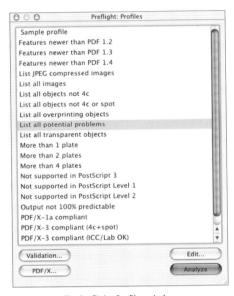

Figure 11.5 The Preflight: Profiles window

3. Select the preflight profile you would like to use to check your document. Here I've selected List All Potential Problems.

 Note: A preflight profile can be extensive and inclusive, such as List All Potential Problems, or specific and restrictive, such as List All Objects Not 4c Or Spot.

4. Click the Analyze button. The Preflight: Results window appears (Figure 11.6) with a list of the results of the preflight analysis.

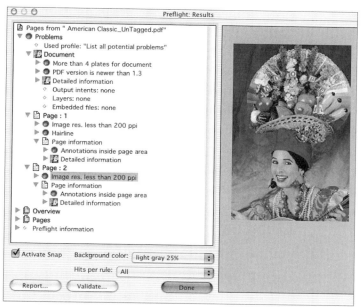

Figure 11.6 The Preflight: Results window

In this case, since we applied the List All Potential Problems profile, the first list item is Problems. Each item in the results list has a display tag; you can click the tag arrow to display the contents of that item.

5. Click the Problems tag arrow. You will notice that there is a Document list item that contains general information about the whole document, such as the PDF version. There are page-by-page lists of items as well.

6. Click the Page 2 tag arrow to view the list of potential problems in page 2.

7. Select the Page 2 list item arrow Image Res. Less Than 200 ppi.

8. Check the context-sensitive Activate Snap box at the bottom of the panel. The image will be displayed in view window to the right.

9. You can change the background of the displayed image by selecting one of the choices from the Background Color drop-down list: white, black, or grays of 25%, 50%, or 75%. Changing the background of an image will provide you with a different perspective on the image, especially around the image edges. This would be helpful if you were printing the image on a light or dark substrate, which you could approximate in this view.

You can see a very detailed description of any document component in your PDF by navigating through the various Preflight list items.

10. Click the Overview tag to view a list of all of the items in the document.

11. Click the Pages tag to view a page-by-page list of all of the items in the document.

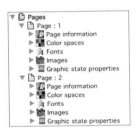

12. You can create a report of the preflight results by clicking the Report button at the bottom of the panel. This will activate the Report window, which allows you to specify the document format and the location of the report you will create (Figure 11.7), as well as the pages to report on.

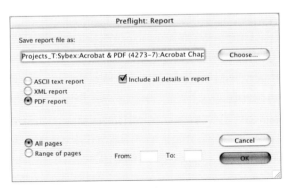

Figure 11.7 The Preflight: Report dialog

The preflight results and report can be used to guide the operator toward any corrections or adjustments that may need to be made to the PDF document. You can make these corrections in the PDF itself using some of the editing tools we cover in Chapter 12, or you might decide that the changes are best made in the original page layout document. This preflight procedure can be run as many times as necessary and should be performed on any corrected version of a PDF.

Validating PDFs

Once a PDF has been preflighted and corrected, the operator in charge of the preflight process can validate the PDF. This may be done to signify that a particular PDF has cleared preflight and is ready for the next step in the production process. Here is how to apply and check validation:

1. Open, preflight, and correct a PDF.

2. In the Preflight: Results window (shown back in Figure 11.6), click the Validate button 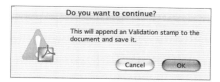 .

3. A dialog will appear informing you that a Validation stamp will be applied to your PDF; click OK.

4. Click Done in the Preflight: Results window.

5. To view the Validation(s), return to the Preflight: Profiles window (back in Figure 11.5) and click the Validation button (Validation...) . The Preflight: Validations window appears (Figure 11.8).

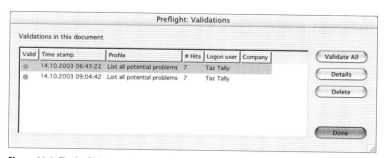

Figure 11.8 The Preflight: Validations window

Any Validations that have been applied to this PDF will be listed, along with a time stamp, the Preflight Profile used, and the Profiler or Logon User. You accept these Validations by selecting them and clicking the Validate All button ⟨ Validate All ⟩. Green bullets will appear next to each of the validated profiles.

To view any validated preflight profile results simply click the Details button ⟨ Details ⟩ in the Preflight: Validations window.

PDF/X-Specific Preflighting and Modifications

Because the PDF/X formatting is increasingly becoming an accepted and used standard for commercial printing, Acrobat 6 has added some PDF/X-specific preflighting tools. There are PDF/X profiles in the regular Preflight: Profiles window, and there is a set of PDF/X-specific tools as well. Here is how they function:

Note: It is a good idea to make a copy of any PDF file prior to applying any of these PDF/X-specific procedures.

1. Open a PDF that you would like to verify meets the PDF/X-1a or PDF/X-3 standard, or open one that you want to modify to meet this standard.

2. Select Document > Preflight. The Preflight: Profiles window appears (Figure 11.9).

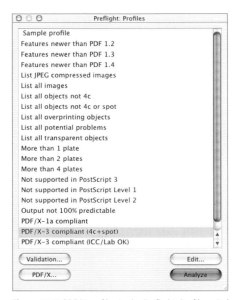

Figure 11.9 PDF/X profiles in the Preflight: Profiles window

3. For PDF/X-oriented preflighting you can proceed in one of two ways. You can select the appropriate PDF/X Preflight profile from the standard list and click the Analyze button, as we did in the preceding section. Or you can instead click the PDF/X button at the bottom of the Preflight: Profiles window. Let's proceed with this method; the Preflight: PDF/X window will appear (Figure 11.10).

```
                    Preflight: PDF/X

  Use PDF/X-3 specification                        [ : ]

  "Save as PDF/X-3..." will preflight your PDF file,
  ask you for an ICC printer profile and then      (  Save as PDF/X-3...  )
  convert your PDF file to PDF/X-3.

  "Verify..." will preflight your PDF file and check
  whether or not it is a valid PDF/X-3 file.        (       Verify...      )

  "Extract ICC profile..." will let you extract an
  ICC output intent profile that has been embedded (  Extract ICC profile...  )
  into a PDF/X-3 file.

  "Remove PDF/X..." removes all PDF/X specific
  information, for both PDF/X-3 and PDF/X-1a files. (   Remove PDF/X...    )

  Through "PDF/X-3 Sets..." you can configure your
  settings for the PDF/X-3 conversion.             (   PDF/X-3 Sets...    )


                                                   (        Done         )
```

Figure 11.10 Preflight: PDF/X window

4. At the top of the window, select the PDF/X format you want to use, PDF/X-1a or PDF/X-3.

Note: The buttons in this window are context-sensitive to whichever PDF/X format you select.

Once you've done this, the Preflight: PDF/X window provides five different PDF/X-related manipulations that can be performed on your PDF document. Click one or more of these buttons:

Save As PDF/X This button not only preflights your PDF but also converts it into a PDF/X-compliant PDF (Figure 11.11). This procedure will ask you for an ISS print profile if one is not included in your PDF. The conversion process can add or change some components, such as missing art and bleed boxes, but cannot alter others, such as graphics files, or change font formats. This process allows you to select a specific PDF/X set of preflight criteria and some non-PDF/X criteria, such as maximum and minimum resolution values, as well.

Verify This button runs a preflight that will verify that the opened PDF is PDF/X-compliant. If it's not, Acrobat will provide an alert (Figure 11.12), informing you of the failed verification and allowing you to view the preflight report. This same message will appear when you click any of the buttons if the preflight tests are failed.

Extract ICC Profile This process allows you to extract any ICC profiles that may be in your document. This step may be required if a specific profile is not wanted or needed or if the PDF workflow being used does not support the embedding of ICC profiles.

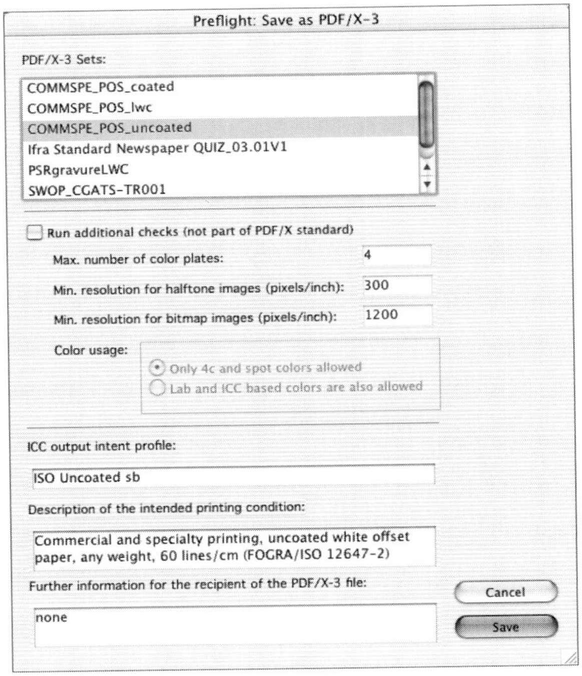

Preflight: Save as PDF/X-3

PDF/X-3 Sets:

COMMSPE_POS_coated
COMMSPE_POS_lwc
COMMSPE_POS_uncoated
Ifra Standard Newspaper QUIZ_03.01V1
PSRgravureLWC
SWOP_CGATS-TR001

☐ Run additional checks (not part of PDF/X standard)

Max. number of color plates: 4

Min. resolution for halftone images (pixels/inch): 300

Min. resolution for bitmap images (pixels/inch): 1200

Color usage:
⦿ Only 4c and spot colors allowed
○ Lab and ICC based colors are also allowed

ICC output intent profile:

ISO Uncoated sb

Description of the intended printing condition:

Commercial and specialty printing, uncoated white offset paper, any weight, 60 lines/cm (FOGRA/ISO 12647-2)

Further information for the recipient of the PDF/X-3 file:

Cancel

Save

Figure 11.11 Save As PDF/X criteria dialog

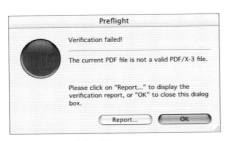

Preflight

Verification failed!

The current PDF file is not a valid PDF/X-3 file.

Please click on "Report..." to display the verification report, or "OK" to close this dialog box.

Report...   OK

Figure 11.12 Failed verification

Remove PDF/X This button allows you to remove PDF/X-specific contents, such as art and bleed box information, that are required by PDF/X-based workflow but not useful for other PDF uses. This remove function can be useful for simplifying PDF/X-based PDFs that you would like to use for other purposes, such as for display on the Web.

PDF/X Sets This button allows you to access and fine-tune any of the PDF/X sets of preflight criteria included in Acrobat (Figure 11.13). You can edit, delete, duplicate, or even create a new set.

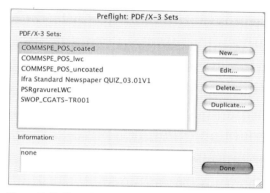

Figure 11.13 Managing PDF/X sets

Third-Party Preflighting Tools

Many companies make PDF-oriented software, and although it isn't possible to mention them all, there are two companies that, through the development of their PDF-related products, have made long-term and particularly important contributions to Acrobat's capabilities and PDF workflow:

Note: I've included trial versions of both PitStop and FlightCheck on the companion CD.

PitStop (Enfocus) PitStop has both PDF preflighting and editing capabilities. Although Acrobat 6 offers much-improved functions, PitStop's tools are still welcome. PitStop has been a constant companion of mine, and numerous others, for many years of working with PDFs. If you need to preflight, and particularly edit PDF documents, I consider this a must-have tool. Enfocus makes this as a plug-in for Acrobat (both Mac and Windows) and offers a server-based version as well. They offer a range of capability levels. Visit them at www.enfocus.com.

FlightCheck (Markzware) FlightCheck is by far and away the leading (most capable and most used) set of preflighting tools available. If you took away my FlightCheck, I would refuse to create documents! Markzware offers both Mac and Windows versions of its software with various levels of capabilities. I use FlightCheck on my native page layout documents (they support a dizzying array of applications), my PostScript files, and my PDFs. Visit them at www.markzware.com.

Preflighting: Who, What, Where, and When

Preflighting certainly needs to be performed by whoever is going to output the final PDF, typically a prepress production staff member in the case of PDF/X files or a webmaster in the case of a PDF destined for a website. But it is also a good idea for document creators to preflight their own files as well. Preflighting a document before converting into a PDF, and then preflighting the PDF prior to sending it out for final output, will help find potential problems before the document enters the production process. Fixing native files is typically much easier and faster (and therefore less expensive) than fixing PDF documents. Don't be afraid to ask your prepress manager or webmaster, who is responsible for the final output, for instructions on preparing and preflighting your PDFs. This is particularly true when you are preparing a file for a PDF/X-based workflow.

Editing PDFs

Although PDF documents are not primarily intended to be used to construct and edit contents, we do in fact have extensive editing capabilities for PDFs. Indeed, the distilling process—converting a page-layout document to a PDF—includes and isolates each text and graphic component of a document. The result is that every part of a PDF document is selectable and editable.

Chapter Contents

The question is often not "can we edit the PDF?" but rather "should we edit the PDF?" The isolation of each document component can make editing a slow and painful process. For instance, each word in a document is a separate document component so that the edited type does not reflow. However, in those cases where you do not have access to the original page-layout document, being able to edit the PDF can be a "bacon saver." Editing tools and capabilities can be found both within Acrobat and in third-party software.

Reducing and Simplifying PDFs

The process of opening and manipulating a PDF document can add numerous document elements to your PDF file. You can add comments, bookmarks, previously used fonts, and more to your document. Following are some techniques that will help you simplify and reduce the size of your PDFs.

 Note: While a PDF is open, you can find out its size by choosing File > Document Properties > Description.

If you have added and or removed document pages or cropped your document, just choosing File > Save As will often significantly reduce the file size.

Beyond Save As, Acrobat also provides a one-step file-size-reduction tool, which removes unused items and compresses uncompressed objects in your PDF document. To apply this tool, simply choose File > Reduce File Size, select a PDF version for compatibility; then click OK.

I have seen reductions of as much as 87 percent from the Reduce File Size command, but this method reduces the size of the PDF files mostly through bitmap resampling at a much lower resolution than the original. As such, the results are not as controllable as adjusting file sizes through the optimization methods covered in the next section and the next chapter.

Optimizing PDFs

Acrobat allows you to optimize your PDF for specific uses while reducing the file size at the same time. The tool of choice here is the PDF Optimizer, which allows you to control the reduction and simplification processes that will be applied to your PDF. Here is how it works:

1. Open the PDF you would like to optimize.

2. Choose Advanced > PDF Optimizer. The PDF Optimizer dialog appears (Figure 12.1), with three tabs: Images, Fonts, and Cleanup. The Images tab opens first by default.

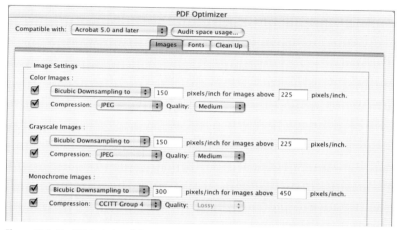

Figure 12.1 The PDF Optimizer dialog, Images tab

3. Before proceeding, it is a good idea to take a look at what is in your PDF document. To do this, click the Audit Space Usage button [Audit space usage...] .

This will bring up the Space Audit dialog (Figure 12.2), which gives a complete summary of what is in the PDF document and how much space each document element occupies. For instance, in the document I have opened here—the June 2003 copy of *Design Tools Monthly*—you can see that the images, which often make up the lion's share of space in a PDF document, occupy only 16.8 percent of the space, while the content streams (copy) occupy the most at 37.85 percent. You can also see that this document contains comments, which occupy only 0.8 percent of the document. The total file size is listed at the bottom of the window (here, 653,695KB). Viewing and evaluating this window can provide you with some clues as to what you might discard or compress to reduce the file's size.

4. When you are through looking at the Space Audit, click OK to close this dialog and return to the PDF Optimizer dialog.

5. At the top of the Images tab, select the version(s) of Acrobat you would like your PDF to be compatible with. Note that the more recent the version, the smaller the PDF will be, because backward compatibility requires more information and therefore a greater file size.

Space Audit		
Results		
Percentage	Bytes	Description
0 %	0	Thumbnails
16.18 %	105750	Images
1.99 %	13005	Bookmarks
37.85 %	247441	Content Streams
16.92 %	110625	Fonts
5.29 %	34594	Structure Info
0.02 %	122	Acro Forms
2.82 %	18448	Link Annotations
0.80 %	5236	Comments
0 %	0	Named Destinations
0 %	0	Web Capture Information
1.69 %	11076	Document Overhead

Figure 12.2 The Space Audit dialog tells you what's taking up room in your PDF.

Note: This feature is an easy way to create a backward-compatible PDF from one that was set up for a later version only—a way to "fix" PDFs that aren't compatible with earlier versions of Acrobat or Reader.

6. Next you can choose, in the Image Settings portion of the Images tab, to uniformly downsample and compress the images that are in the PDF (see Figure 12.1). These settings work just like the Images tab in Distiller. (☞ Chapter 4, "Creating the PDF You Want," for more information on assigning downsampling and compression settings.) The more you downsample the image (lower the resolution) and the more you compress the image, the smaller your PDF will become. But remember that reducing the resolution and increasing the compression will progressively lower the quality of your images.

Note: Optimizer provides a lossy monochrome compression option known as JBIG2 (not currently available in Distiller) that provides greater compression of line art than CCITT Group 3 or 4 modes.

7. Instead of applying uniform compression, you also have the option to Enable Adaptive Compression by activating the check box in the lower portion of this Images tab. Checking this will deactivate the uniform compression and downsampling options in the upper portion of the window. Adaptive Compression applies a sophisticated compression algorithm that varies the amount of compression depending upon the image area characteristics (with more compression applied to more consistent areas) and helps to remove screens, noise, and patterns from the images. You can adjust the amount of compression that will be applied by moving the Compression/Quality slider. A bit of experimentation will show whether you will want to use uniform or adaptive compression. You can also choose Remove Edge Shadows From Images to reduce or remove any dark image edges created when images are not scanned squarely.

8. Next, click the Fonts tab (Figure 12.3). Here, you can select any fonts that you do not want to have embedded in your PDF from the Embedded Fonts column and move them to the Fonts To Unembed column.

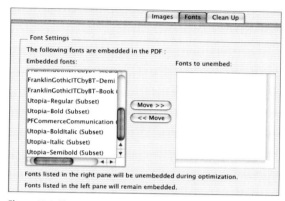

Figure 12.3 The PDF Optimizer dialog, Fonts tab

Note: Any unembedded fonts will be removed from the PDF document. If those fonts are available on the system that will be used for viewing the PDF, you *might* not experience any font substitution–related problems. However, the best way to maintain the font and typesetting integrity of your PDF is to keep the fonts embedded, so unembed fonts only as a last resort.

9. Now click the Clean Up tab (Figure 12.4).

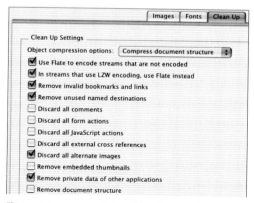

Figure 12.4 The PDF Optimizer dialog, Cleanup tab

10. Select the options you would like to be applied to clean up and reduce the size of your PDF. Some of these options are "safe" and can be applied without fear of losing key content that could affect document functionality; with other options you must be more careful. The following options are safe and can be checked:

- Compress Document Structure
- Use Flate To Encode Streams That Are Not Encoded
- In Streams That Use LZW Encoding, Use Flate Instead
- Remove Invalid Bookmarks And Links
- Remove Unused Named Destinations
- Discard All Alternate Images
- Remove Private Data Of Other Applications
- Optimize The PDF For Fast Web View

On the other hand, be careful about these options (you'll probably want to leave them unchecked):

Discard All Comments Would remove any comments made during collaborative publishing.

Discard All Form Actions Would disable all actions, such as submit-forms actions, associated with any forms.

Discard All JavaScript Actions Would disable any interactive JavaScript functions.

Discard All External Cross References Would delete any links to external files.

Remove Embedded Thumbnails Would disable the use of the Pages tab for viewing, selecting, and organizing PDF pages.

Remove Document Structure Would remove tags from your PDF, limiting its use as an eBook and removing your ability to edit the element order.

Remove Hidden Layer Content And Flatten Layers Would remove all layer content that has been hidden and compress all the visible layer data, thereby removing the editability of any layer except one.

11. Click OK when you have finished assigning your Optimizer settings. Acrobat will perform a Save As function and ask you to specify a location for your new optimized PDF. Your original, unoptimized PDF will remain untouched, in case you need to return to it. The *DTM 06/2003* file I used to demonstrate this process was reduced from an already slim 653,659KB file to 524,952KB using only the "safe" optimizing options.

Reformatting with PostScript

Another method for simplifying a PDF document is to convert the PDF back into Post-Script and create a new PDF though Distiller. This method is especially useful when the Optimizer is not getting the job done or you are having troubles outputting a PDF and want to start from scratch. Here is how it works:

1. Open the troubled PDF.
2. Choose File > Save As. The Save As dialog appears.
3. Locate the watched folder into which you would like to save the PostScript file. (☞ Chapter 4 for information on setting up and using watched folders.)
4. Select PostScript from the Format menu.
5. Click OK.

Your current PDF document will be converted into a PostScript file, which in turn will be re-created as a new PDF document using the Distiller Settings assigned to your chosen watched folder.

Reflowing (Changing the Order of) PDF Contents

Reflowing the order in which a PDF document occurs is really necessary in only a couple of circumstances. Two common reasons for reflowing contents are:

- To adjust the order in which PDF document components are accessed by an eBook reader
- To adjust the order in which form fields and other tabbed objects are accessed

In either case, it is advisable to have all of the structure in your PDF identified or "tagged" first.

Open the PDF whose structure you would like to view and edit, then choose Advanced > Accessibility > Add Tags To Document.

Once you have added tags to a document, you can use them for reordering tasks.

Changing the Read Order

The order in which file contents are accessed or processed is known as read order. Read order is very important in circumstances such as form fields, where the read order control the order in which the form fields will be navigated when a form user tabs through the form, or in the case of a eBook readers where the read order controls the order in which document contents are accessed and presented by the reader.

1. Open the PDF whose content read order you would like to adjust. To demonstrate, I'll use the American Classics document I mentioned in the previous chapter; AmericanClassic.pdf is included in the Chapter 11 folder on the companion CD.

2. Choose View > Navigator Tabs > Content. The Content tab will appear.

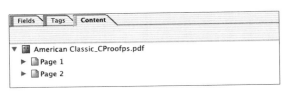

3. Expand the Content view for the page whose order you would like to control (Figure 12.5 shows Page 1 expanded). You will be able to see all of the contents of this document.

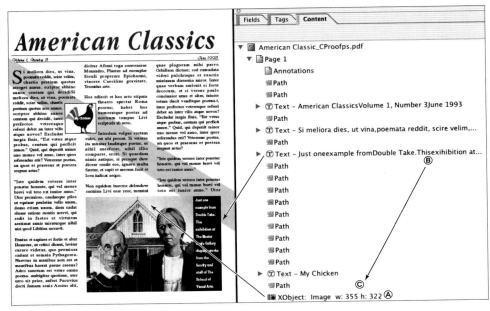

Figure 12.5 Page 1 and its contents

You will notice that the "Farmer and Wife" image (A) (which occurs first in column 2) and its associated text (B) (which has been placed in a separate text box in column 3) are clearly separated by other document contents in the Content list. This means that they will likely not display together if this document is reflowed in an eBook reader. So we will move the position order of the copy to a new position closer to the image.

4. Click the Text content item (B) to select it.

5. Drag the selected Text content item (B) down to its new position (C).

```
▶ ⓣ Text – My Chicken
   ▦ Path
▶ ⓣ Text – Just oneexample fromDouble Take.Thisexihibition at...
   ▣ XObject: Image  w: 355 h: 322
▶ 📄 Page 2
```

The related text will now be displayed near the graphic when the document is reflowed in an eBook reader.

Changing the Tab Order of Objects

Adjusting the tab order of PDF contents, such as form fields, links, and annotations, involves making sure that all document components are "tagged" and then accessing and adjusting the position of the content tags in the PDF. There are two methods—the Rule method and the Edit Tags method—to control the tab order of objects.

Some documents, especially those with complex forms, may not lend themselves to the simple use of tabbing rules, explained in the following section. In those cases, you can edit the tabbing order object by object, which is described in the section after that, titled "Edit Tags Method."

Rule Method

You can specify how tabbed objects, such as form fields or annotations (comments), will be accessed by assigning a rule to control how these objects will be accessed on the page:

1. Open the PDF whose content read order you would like to adjust. Here I'm using the order form, CompletedForm.pdf, from the Chapter 8 folder on the CD.

2. Add tags to this PDF if they are not already present (see the section "Tagging Your PDFs" earlier in this chapter.

3. Click the Pages tab to activate the thumbnail views of the pages.

4. Click the page thumbnail to select the document page where you would set the tab order.

5. From the Options menu or from the context menu (Control+click/right-click), choose Page Properties.

6. Click the Tab Order tab in the Page Properties dialog.

7. Select an option to control the order in which tabbed items will be selected. Here are some tips on each option:

Use Row Order Select this option if your document contents are arranged horizontally and you want to tab through your document from binding to page edge (left to right or right to left). This is a good choice for many forms.

Use Column Order Select this option if your document contents are arranged vertically and you want to tab through your document from top to bottom as well as from binding to page edge. You would select this for multicount text pages and spreadsheets.

Use Document Structure This setting uses the built-in (tagged) document structure to control the tab order (the most common choice for tagged documents).

Unspecified This option will be the default setting if the PDF you have opened has been created in an earlier version of Acrobat. Select one of the other choices. You first might want to structure/tag your PDF and then select the Use Document Structure option as a starting place.

8. Click the Close button when you have finished.

Edit Tags Method

For more control, Acrobat allows you to set the tabbing/structure order of each document element in a PDF file individually:

1. Open and save a copy of a PDF document with a complex structure, such as a form, with a tab order that does not work properly. You can try this with a filled-in version of my order form, in the Chapter 12 folder on the CD, named CalibrationForm.pdf.

2. Add tags to this PDF if they are not already present (Advanced > Accessibility > Add Tags To Document).

3. Choose View > Navigation Tabs > Tags.

4. In the Tags tab that opens, display the content tags until you find the content items you want to edit. Figure 12.6 shows the content items that belong to the fields at the bottom of the order-form page. You will notice that the proper order of the form should be Name, Address, City, etc. But, as is evident in the Tags tab, the Name (A) is in the proper location, but the Address (B) and City (C) are reversed. This commonly happens when form fields are created out of order or are edited or replaced.

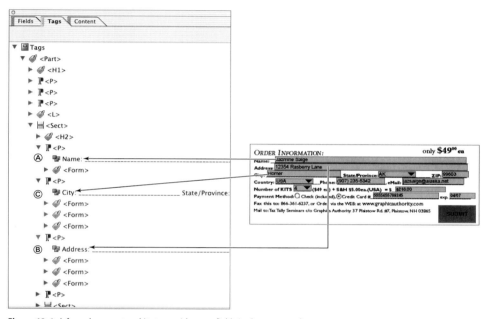

Figure 12.6 A form document and its tags with some fields in the wrong order

Note: The result of the misordered tags is that someone using the Tab key to move through the form fields would skip from the Name field to the City field and then back to the Address field.

5. To correct the tabbing order, simply drag the tags up and down; here, drag the Address tag up between the Name and City tags.

Note: You might find that the dragging process proceeds a bit more smoothly if you close the tags prior to moving them. Then reopen the tags to check that the order is correct.

6. View the new tag order (Figure 12.7) and try the tab sequence in the document to make sure it works properly.

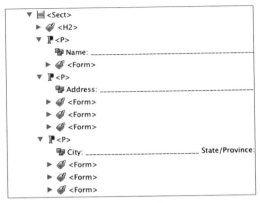

Figure 12.7 The new, corrected, tag order

Adding Alternative Text to Enhance Accessibility

In addition to the enhanced accessibility functions we covered in Chapter 5, "Controlling Acrobat and Access to Your PDFs," Acrobat lets you provide alternate text to take the place of content (such as a graphic or movie) so that the visually impaired can have access to a description that the Read Out Loud function can read. Here is how to add alternate text to an image:

1. Open the file to which you would like to add alternate text (here I will again use my calibration order form).

2. Choose View > Navigation Tabs > Tags to show the Tags tab (Figure 12.8).

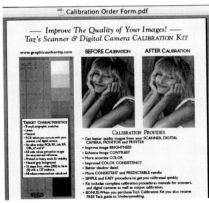
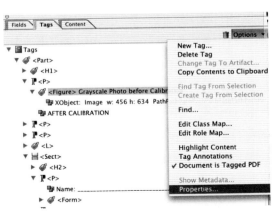

Figure 12.8 Viewing the document tags

3. Expand the display of the tags content until you find the tag for the element to which you would like to add some alternate text. Here I'll work with the BEFORE Calibration graphic.

4. Click the tag for that content (here labeled Grayscale Photo Before Calibration) to select the tag.

5. From the Tags tab's Options menu, or from the context menu (right-click/Control+click), select Properties. The TouchUp Properties dialog appears.

6. Click the Tag tab, which provides Type, Title, Actual Text, Alternate Text, and Language fields.

7. In the Alternate Text field, type in the description of the content. Be as explicit as you can—for instance, say what you were trying to show with a graphic.

8. Select the Language you would like to be used.

9. Click the Close button when you are through.
   This alternate text will then be read when the Read Out Loud function is used.

Editing Text in PDFs

Acrobat provides the ability to select and edit all text elements in a PDF document. Be aware, however, that this is not text editing as usual. During the distilling process, each word is isolated as a separate document item so that text copy no longer flows as it does in a standard page layout document. As a result, text editing can be a slow and cumbersome process. This is why Adobe specifically refers to its built-in editing tools as text and graphic TouchUp tools. But if all you have is the PDF, it's nice to at least have the editing option. Here is how text editing is accomplished:

1. Open and save a copy of the PDF document you would like to edit. Here I will use the American Classic document from Chapter 11.

Note: It is always a good idea to work on a copy of the PDF when you are editing.

2. Display the Advanced Editing tools (by selecting Advanced Editing Toolbar from the Advanced Editing icon of the main toolbar palette).

3. From the right end of the Advanced Editing toolbar, choose the TouchUp Text tool.

Embedded vs. Computer Station Fonts

There may be two sets of fonts in your list, separated by a blank space. The top set of fonts is the fonts embedded in the active PDF document. The second font list is the active font set available through the computer station on which this PDF is opened. Any font that is selected from the computer station list should be embedded to ensure that these new font files will accompany this PDF wherever it is sent.

Subsetting the new fonts will restrict the number of font characters embedded to those used in the actual copy. So subsetting will reduce the file size addition of the new embedded font files but will limit editability to include only those embedded characters. As we discussed in Chapter 4, subsetting can also help guarantee that the embedded fonts will always be used during printing.

4. Select the text characters you would like to edit (here I am selecting the headline "American Classics"). You can select as many or as few text characters as you like, but remember that text does not reflow when it is edited. Text will only expand or contract to accommodate the changes you make.

5. Right-click/Control+click anywhere in the active Document pane, and choose Properties from the context menu. The Touchup Properties dialog appears.

6. Click the Text tab.

7. The currently used font for the selected text is indicated in the Font drop-down menu. To change the font used, click this menu and select a new font from the list.

8. Choose to Embed and Subset any new computer station font files in your PDF by clicking those check boxes.

9. Adjust any of the standard font characteristics, such as size, character and word spacing, horizontal scaling, fill color, and baseline offset, by changing the values in the Text tab. Two adjustments you can make to your type characteristics that are not commonly available in most page layout applications are the stroke color and width.

Note: The reason you can edit the character strokes is that the process of distilling places the complete scalable vector font data front and center in the PDF, thereby providing you editing access to the actual vector paths rather than just low-resolution raster screen font data.

Note: Be careful not to assign too thin a stroke (0.25pt or less), because that may not print reliably on some devices.

10. When you have finished setting your font character values click the Close button to apply the new values.

At the risk of beating a dead horse, I remind you that your type will not reflow; it can only expand or contract, so line breaks will occur on the same words, but their positions will change. You will often find that when adjusting body copy you'll need to adjust at least the word spacing to keep the position of line breaks similar to their original position.

Adding Text to PDFs

You can use the same TouchUp Text tool you used to edit text already present in a PDF document to add text to a PDF as well. This tool is typically used to add small amounts of text, not whole paragraphs. You can edit text added with the TouchUp Text tool in the same way as any other PDF text:

1. Zoom in to the area where you would like to add some text (here I have zoomed into the top of the farmer and wife image).

2. Select the TouchUp Text tool ![T] to activate it.

3. Option/Ctrl+click where you would like to add your new type; a New Text Font dialog appears.

4. Select a font and a mode (vertical or horizontal type).

5. Click OK. A new text field will appear.

6. Type in the copy you want (here I have added "The Third Eye Farmer"), and hit the Enter key when you have finished.

Editing Objects in PDFs

Acrobat allows you to edit whole objects in a PDF files as well as type characteristics. Objects include any elements within a PDF page, such as graphics, lines, borders, and even type objects.

Moving Objects

To move an object around in your PDF file, follow these steps:

1. Select the TouchUp Object tool .

2. Click the object you would like to move. Here I will select the Type Object containing the "American Classics" headline. A thin blue (bounding box) line will surround the selected object.

American Classics ——— Selection bounding box

Volume 1, Number 3   June 1998

Note: Note that when I selected this Headline text object, the small "Volume," "Number," and "Date" copy was selected as well. Similar local objects are often grouped together in the distilling process.

3. Click within the bounding box, and drag the object to whatever new position you like.

Editing Object Contents

You can edit the content of individual objects by accessing an appropriate application through Acrobat. Here's how:

1. Select the object you would like to edit.

2. Right-click/Control+click the object, and from the object's context menu choose the Edit command (which would be Edit Image for a graphic).

An application appropriate for the selected object will be launched and the selected PDF object will open. If you choose to edit a bitmap, you'll likely launch Photoshop because of the pixel-based nature of the selected image. If you were to select text, Illustrator might be used.

3. Edit the object with the application.

4. Save and close the image in the graphic application.

5. Wait a few minutes while the new version of the image is being updated into the PDF.

Opening and Editing PDFs in Illustrator

Since a PDF document is really a special version of a PostScript file, it can be opened and edited in Adobe Illustrator, which is essentially a drawing program that can open and edit PostScript-based objects.

Note: Any pixel-based graphic will behave as if it had been placed in Illustrator, so any significant editing of these graphics should be performed in Photoshop.

Be sure you make a copy of your PDF before you open it in Illustrator, because any changes to the document, either during opening in Illustrator or through editing in Illustrator once it is opened, are saved back into the original PDF. Here is how it works:

1. Make a copy of the PDF you intend to open in Illustrator. Here I will open a copy of the American Classic document from Chapter 11 to edit the chicken graphic.

2. Launch Illustrator and choose File > Open. Select the PDF copy you made in Step 1 and click Open.

3. In the untitled page-selection window that appears, select the PDF document page you would like to open, and then click OK. The chicken is on Page 1, so I'm opening that page.

4. When your selected PDF page opens in Illustrator, perform a Select All with one of the Selection tools. You will see all the page elements selected. Any of the PostScript page elements, such as type and vector graphics, can be selected individually and edited using Illustrator's tools.

Sometimes, not all of the PDF page elements are interpreted and opened properly in Illustrator. For instance, here the spot color portions of the chicken were not properly recognized by Illustrator and therefore do not appear in the PDF when it is opened in Illustrator. If you were to simply save this opened PDF, these unrecognized elements would be removed from the newly saved PDF. This is one reason why you always want to work on a copy of the PDF document when you open it in Illustrator.

5. When you have finished editing your PDF page in Illustrator, choose Save or Save As from the File menu. Your opened and edited PDF will be saved back out as a PDF again with any changes that occurred to it during the opening and editing of the PDF in Illustrator.

Where and When to Edit PDFs, and Version Challenges

Clearly, after having read though this chapter, you can see that any element of a PDF document can be edited. So as I said at the outset, the question is not whether we *can* edit in PDF but whether we *should*. Some editing functions (such as editing an individual graphic file, discussed earlier in this chapter) can be accomplished easily and quickly though Acrobat. Other editing chores—such as extensive text editing—can be very laborious and time consuming and are best handled in the original page layout application, followed by the creation of a new PDF (and if you are in the habit of using watched folders for creating PDFs, the prospect of creating a new PDF should be fast, accurate, and nonthreatening).

Another important consideration to keep in mind when trying to decide whether to edit a PDF or its source file is the ability to replace pages (discussed in Chapter 7). If you edit the source file (often only some page requires changes), then create new PDF pages, and then replace only those pages in the original PDF, all of the fields, bookmarks, and comments will be retained as the under-lying PDF is replaced. This is a handy feature and capability to remember if you are working with commented and/or bookmarked PDFs.

But even if you decide to perform an edit in a PDF (which you may do for reasons of production or workflow speed), there is an additional challenge to consider: versioning. By performing an edit on a PDF document, you are creating a new and unique content version of that document. So if you edit PDF documents, and especially if you edit client files, you should establish a feedback process whereby any edits made in a PDF document will somehow be communicated back to whomever has access to the original page layout document, so that those changes can be updated there as well.

Third-Party PDF Editing Tools

While Acrobat provides some basic editing capabilities, if you need to regularly open and perform extensive edits to multiple objects within numerous PDF documents, then you should consider acquiring a third-party extension designed specifically for this purpose.

There are numerous editing plug-ins for Acrobat, but the one with which I am most familiar and have had much success is PitStop from Enfocus. PitStop provides a wide and deep range of global, page-based, and individual-object editing tools, including a complete preflighting and correction tool set, automation functions, a certification tool for prepress and PDF/X standards, and even a server-based versions of its tools. If you need to edit a lot of PDFs, get PitStop. I've included a trial copy of this software on the book's companion CD.

Outputting PDFs and Their Contents

PDF documents and their components can be output from Acrobat and/or imported into other applications in a variety of ways. You can print PDF documents, or you can export them in a wide variety of file formats and even open them in other applications. You can also copy and paste text and graphic elements or export them. In addition, you can import graphic elements into other applications such as Photoshop.

13

Chapter Contents

Previewing PDF Prints

Acrobat 6 offers useful print preview capabilities, including several commercial print previews that allow you to preview separated colors and even simulate how documents will look on different types of papers. At any time before or during the printing process, you can ask Acrobat to provide you with an on-screen preview of what your document will look like when it prints.

The first step in getting an accurate preview is to tell Acrobat what the print conditions will be. Here's how it works:

1. Open the document you want to print.

2. Choose Advanced > Proof Setup > Custom. The Proof Setup dialog appears.

3. From the Proofing Space menu, select the type of printer/press and paper that will be used—here, U.S. Web Coated (SWOP) v2.

4. Check the Ink Black and Paper White check boxes.

5. Click OK.

6. Choose Advanced > Proof Colors.

7. Choose Advanced > Overprint Preview.

Acrobat will provide an on-screen simulated preview of how both the black and colored inks will look, including any overlaps, given the print conditions you have assigned. This preview is not 100 percent accurate, but it provides a good representation of how various printing conditions, such as coated vs. uncoated stock, will affect the final look of your printed piece.

Previewing Color Separations

Acrobat provides an on-screen preview of how your colors are assigned and how they will separate. To see this, choose Advanced > Separation Preview. The Separation Preview dialog (Figure 13.1) will appear with a list of all the colors present in your document.

Uncheck the colors you do not wish to preview. In the second image, I have unchecked the CMYK process plates so that only the spot colors will be visible on screen.

Figure 13.1 Preview of a PDF with composited colors

Printing PDFs

PDF documents can be printed out of Acrobat with many variations. The print options available depend upon the printer driver you select because each device supports different types of output. Many desktop non-PostScript printers, for instance, support only composite printing and no separations. Here I will use the Adobe PDF printer driver, because it includes a wide range of options, to demonstrate the printing process, and I will discuss some common variations along the way. As I proceed, I'll focus on the print variables that are of special interest to printing PDF documents and provide brief comments on standard printing choices.

1. Choose File > Print. The Print dialog appears (Figure 13.2).

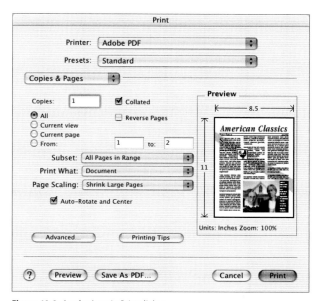

Figure 13.2 Acrobat's main Print dialog

2. The first step in this dialog is to select a printer driver. This is a critical initial step because the printer driver you select will determine which print capabilities and variables will be available. From  the list of available drivers (here, the Printer drop-down menu at the top of the dialog), choose the output device on which you intend to print your PDF. Here I will select Adobe PDF as if I will print this to another PDF file.

 Note: The look and actual content and arrangement of the menus, check boxes, and fields will depend upon which operating system (Windows or Mac), which version of the OS, and which specific printer driver you have selected. Some terminology will be different as well. On a Mac you may have PDF or Print "Options," while in Windows the terminology may be "Preferences" or "Properties." And different versions of Windows and Mac operating systems will look different as well. You will likely have to root around a bit to get used to the specific look and organization of your Print windows.

3. From the unnamed drop-down menu, choose the Copies & Pages option.

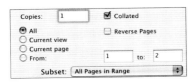

4. Specify the number of copies and which page(s) to print, but also notice that you have the choice of printing either the Current Page (active view) or just the Current View (such as a zoomed-in view) in addition to standard pages.

5. Acrobat also provides a Print What menu, which allows you to select from a list of possible PDF document components such as comment and form fields in addition to the standard document. The contents of your choice will be displayed in the Preview window to the right.

 Note: A separate Print With Comments command is covered later in this chapter.

6. The Page Scaling menu provides the ability to not just scale all pages but scale and tile individual pages, such as oversized pages. This is a handy feature, since a PDF document can support pages of various sizes.

7. Check the Auto-Rotate And Center check box if you have pages with different orientations and would like them to all print in one orientation. This too is a handy option, since a PDF supports multiple page orientations.

"Printing" to a PostScript File

At some point, you need to tell the Print dialog box whether you want to actually print out a document or save the document as a file, such as a PostScript file (often known as "print to disk"). These settings are typically found in a menu associated with the main Print window.

To print to a PostScript file, in the main Print dialog, click the unnamed drop-down menu and choose Output Options, as shown in Figure 13.3.

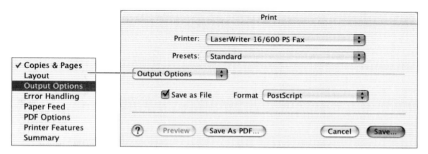

Figure 13.3 Print dialog Output Options

> **Note:** You can still change the printer driver in this dialog, but as I mentioned earlier it is best to do this at the beginning of the print setup.

To save your file to disk, select the Save As File check box and then, from the Format drop-down menu, choose PostScript. You can save the resulting PostScript file directly into a watched folder for reprocessing into a PDF, open it in Distiller separately, or simply save it for other uses (such as printing on older devices that do not accept PDF documents).

"Printing" to a PDF File

The Format menu (in the Print dialog Output Options) also offers another choice: PDF. Although the Print dialog supports saving a PDF out as a file, this is usually not recommended if you want to create a dependable PDF file. If you want to "save" a

PDF document out as another PDF file, it is best to use the File > Save As command, covered later in this chapter.

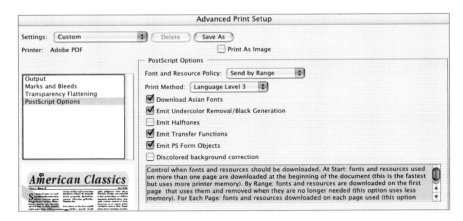

Note: PDF documents can also be saved as PostScript files from Save As, as we did in the Chapter 12, "Editing PDFs." However, the Print method, which I am using here, provides more control of the output, but both are viable methods.

If you do select to print this PDF as another PDF—which you might want to do to change the look and content of the PDF (such as printing proof separations)—you will want to assign the Distiller setting to be used. Here's how:

1. In the main Print dialog, click the unnamed drop-down menu and choose PDF Options. The PDF Options dialog appears (Figure 13.4).

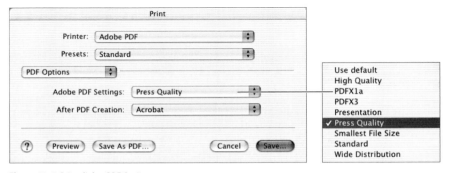

Figure 13.4 Print dialog PDF Options

2. From the Adobe PDF Settings drop-down menu, choose the Distiller setting you want to be used for the creation of the PDF document. (See Chapter 4, "Creating the PDF You Want," for more information on PDF Settings.)

3. From the After PDF Creation menu, choose whether you would like to have your new PDF opened and, if so, by which application, Acrobat or Reader. This is a handy timesaving option, since it is always a good idea to take look at your PDF after you create it.

Fine-Tuning Print Settings

After you have set up the main Print dialog, you can choose to either go ahead and print your document (or save it to a file) or fine-tune your output. If you are outputting in a commercial print environment and printing directly from Acrobat, or if you want to print separations for proofs or to control the colors that will print, you will likely want to further fine-tune your output.

In the main Print dialog, click the Advanced button. (This may be called a Preferences or Properties button in your dialog.) The Advanced Print Setup dialog appears (Figure 13.5). The list on the left side of this dialog provides several categories of options you can tweak.

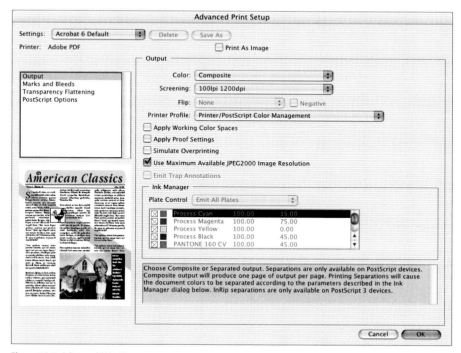

Figure 13.5 Advanced Print Setup

The next few subsections cover the options in each of the categories. When you are through configuring all the print settings, you can save your choices to be loaded again in the future as a set by clicking the Save As button to create a new custom setting.

Note: If you are unsure of how to apply a particular setting in a specific circumstance, click the option in question and read the description that appears in the very helpful text window at the bottom of the dialog.

When you have finished with the Advanced Print Setup, click OK and complete the printing process.

Output Options

Select Output from the list on the left. A variety of color and screening-related characteristics will appear. Here are tips on configuring some of these:

Color From this menu, choose whether you want your colors to print as a type of composite (Composite or Composite Gray) or as a type of separation (Separations or In-RIP Separations).

> **Composite** All colors present will be output together as one composite page of output for each document page.

> **Composite Gray** All colors will be converted to grayscale and output as one composite page of output for each document page.

Note: If you select one of the Composite settings, you will have the option of activating two proofing-oriented check boxes: Applying Proof Settings (both Composite modes) and Simulate Overprinting (Composite only), both of which rely on Acrobats 6's new on-screen proofing capabilities. See the section "Previewing PDF Prints" at the beginning of this chapter for instructions on controlling on-screen proofing settings.

> **Separations** Each color used will be separated and output as a separate output page for each color present on each page.

> **In-RIP Separations** Pages will be output initially as composite pages but with each color prepared for separation at a printing device (RIP). In-RIP Separations are supported only on PostScript level 3 devices.

Ink Manager If you select Separations from the Color menu, the Ink Manager area will become accessible. You can control which inks, typically process (CMYK) and Pantone spot colors, will print, as well as which color conversions (such as spot to process) you may want to occur. If you select Custom from the Plate Control menu, you can control the fate of each color separately.

Color management: Printer Profile In the middle of the Print dialog, you can choose to either use the color management controls here or ignore them. Which options are available here will depend upon your choices in the Color menu. Whether you control your color here or in a previous environment such as Photoshop will largely depend upon your workflow. If you, like me, create and control most of the images that go into your documents, and you create most of your own page layout documents, then you will likely control your colors during image capture in Photoshop and/or your page layout application. In other words, you don't want Acrobat mucking around with your colors. In this kind of front-end-controlled color workflows you will want to select Same As Source (No Color Management).

If, on the other hand, your workflow involves lots of documents and images arriving from various sources (such as in a newspaper or other multisource publication), and you are putting them all together in a PDF for output, then you might want to control the color in Acrobat in order to attempt to apply some semblance of color consistency to the color chaos. So you might select a print profile consistent with your output device, such as U.S. Web Uncoated v2.

Apply Working Color Spaces If your workflow and color management system require that every color object be assigned (tagged with) a color profile, you can click this check box to apply the color profile you selected from the Printer Profile menu as your source profile for untagged color objects.

JPEG2000 Check the Use Maximum Available JPEG2000 Image Resolution check box if you want your JPEG2000 (J2K) format images to print at their highest resolution. The JPEG2000 image format supports multiple resolutions, and checking this box will ensure that the highest-available resolution is used. Select this for the highest-quality output devices, such as for prepress, or if you are not satisfied with the default results.

Color Assignments

The fate of any nonprint colors such as RGB or index colors that may still be in the PDF is uncertain during printing. They may be converted to process, typically CMYK (using who-knows-what algorithm), converted to grayscale, or not printed at all. Even the spot-to-process conversion presented here is suspect, since there is no agreed-upon set of spot-to-process conversion values. So for the most dependable and predictable results, it is a good idea to have all colors previously assigned to either the process or spot colors you want, prior to printing. Acrobat plug-ins such as Enfocus Pit-Stop can make the reassignment of color values in a PDF a relatively fast and easy process.

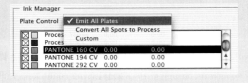

Marks And Bleeds Options

To see the next category of options, choose Marks And Bleeds from the list on the left side of the main Print dialog (Figure 13.6).

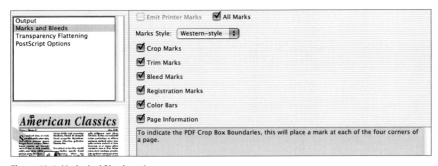

Figure 13.6 Marks And Bleeds options

Select the items you would like to have printed; check All Marks if you want them all. Again, if you are not sure what an item is, click it and read about it in the text information area at the bottom of the window.

Note: One of the terrific features of a PDF document is that the document and its contents can be "printed" at 100 percent as a PDF file, regardless of what marks or color bars you want to show. You are not restricted to an 8.5″×11″ page with a $\frac{1}{4}$″ margin as you are with many desktop printers.

Transparency Flattening Options

Next, choose Transparency Flattening (Figure 13.7) from the category list on the left side of the main Print window. Here are some tips on setting up these options:

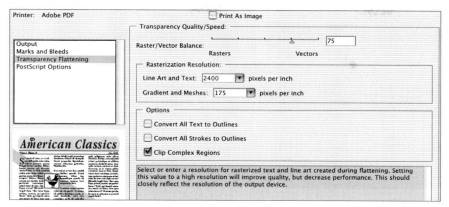

Figure 13.7 Print dialog Transparency Flattening options

Raster/Vector Balance Many graphics and even page layout applications now support saving images with both vector- and pixel (raster)-based elements along with transparency. These combination graphics can be very complex and sometimes difficult to output. Flattening these complex images can reduce printing complexity. The Rasters/ Vectors slider allows you to determine how much vector information, and therefore complexity, will be allowed into the final version of the PDF or print. The higher this value is, the higher the quality of the final output (and the more RAM and processing time are required). This value should be between 75 and 100 for the best results. If you are generating PostScript errors from your print output device, you can lower this value; if complex areas of your pages are not printing well, you may want to raise it. If your output device just refuses to print your PDF, try checking the Print As Image check box, which will convert everything to pixels (100 percent raster) to minimize the document complexity.

Rasterization Resolution These two menus in this section are used to control the resolution at which various types of vector elements will be rasterized, such as vector (PostScript) text, line art gradients, and meshes. For the highest-quality text and line art edges, select the maximum optical resolution of your output device (1200 for desktop, 2400–3600 for commercial printing). Gradients and meshes should be set to output at the line screen at which other raster images will be printed (85–120 for desktop devices and 150–175 for commercial printing). If your Raster/Vector Balance is set to 100, a minimum amount of rasterization of vector elements will occur.

Convert All Text To Outlines and Convert All Strokes To Outlines Checking these boxes will simplify PostScript-based images (text and stroked art) when an image is flattened, thereby simplifying the printing process. However, converting to outlines may result in the fattening of text and line art edges, particularly if the edges are thin and/or serif-like. I avoid selecting these options unless I am receiving PostScript errors during printing.

Clip Complex Regions I select this option if I have complex overlapping vector and raster art and the edges of my overlapping artwork and images are not printing accurately. But be aware that checking this box may result in slower printing or PostScript errors because of the complexity of the paths created.

PostScript Options

For the next category of options, choose PostScript Options from the list on the left side of the main Print dialog (Figure 13.8). The settings in this window determine which elements will be downloaded to the printer memory and when. Here are some guidelines on setting them up:

Font And Resource Policy This option controls when fonts and other repetitive resources are downloaded to the printer. I typically select Send By Range because this will download font and other data initially and then remove the data once it is no longer needed.

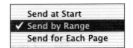

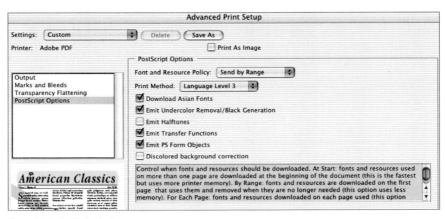

Figure 13.8 PostScript Options

Print Method Here you set the level of PostScript code to be used during printing. Historically there are three levels, although only two appear here. Most newer PostScript printers will be Language Level 3. When in doubt about a printer or if you repeatedly receive PostScript errors, choose Language Level 2.

The remaining options are a checklist of items and information to be included. I typically check all of these except Emit Halftones (halftoning should be determined at the RIP) and Discolored Background Correction (I turn this on only in rare cases with certain desktop printers that create background color casts). Remember that if you are unsure of the meaning of these various choices, click a selection and read its description in the lower text information window.

Printing over the Internet

Acrobat 6 provides the ability to print your PDF files over the Internet through a service called PrintMe. This service allows you to print to PrintMe-enabled devices from any Internet-connected device. Here's how to get started:

1. Open the PDF document you would like to print over the Internet.
2. Make sure you're online.
3. Choose File > PrintMe Internet Printing. The initial PrintMe signup/login window appears (Figure 13.9).
4. Click the Signup Now button and follow the instructions.

Figure 13.9 The PrintMe login dialog

Importing and Exporting PDF Documents and Contents

There is a wide variety of tools and methods for moving contents, including text and graphic components, into and out of PDF documents. Following are some of the more useful tools and techniques.

Changing the Format of PDF Documents

Because a PDF document is a form of PostScript, you can change it into a wide variety of file formats for use in various circumstances and by various applications.

File Formats

The concept of file formats is easily understood if you divide any document into two parts: its contents and the container that holds those contents. Contents are document elements such as text and graphics. File formats are the container into which you place your document contents.

You employ different file formats (containers) for different uses. A PDF is one file format, and a PostScript file format is another. Both may have essentially the same content stored in different containers bound for different uses. A PDF document can be saved out as an integrated text and graphic document, such as another PDF, EPS, HTML, or XML; as a text-based file, such as a Word DOC; or as a graphics file, such as TIFF or one of the JPEGs, depending upon how you might want to reuse the content of your PDF.

One of the easiest ways to change a PDF's file format is to use the Save As function in Acrobat. Here's how:

1. Open the PDF whose file format you would like to change.

2. Select File > Save As. The Save As window will appear (Figure 13.10).

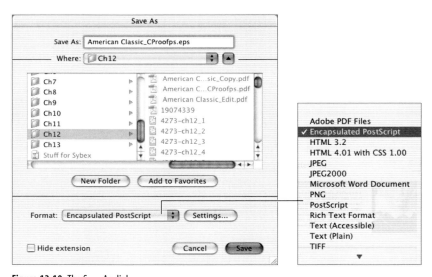

Figure 13.10 The Save As dialog

3. Click the Format menu and select a file format. Here I have selected Encapsulated PostScript (EPS).

4. After you have selected the file format, be sure to click the Settings button so that you can configure your new format to match your needs for this new file.

Each file format will have its own unique Save As Settings dialog, like the one in Figure 13.11 for EPS format. (Note here that the EPS Save As Settings dialog is similar to the Advanced Print Setup one we used in previous sections.)

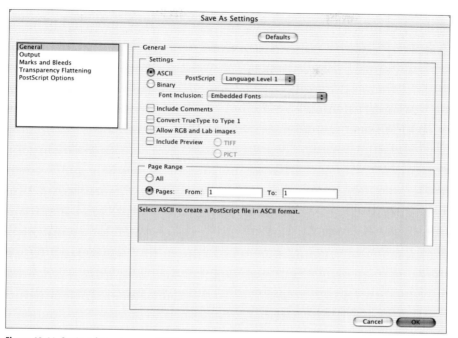

Figure 13.11 Settings for saving as an EPS file

Note: Acrobat will automatically add the appropriate three-character extension onto your new file (in this case it is .eps). You can choose to either hide or show this extension. I recommend as a matter of course that you show it, so that the document's format can be easily recognized at a glance without having to open the document.

5. When you are through configuring your file format settings, click the OK button in the Save As Settings dialog; then click the Save button in the Save As dialog to create your new file.

Exporting or Saving Contents

Text can be easily exported from a PDF document in various ways. You can export all the text in your PDF, export all the images at once, or copy and paste selected content.

Exporting All Text or All Images

To export all the text in your PDF file, choose File > Save As and select one of the many text file formats available there (see the preceding section).

Instead of accessing one image at a time, you may need to export *all* images from a PDF document with the same format and with the same settings. To do so, open the document from which you would like to export all of the images and choose Advanced > Export All Images. Configure the next dialog (Figure 13.12) as follows:

1. Select a file Format for the images.

2. Click the Settings button, assign the settings for the format you chose (as described in the preceding section), and then click OK to return to the Export All Images dialog.

3. Establish a base name for your images using the Save As field. Acrobat will create a sequence of images using this base name.

4. Leave Hide Extension unchecked so that the three-character file extension (in this case .jpg) will be visible at the end of all the exported graphics filenames.

5. Click the Save button to complete the process.

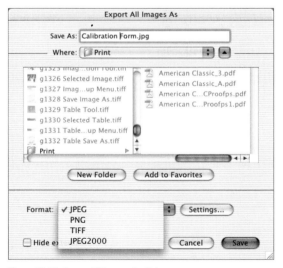

Figure 13.12 Export All Images As dialog

Pasting Selected Text

It's easy to copy and paste selected portions of the text in a PDF document. Here's how:

1. Expand the Selection toolbar to show all three selection tools (Text, Table, and Image; Figure 13.13).

Figure 13.13 Showing the Selection toolbar

2. Click the Select Text tool ⒯ .

3. Click and drag over the text you want to select.

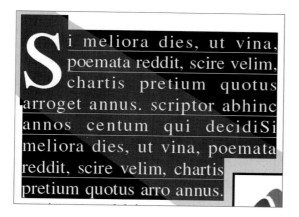

4. Copy this selected copy by doing *one* of the following:

- Choose Edit > Copy.
- Press ⌘/Ctrl+C.
- Control+click/right-click the selected text to activate the context menu (my choice here) and choose Copy To Clipboard.

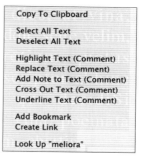

5. Move to the application and document into which you would like to insert your selected and copied text, and paste it.

Pasting an Image

To copy and paste a single image:

1. Expand the Selection toolbar to show the selection tools (Text, Table, and Image).

2. Click the Select Image tool .

3. Click the image you want to select. A negative view of the image will appear, indicating that it is selected.

4. Copy this selected image by doing *one* of the following:

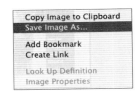

- Choose Edit > Copy.
- Press ⌘/Ctrl+C.
- Control+click/right-click the selected text to activate the context menu (my choice here) and choose Save Image As.

5. Select a location and a file format for your image in the Save Image As window.

> **Note:** ↪ Chapter 12, "Editing PDFs," and the sections later in this chapter for more information on opening images in Photoshop.

Exporting or Pasting a Table

You can export a table, open it in another application, or copy and paste it:

1. Expand the Selection toolbar to show the selection tools (Text, Table, and Image).

2. Click the Select Table tool ▦ .

3. Click and drag over the table you want to select. A bounding box will appear around the table, indicating that it is selected. You can resize this box to make sure the entire table is selected.

4. Copy this selected table by doing *one* of the following:

> Copy Selected Table
> Save Selected Table As...
> Deselect
> Open Table in Spreadsheet
> Select Table Uses Document Tags

- Choose Edit > Copy.

- Press ⌘/Ctrl+C.

- Control+click/right-click the selected text to activate the context menu (my choice here) and choose one of the copy or export options: Copy Selected Table, Save Selected Table As, or Open Table In Spreadsheet.

> **Note:** An icon for the preferred spreadsheet application (Excel here) will appear next to the Open Table In Spreadsheet menu selection.

5. If you chose Save Selected Table As, select a location and a file format for your image in the Acrobat Save As dialog. If you chose Copy Selected Table, move to the application and document into which you would like to insert your selected and copied table, and paste it.

Using Snapshots of PDF Contents

If you ever need to show just a portion of a PDF document page, Acrobat provides a screen capture tool just for this purpose, and it's easy to use. Here's how:

1. Zoom in on the portion of the PDF document page you would like to capture.

2. Select the Snapshot tool ▣ (just to the right of the selection tools).

3. Make a snapshot selection in *either* of two ways:

- Click just once on the active PDF document window, and the entire visible area of the PDF document panel will be captured. (This is why I had you zoom in to just the area you wanted to capture.)

- Click and drag across the area you would like to capture (as I've done in Figure 13.14), and a thin, dashed selection rectangle will be drawn around your snapshot area.

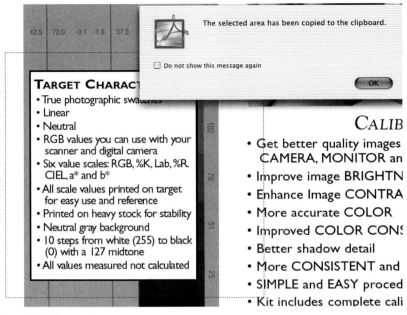

Figure 13.14 The snapshot area

In both cases, a message will appear informing you that the selected area has been copied to the Clipboard. (You can disable this message by clicking the Do Not Show This Message Again check box.)

4. You can now paste this image into any PDF document by clicking the Paste Clipboard Image icon ▮ and then doing *one* of the following:

- Click anywhere on a PDF document page to have the screen shot pasted at 100 percent.
- Click and drag to define the size of the pasted image (usually the best option).

In either case, you can resize the pasted image by dragging the black square control points on the edges of the pasted image.

You can also paste a Snapshot image from the Clipboard into any application—such as Photoshop or a page layout program's graphic box—that will accept a graphic image

Note: If you paste this screen capture into a page layout document, it will embed rather than link this image. So if you need to use only linked images, copy this screen grab into Photoshop first, save the image out of Photoshop, and then place that image as a linked image into your page layout document. When copying a PDF snapshot into Photoshop, simply select File > New (the new image will have the same dimensions as the snapshot) and then paste the snapshot into the new image (which will paste the snapshot into a new layer). Finish up by flattening the image.

Working with PDFs in Photoshop

In Chapter 12 we discussed using Illustrator as a PDF editing tool. Although Photoshop is not strictly speaking a PDF editing tool (because Photoshop works with pixels rather than PostScript data), there is a good deal of useful functionality among Acrobat, PDF files, and Photoshop. Following are some of the key tools and techniques for using Photoshop and PDF documents together.

Adding Notes to Photoshop Images

Just as in Acrobat, you can add a note or PDF-like note comment (known as an annotation in some versions of Photoshop) to any Photoshop image. Then when you save this image out of Photoshop as a PDF (which we'll do in the next section), you can open the comment/annotation and use it in Acrobat just like any other note-commented PDF file:

1.   In Photoshop, open the image on which you would like to comment. Here I will use a photograph I took in the Yukon to which I have added some text in Photoshop.

2.   Click the Notes tool ▣ to select it (or simply type **N**).

3.   Click the image at the location where you would like the note to be placed. You will see that you can add either a text note or an audio note.

4.   Type in the note message (or speak the audio note) you want. A little Note icon will be placed on the image.

5. When you save the image, be sure to select the Save Annotations check box so that the note will be saved along with the graphic image. (I have also saved the layers as well to retain the editable text layer.)

Saving PDFs from Photoshop

A Photoshop image can be saved as a PDF document and then opened in Acrobat just like any other PDF file. Here's how:

1. In Photoshop, open the image you would like to save out as a PDF. Here I will use the annotated Yukon image with the saved editable text layer from the preceding section (Figure 13.15).

2. Choose File > Save As; the Save As dialog (Figure 13.16) will appear.

Figure 13.15 The Yukon image with a text layer

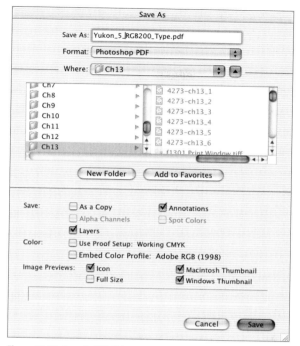

Figure 13.16 Save As PDF dialog

3. Configure this dialog as follows:

   a. Choose Photoshop PDF from the Format menu.

   b. Check the Save Annotations check box to preserve any note you've created.

   c. Check the Save Layers check box if you want to preserve editable layers.

   d. Check Use Proof Setup and Embed Color Profile to include any information you may need.

   e. Check the previews you want.

4. Click Save. The PDF Options dialog will appear (Figure 13.17).

Using PDF Security to Secure Your Images

If you are a photographer or someone else who is concerned about the security of your images, saving and distributing your images in PDF format is an easy and secure way to protect your images. You can easily allow anyone to see your images but prevent them from accessing them. ∞ Chapter 5, "Controlling Acrobat and Access to Your PDFs," for more information on security and Chapter 8, "Building Presentations and Forms," for some ideas on creating secure image presentations.

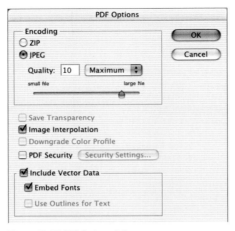

Figure 13.17 PDF Options dialog

5. Configure this dialog as follows:

   a. Select either ZIP or JPEG encoding depending upon which type of compression you would like applied to your image

Note: ZIP will apply lossless compression, which will preserve the quality of you image but will provide limited compression (50% max). JPEG will provide more (lossy) compression capability but with a progressive loss of image data and therefore quality. If you select JPEG, choose a high quality (8–12) if you want to preserve image quality.

   b. If you selected JPEG, assign a quality/compression factor. I typically choose 10–12 to preserve maximum image quality.

   c. If you have layers with transparency, check Save Transparency to preserve that.

   d. Check Image Interpolation if you have a low-resolution image that you intend to print. This will provide an anti-aliased edge to improve its look when printing.

   e. Apply a PDF Security option if you like.

   f. If you have any vector data (type of vector line art), you will need to decide whether you want to include that data or not. In the case of the fonts, decide whether or not you want the fonts to be included as embedded fonts or as vector outlines. If you do not include the vector data, it will all be flattened and become part of the background image.

If you include the font data, either as vectors or as embedded font files, your text will be separated within the PDF as a selectable object. The type of formatting/styling you have applied to your text will determine how editable it is in the PDF. But you will be able to at least select and move the text object, if not all of its formatting/styling, some of which, such as drop shadows, will be treated as part of the background image.

Using PDF Pages in Photoshop

There are two easy methods for working with PDF document pages in Photoshop: You can either Open or Place a page. Which method you use depends upon whether you want to use the PDF document page as a separate file or to insert a PDF document page in an already-opened Photoshop image.

Opening PDF Pages As Separate Photoshop Images

Opening a PDF in Photoshop is mechanically similar to opening any other image, but with just a few additional options to consider:

1. Choose File > Open.

2. Browse to and select the PDF you would like to open. The file Format indicator will recognize a non-Photoshop PDF as Generic PDF. Click the Open button.

3. In the PDF Page Selector dialog (Figure 13.18), navigate (using either the Go To Page button or the vertical slider) to the page you would like to open in Photoshop and click OK.

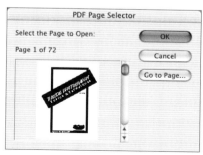

Figure 13.18 The PDF Page Selector

The Rasterize Generic PDF Format appears (Figure 13.19). At this point the PDF page you are opening is still in PostScript (that is, resolution-independent, scalable form). So now is the time to assign the dimensions and resolution at which you want to use this PDF document page in Photoshop. You can choose any combination you like, but do this now while it is still scalable. Once the PDF page is rasterized (converted into pixels), any scaling or resolution adjustments you make can lead to significant interpolation and lowering of image, and especially edge, quality.

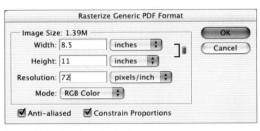

Figure 13.19 PDF Rasterize Settings

4. The initial rasterization setting are 8.5″×11″ at 72 ppi in RGB color mode. Configure the Rasterize Generic PDF Format window to suit your needs as follows:

    a. Make sure the Constrain Proportions check box is checked (a link will be placed between the Width and Height fields) so that all dimension adjustments will be proportional.

    b. Adjust either the Width or Height dimension (the other field will change automatically because of the proportional constraint established in Step a). You can also set dimensions in units other than inches, such as percentage, by accessing the unit menus next to the Width and Height fields.

    c. Assign a Resolution value—300 ppi is common.

    d. Select a color mode. Typically I will use either RGB or Lab even if I ultimately want a CMYK image, because I prefer to tailor my RGB/Lab-to-CMYK conversion to specific output devices.

    e. Be sure to check the Anti-aliased box so that all your graphic edges will have smooth, gradual transitions (a key to good-looking edges in pixel-based images). If you want a hard, abrupt edge for some reason, then uncheck this feature.

5. Click the OK button to complete the opening and conversion process.

    The PDF will be converted into a pixel-based image with the anti-aliased edged objects on a transparent background (Figure 13.20). Zoom in on one of the object edges to see the anti-aliasing.

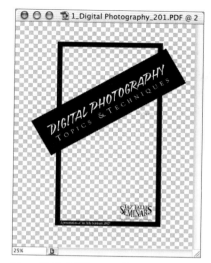 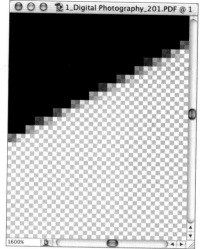

Figure 13.20 A PDF page with transparency, and a zoomed-in view of an anti-aliased edge

Note: I like to keep one copy of the converted PDF page with the transparency intact in case I want to use these page elements somewhere else in the future. The transparent background makes the selection and use of such elements far easier.

Placing PDF Pages in Other Photoshop Images

If you already have an open Photoshop image to which you would like to add a PDF page, your best bet is to simply place the PDF. Here's how to do this:

1. Open the image in which you would like to place a PDF page. Here I am using one of my Yukon photographs as a background.

2. Choose File > Place.

3. Locate, select, and open the PDF document that has a page you would like to place (here I am using a PDF copy of my digital photography manual).

4. In the PDF Page Selector dialog (shown back in Figure 13.18), select the page you would like to place, and then click OK. The chosen PDF document page will be placed as a transformable object with resizing/reshaping control points around its border (Figure 13.21).

Figure 13.21 Inserting a PDF page

5. Examine the Transform options bar to make sure that Anti-alias is checked, so that when a transform is applied, all object edges will be smoothed with anti-aliasing.

6. Using the control points and the mouse or the Transform palette, resize or reshape the placed PDF page image to suit. The placed PDF page is still a Post-Script object and is therefore scalable and skewable, as shown in Figure 13.22.

7. Hit the Enter key (or double-click the transformed image) to apply the transform and rasterize the PDF document page. This will also create a new layer containing the PDF document image.

8. Zoom in on an object edge to make sure it is anti-aliased. You can see how the anti-aliasing allows the PDF image to blend in with its background.

Extracting PDF Images with Photoshop

In Chapter 12 you learned how to access, edit, and replace a pixel-based image in a PDF document with Photoshop (by Control+clicking/right-clicking with the TouchUp Object tool on the image in the PDF file). You can also just suck that image right out of the PDF file directly through Photoshop. This is a handy technique to use if you want to access an image embedded in a PDF document for other uses. Follow these steps:

1. Choose File > Import > PDF Image.

2. From the Select PDF For Image Import dialog, browse to the document that contain the graphic(s) you would like to import, and click Open.

3. In the PDF Image Import dialog (Figure 13.23), scroll through to find the image you want to import. Then click the OK button.

Figure 13.22 (left) Resizing a placed PDF page; (right) the committed transform which is placed in its own layer

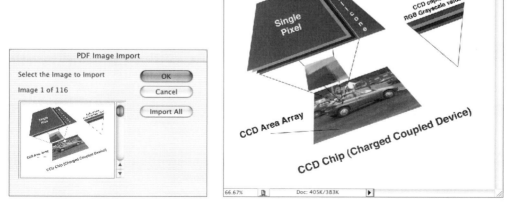

Figure 13.23 Selecting an image from a PDF file; (right) the image imported into Photoshop

Note: You can also click the Import All button to import all the pixel-based images in the PDF, but be careful what you ask for. Some PDFs—like this one—have more than 100 images!

Your image(s) will be opened in Photoshop. These images will have the same dimensions, resolution, and color space in which they were included and stored in the PDF. Once they are imported, you are free to handle the images like any other Photoshop image.

Automating
Acrobat Tasks

14

Acrobat offers a number of automation functions to help make repetitive tasks proceed with greater speed and fewer mistakes. Acrobat automation tools include batch functions, page and document functions, and access to JavaScript.

Chapter Contents

Running batch sequences

Creating custom batch sequences

Creating automatic events with actions

Running Batch Sequences

Batch functions are sequences of processes or commands that are applied to multiple documents. Batch processing can relieve repetitive drudgery and save you time. Here is how to make Acrobat's batch sequences work for you:

1. To begin a batch processing session, it is a good idea to gather all the PDF documents on which you would like to perform a batch sequence and place them in one folder.

2. In Acrobat, choose Advanced > Batch Processing. The Batch Sequences dialog appears (Figure 14.1). This contains a default list of batch sequences that can be run.

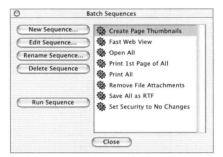

Figure 14.1 Control your batch sequences from this dialog.

3. Select one of the batch sequences listed in the right pane. Here I have selected the Create Page Thumbnails batch sequence.

4. Click the Run Sequence button.

5. In the dialog that appears (Figure 14.2), check the list of all the commands that will be applied (in this case, one) to the files that you will select.

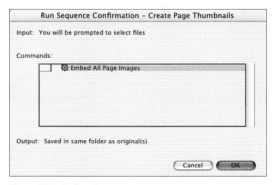

Figure 14.2 Confirm the run sequence.

6. Click OK.

7. In the Select Files To Process dialog (Figure 14.3), locate and select all the files you would like to include in this batch process. Use Shift+click to select a continuous series of files, and then click Select.

Figure 14.3 Select the files to batch process.

The batch process will commence, showing a progress bar that tracks the batching.

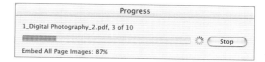

Creating Custom Batch Sequences

Any task or sequence of tasks that you perform regularly is a candidate for creating and using a batch function. Here is how to create your own batch sequence:

1. Choose Advanced > Batch Processing; the Batch Sequences dialog (shown back in Figure 14.1) appears.

2. Click the New Sequence button.

3. In the Name Sequence dialog (Figure 14.4), type in the name of the sequence you would like to create, and then click OK.

Figure 14.4 Name your sequence and click OK.

4. The Batch Edit Sequence dialog appears (Figure 14.5); click the Select Commands button.

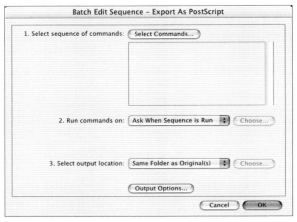

Figure 14.5 The Batch Edit Sequence dialog

5. A list of all the available Acrobat commands appears in the Edit Sequence dialog (Figure 14.6). In the *left* pane, select a command you want to include in your batch sequence (here, I first added Rotate Pages), and then click the Add button. That command will appear in the list on the *right*.

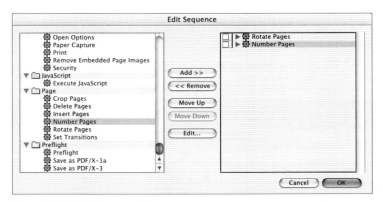

Figure 14.6 The Edit Sequence dialog

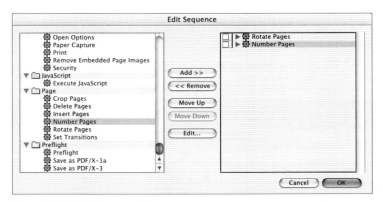

6. To set up the exact operation of a command within the sequence, select the command from the list in the *right* pane and click the Edit button. A dialog specific to that command appears (Figure 14.7 shows the dialog specific to the Rotate Pages command).

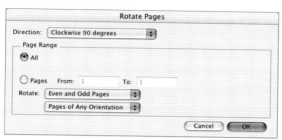

Figure 14.7 Configuring the Rotate Pages command

7. Configure the dialog to suit you (here I've set all pages to be rotated clockwise 90 degrees) and click OK.

8. Repeat Steps 5–7 for each additional command you want to include in the sequence. Here I've also added the Number Pages command.

9. If you want to be able to input data and or make adjustments at any step during the process, you can make a command step interactive by clicking the check box to the left of the command in the right pane. A small interactive symbol will appear in the check box. If this is activated (which is not necessary in our current sequence), then the batch process will pause during this implementation of the command step to allow you to make any adjustments you like.

10. Set the order of the commands in the sequence, or delete any you don't want, by highlighting a command in the right pane and clicking Move Up, Move Down, or Remove.

11. Click the OK button in the Edit Sequence dialog to complete the editing process and return to the Batch Sequences window.

12. You can now activate a batch process by selecting one of the sequences and clicking the Run Sequence button, or you can select one of the other Batch Sequences options.

13. Click the Close button in the Batch Sequences dialog to exit the batch processing features.

Determining Which Files the Batch Runs On

Once you have created the batch command sequence, you should assign a Run On command that will determine how you will designate which files the sequence will work with. Here's how:

1. In the Batch Edit Sequence dialog (shown back in Figure 14.5), click the Run Commands On drop-down menu.

2. Choose an option: Selected Files, Selected Folder, Ask When Sequence Is Run, or Files Open In Acrobat. If you choose Selected Files or Selected Folder, controls will appear to allow you to identify the files or folder.

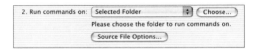

3. Control the format of the source files that will be processed by clicking the Source File Options button and checking the desired formats.

Your new batch sequence is now ready to run.

Assigning Output Location

After you have created the batch command sequence and a Run On determination, you must assign your output location. To do so, in the Batch Edit Sequence dialog (shown back in Figure 14.5), click the Select Output Location drop-down menu. Your options are Specific Folder, Ask When Sequence Is Run, Same Folder(s) As Original, or Don't Save Changes. If you select a specific folder location, you will need to click Choose to locate that folder.

Selecting a Name and File Format

The final step is to assign a file format and a naming structure to your batch-processed files. In the Batch Edit Sequence dialog (shown back in Figure 14.5), click the Output Options button (Output Options...) . The Output Options dialog appears (Figure 14.8).

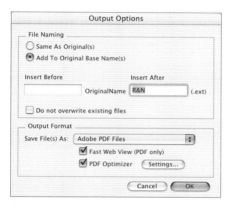

Figure 14.8 The Output Options dialog

Configure this window as follows:

File Naming You have the option of either keeping the original name of the file or adding a prefix or suffix to the filename. Here I have chosen to add the suffix R&N (for "rotate and number").

Do Not Overwrite Existing Files If you want to keep the original file intact, check this box.

Output Format Select the file format you would like the batched file to acquire. The default file format is PDF.

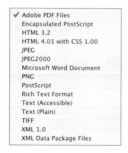

Fast Web View As a matter of routine I always select this anytime I create a PDF. This allows the PDF to be served up a page at a time over the Web.

PDF Optimizer If you would like to reconfigure your new PDF, check this box and then click the Settings button. You can then set up your PDF settings (in the dialog shown in Figure 14.9), just as you have done previously (☞ Chapter 4, "Creating the PDF You Want," for more detailed information on Distiller settings). Click OK when you have finished.

Your new batch process is ready to run anytime you want to use it!

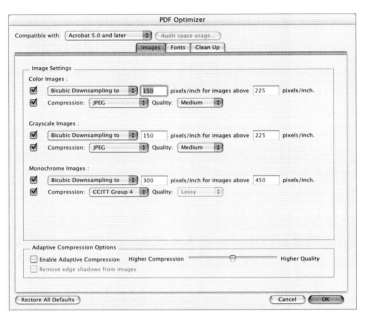

Figure 14.9 Check PDF Optimizer and click Settings to access this dialog.

When to Use Batch Processing

Batch processing is a useful way to automate any task or sequence of tasks that needs to be performed on a regular basis. Using a batch function not only helps speed up those tasks but also helps ensure that they are performed the same way with the same settings each time. Similarly, batch functions can be used to establish consistency in the way the same tasks are performed by multiple people. If all the people in a work group use the same batch function to accomplish a task, then all members will perform that task the same way. This is particularly useful when performing tasks with many options, such as printing or assigning security controls.

Batch processing is also a handy way to update previously created PDF documents into newer formats or resave PDFs into other file formats. As you develop your own workflows, always keep a lookout for which repetitive tasks could be automated with a batch process.

Creating Automatic Events with Actions

Another type of automation that Acrobat supports is an event (known as an action) that automatically occurs when it is triggered by some other event (known as the trigger). For instance, you could have a sound or movie play whenever a specific page is opened. There are literally an unlimited number of events or actions that can be defined. Once you make your first action, you will have all sorts of ideas about how to use them.

As an example, let's make a sound play every time someone opens a specific document page:

1. Click the Pages tab to activate the thumbnail views of your document.

2. Click the thumbnail of the page to which you would like to add an action.

3. Choose Options > Page Properties (or Control+click/right-click and choose Page Properties).

4. Click the Actions tab (Figure 14.10), where you define the combination of trigger and action. In this case, do the following:

  a. Click the Select Trigger menu and choose Page Open.

  b. Click the Select Action menu and choose Play A Sound.

  c. Click the Add button. Navigate to where the sound file that you would like to be activated as part of this action is located. Highlight this sound file and click Select.

When you are returned to the Page Properties dialog, you will see that your newly selected sound file is added to the Actions list (Figure 14.11).

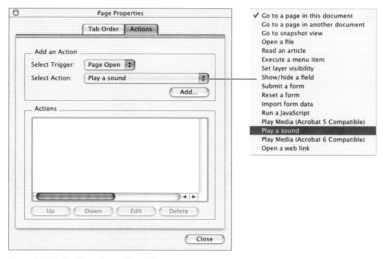

Figure 14.10 The Page Properties dialog

Note: Acrobat supports two kinds of sound files for actions: uncompressed .aif and .wav sound files. If you have a sound file that is not in either of these formats, open the file in any sound or movie editing application, such as QuickTime Pro, and export it in either AIF or WAV format. You will also find that Acrobat likes to have any sound (or media) file that you use as an action to already be linked to the PDF document as a linked resource (with the Link, Movie, or Sound tool). I've included a sample uncompressed sound file, FireIceSong.wav, in the Chapter 14 folder on the CD for you to experiment with.

Figure 14.11 The action has been added.

5. Click Close to complete the creation of the action. The next time that page is opened, the sound file will automatically play.

Variety of Automatic Actions

You can use the same process we used to create the page-open sound action here to create a wide variety of actions (as the complete Actions list in Figure 14.10 shows). Actions can be accessed with wide range of triggers, including mouse up and mouse down, thumbnails, bookmarks, articles, comments, and even form fields. You can also use actions to access Java Scripts. Once you get the hang of creating actions, you will use them for all sorts of cool links. Adding sounds and movies with actions is a snap and is a great way to spice up a PDF presentation.

Index